Japanese Outbound Acquisitions

Shigeru Matsumoto

Japanese Outbound Acquisitions

Explaining What Works

palgrave
macmillan

Shigeru Matsumoto
Graduate School of Management
Kyoto University
Kyoto, Japan

ISBN 978-981-13-1363-9 ISBN 978-981-13-1364-6 (eBook)
https://doi.org/10.1007/978-981-13-1364-6

Library of Congress Control Number: 2018951791

Cover Design by Akihiro Nakayama

This Palgrave Macmillan imprint is published by the registered company Springer Nature Singapore Pte Ltd.
The registered company address is: 152 Beach Road, #21-01/04 Gateway East, Singapore 189721, Singapore

Preface

Although a company has taken all the necessary steps before an acquisition, they still fail in managing the target after the transaction. Why do Japanese companies repeatedly fail in their cross-border M&As, and how can they succeed in these acquisitions? This book aims to answer these questions.

I have 20 years of experience in advising on M&As, proposing deals to clients in Japan and overseas, and assisting in related negotiations. On many occasions, I have accompanied clients overseas and negotiated with local target companies and their shareholders. While there have been deals that were successfully negotiated from start to finish, there have also been deals where the negotiations failed at the last minute. Overall, the hurdles to be cleared before closing a deal are much higher in cross-border than domestic transactions because the business environments of the two parties to the deal are different.

Even when the other party is initially considered a good target, many potential deals fall through for reasons such as poor chemistry between management, feasibility of synergy is lower than anticipated, local regulation issues around the target company's business, and, of course, an irreconcilable gap between a seller's expected price and the price a buyer can justify (this gap is particularly high in emerging countries).

Japanese companies carefully consider acquisition opportunities. Therefore, the deals for which they are able to reach an agreement are those for which they have carefully carried out their due diligence, using professionals such as accountants and lawyers, and conducted negotiations until they were satisfied. Thus, for such acquisitions in which all the necessary steps were taken, potential synergy was identified, and the acquisitions were conducted with the confidence that they would be successful.

However, even when these companies have taken all the necessary steps, in many cases companies are not able to deliver what they anticipated. There has been a constant stream of failures in which the acquiring company incurred a major loss. The acquiring company is placed under the spotlight by the media and markets at the announcement of the acquisition, but it is not unusual for the company to find itself under the spotlight once again, this time, when it records an extraordinary loss on the impairment of goodwill, or when it decides to withdraw from the business they acquired.

As a banker who proposes the benefits of outbound acquisitions to clients, I am extremely concerned with the question of why businesses fail after an acquisition. Bankers are involved only until the acquisition is completed, but they do not participate in the business after that. Once the overseas acquisition is completed, what path will it take and what will the outcome be? Explain what works. Alongside my continuing work, finding the answers to these questions was my motivation for embarking on my Ph.D. research at Kobe University.

At the start of this research, I collected data on the outcomes of 116 outbound acquisition deals conducted by Japanese companies, specifically those with an acquisition price of 10 billion yen or more and those for which at least 10 years have passed since the acquisition. I found that in 51 cases out of 116, or nearly half, the acquiring company had already sold or withdrawn from the business, with a total of 2.8 trillion yen spent on the acquisitions for these failed businesses. When also considering the management resources invested after the acquisitions, failed acquisitions come at a high cost to acquiring companies.

Many M&A-related books provide guidance on the practical and technical aspects of conducting an acquisition, such as due diligence, valuation, and financing. However, in this book, I attempt to focus not on those techniques but on post-acquisition management, especially in the cross-border transactions from my research results. It would seem that the high probability of failure in overseas M&As cannot be improved merely by gaining expertise in practical aspects of transactions.

Acquiring companies invest enormous amounts of resources into an acquisition, so for the investment to be worthwhile, the business needs to succeed with significant profit growth, not just break even. While the processes and practices at the time of the acquisition are important, they focus on how to avoid failure, but what is required to achieve success is the ability of the management to go beyond those transaction skills.

This book starts Part 1 by questioning the conventional rationale of overseas M&As. The many failures indicate the potential for major misunderstandings during discussions or negotiations about the benefits that acquisitions can provide. Further, through a long-term evaluation of Japanese overseas acquisitions up to the present time, I attempt to divide the cases into successes and failures and to identify the fundamental factors behind the failures.

In Part 2, I explain the points in common among Japanese companies that have used their acquisitions to successfully develop a global business. Further, I consider strategies of successful companies, using the example of IBM as a "local company" that has achieved significant profit growth by utilizing M&As.

Finally, in Part 3, I summarize the lessons learned from the overseas M&A successes and failures that have been considered in this book thus far.

Kyoto, Japan Shigeru Matsumoto

Contents

Intended Readers

This book is intended for the following readers.

1. Company executives

By understanding the points in common among the failures and successes in this book, you will avoid making mistakes in management decisions when conducting overseas acquisitions.

2. Corporate managers working on strategy, finance, and overseas business development

By understanding the traps that lie in wait within the rationale for overseas M&As, such as buying time and capturing global market share, you will avoid strategic mistakes when proposing deals to management. Also, by reading about the success cases that have realized profit growth, you will understand what works.

3. Practitioners, such as bankers, lawyers, and accountants who advise on transactions

By rethinking what it means for an M&A to be a success, you will avoid mistakes when advising clients.

4. Researchers

By learning new approaches to evaluating acquisitions, in cases of both success and failure, you will see the importance of reviewing long-term, post-acquisition performances rather than just the immediate impact of deal announcements upon share price.

5. MBA students

You will learn about the challenges and opportunities of cross-border M&As for your future career.

Despite many failures, Japanese companies are still highly motivated to conduct outbound acquisitions and still have high expectations from them. If instead of wondering, "How is such a transaction completed?" readers ask, "What makes an overseas M&A a success, and what did management do to achieve this?" then I will have achieved half of this book's objective. Further, if this book results in adding just one more cross-border M&A success story, then I think writing this book will have been worthwhile.

Not many business people have experience working on multiple overseas acquisitions. Rather, in the majority of cases, they must take on the challenge of such a major endeavor despite a serious lack of experience.

"If I had been involved in this acquisition, what decisions would I have made?" I hope you read the case studies in this book with this sense of curiosity.

About the Author

Shigeru Matsumoto Professor Shigeru Matsumoto received his Ph.D. from Kobe University. For his doctoral dissertation, he conducted an in-depth study of Japanese cross-border mergers and acquisitions (M&A). He also holds an MBA from Thunderbird School of Global Management, which he attended through the US Fulbright Program. He has 20 years' experience in investment banking and advisory as a managing director at global institutions, including the Hong Kong Shanghai Banking Corp. (HSBC), Macquarie Capital, and PricewaterhouseCoopers (PwC). He has served as an advisor on over 50 Japan-related cross-border M&A transactions in 20 countries, including the US, the UK, France, China, and Vietnam. In 2015, he won the 9th Grand Prize at the Mergers & Acquisition Forum for his recent publication on Japanese cross-border acquisitions.

List of Figures

List of Tables

CHAPTER 1

Introduction

Can Japanese Companies Succeed in Outbound Acquisitions?

1.1 Discussion in the Board Room and the Landscape Outside the Company

When a company considers a deal, its only choice is either to conduct the acquisition or not.

The strategic objective of acquisition is to achieve sustainable profit growth by incorporating external business and then creating synergies. Therefore, the acquiring company should think in advance about how the outbound acquisition can help the company's overseas business take a leap forward compared to its green field investment option.

In reality, it is not possible to find a target that will perfectly meet the acquiring company's requirements; moreover, the company faces time constraints in conducting its due diligence on the proposed acquisition. There are also limits to the access of information before completing a transaction, especially cross-border M&A, because of remote locations and different management environments. After a potential acquirer has clarified the actual situation of the target company and identified any issues it may have through due diligence, using accountants and lawyers, opinions within the acquiring company will sometimes be divided, even for promising deals. The target may have initially been seen through rose-colored glasses; but, upon entering the final stage of a deal, a more cautious opinion may in fact begin to sound more convincing.

S. Matsumoto, *Japanese Outbound Acquisitions*,
https://doi.org/10.1007/978-981-13-1364-6_1

Proponents of acquisitions are keenly aware of actions taken by competitors, and not wanting to miss the opportunity, consider the deal in front of them to be a golden opportunity. They are certain that their company will become a global market leader through acquisition, and they fear that their company will lag greatly behind if a domestic rival acquires the target company. These advocates insist that outbound acquisition is the best tool for the company's growth strategy; especially when the company has budgeted for a potential acquisition as a part of its growth plan, they feel they cannot subsequently back down.

Conversely, the more cautious faction points to problems it will face following the acquisition, saying, for example, "While the target company has an excellent brand, it has become caught up in price competition and its profitability has been going down," "The capacities of its production and research and development are limited; we will need to make a large capital investment after the acquisition," and "If the current target management team resigns, we may not be able to carry out the management ourselves." Both groups tell only one side of the story.

Even if the relevant business unit believes that an overseas acquisition will expand their influence, this may not be true for the other business units. Thus, apart from determining whether an acquisition is a good or a bad deal, deciding to pursue an acquisition is also tied to the power balance within the acquiring company. An acquisition, additionally, can clarify which businesses within the company are priorities and where the respective regions rank in order of priority.

When an acquiring company makes progress in its negotiations, then the company starts to consider financing for the deal. However, voices within the companies sometimes ask, "Why should hard-earned funds from the domestic businesses be generously spent on the acquisition of overseas business, and should not the domestic businesses be rewarded first?" In addition, finance departments worry about their companies' credit rating being downgraded if they take on a large amount of debt to fund the acquisitions.

In the meantime, a new bidder may appear to compete for the acquisition, prompting the seller's shareholders to demand that the acquisition price be raised. The target company's management, which has been friendly since the start of negotiations, may say, "We want you to acquire us, as we do not want to be taken over by the other company." Thus, this sense of obligation to rescue the management of target company is an added complication.

Finally, the significant decision of whether or not to conduct the acquisition is left to the top management. A large-scale acquisition will have a major impact on a company's financial performance, and a highly profiled outbound acquisition will often put a spotlight on the top management responsible, whose capability to fulfill his or her obligations to the company may be called into question if the acquisition does not go well. Thus, an acquisition could either make or break the reputation of the top management. Please refer to Fig. 1.1.

How does this situation appear when viewed from outside of the company? A commercial bank sees a client's potential outbound acquisitions as an excellent financing opportunity. Such large-scale financing would lead to more revenue for the bank and allow the bank greater influence over the client.

Under a monetary easing policy led by Bank of Japan, commercial banks have actively attempted to increase their financing. However, the best companies are cash rich and virtually debt-free, and they are not keen to leverage themselves. Therefore, banks have few other opportunities for lending, so they actively pursue acquisition finance offering significantly attractive interest rates. Presently, a very good environment for raising funds is in place for Japanese companies.

What about the sellers? Recently, more Japanese outbound acquisitions are sourced through private equity. Those financial investors, who have carefully improved target performance after their investment, are always on the lookout for exit opportunities. Japanese companies are interesting acquirers, for while they tend to be cautious up to the time of conducting the deal, they also tend to offer an attractive price once they decide that they want to purchase the target company. Financial investors know their competitors have earned significant gains following sales to Japanese firms. Thus, Western private equities, which are keen on delivering high returns to their investors, welcome the participation of the Japanese in the bidding process.

Apart from a company's motivation for business growth overseas, banks and financial investors play a significant role in increasing the volume and price of Japanese outbound acquisitions.

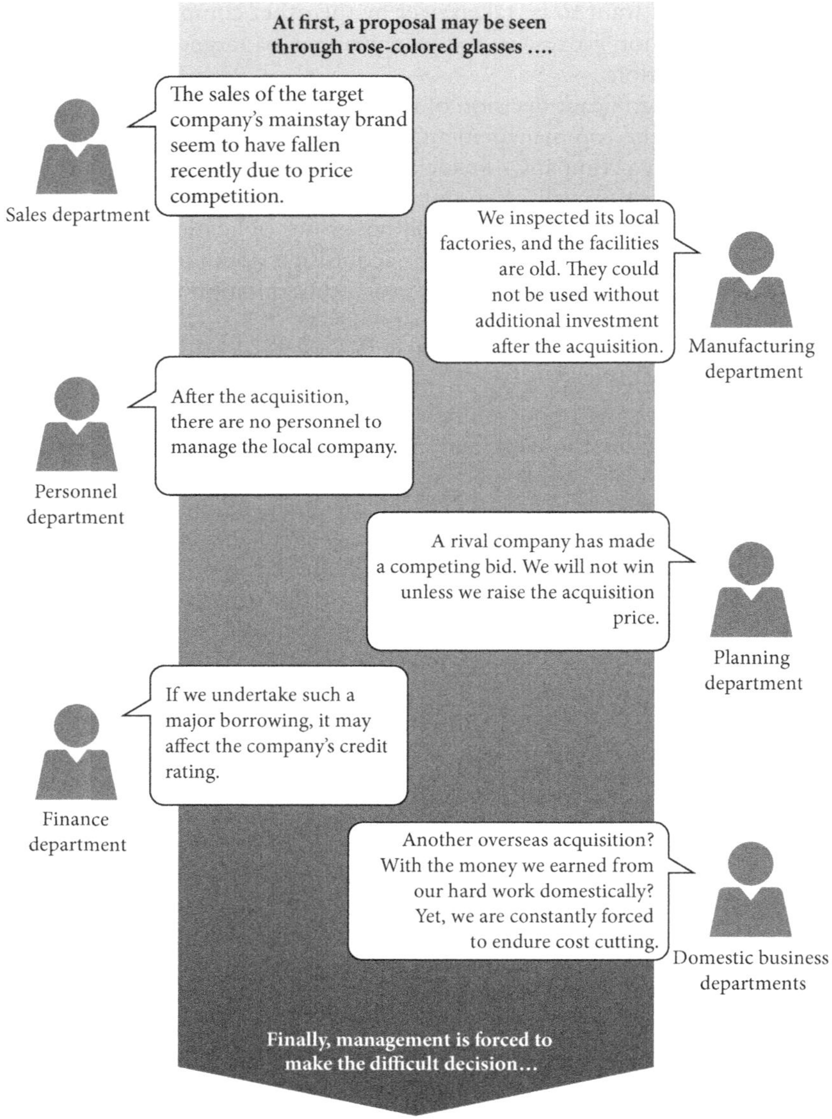

Fig. 1.1 Management decision making process for outbound acquisitions

1.2 Trillion Yen Deals: The Likelihood that an Acquisition Will Succeed

Takeda Pharmaceuticals, SoftBank, and Suntory.

The Points in Common Among One-Trillion-Yen Acquisitions

As Japanese outbound acquisitions increase, large-scale deals of over one trillion yen have become less rare. The acquisition of the major Swiss pharmaceutical company Nycomed by Takeda Pharmaceuticals was worth 1.1 trillion yen (9.6 billion euro),[1] that of the US mobile phone company Sprint Nextel by SoftBank was worth 1.8 trillion yen (21.6 billion dollars),[2] and that of the US liquor and spirits distiller Beam Inc. by Suntory was worth 1.65 trillion yen (16 billion dollars),[3] see Table 1.1. There are great expectations on performance after such acquisitions from both domestic and overseas investors.

These one-trillion-yen acquisitions have three points in common in their backgrounds.

The first point in common is that the acquiring companies are Japan's leading and most profitable players in their respective sectors, such as pharmaceuticals, mobile phones, and beverages. They considered the overseas market to be a new frontier since they have been focused on the domestic market and had not ventured overseas before that time.

The second point is that major Japanese banks have provided significant financing for these outbound acquisitions. The three companies that conducted the one-trillion-yen acquisitions had stable domestic businesses and, thus, were able to secure the funds for the acquisitions at favorable rates. Takeda Pharmaceuticals borrowed 600 billion yen, including from Sumitomo Mitsui Bank. SoftBank obtained 1.5 trillion yen in financing from three banks—700 billion yen from Mizuho Corporate Bank, and 800

Table 1.1 Acquisitions exceeding one trillion yen

Acquirer	*Target*	*Price*
Takeda Pharmaceuticals	Nycomed	1.1 trillion yen
SoftBank	Sprint Nextel	1.8 trillion yen
Suntory	Beam	1.65 trillion yen

Company press releases and Thompson Reuters

billion yen from Tokyo-Mitsubishi UFJ Bank and Sumitomo Mitsui Bank—at the agreed upon rate of 1.4%. For Suntory's acquisition, Tokyo-Mitsubishi UFJ bank provided the largest ever independent financing to a private sector company—1.4 trillion yen.[4] Thus, all three companies were able to obtain low-interest-rate financing to fund their acquisitions, one of the benefits of the quantitative easing policy conducted by the Bank of Japan.

The third point in common is that the main shareholders of the target companies were financial investors, including private equities. The shareholders of Nycomed acquired by Takeda shareholders included Nordic Capital Funds V and VI and DLJ Merchant Banking Partners (a Credit Suisse affiliate).

Nycomed had planned an initial public offering but finally settled on the sale to Takeda. One of Sprint's major shareholders was the investment management company Paulson, which supported the acquisition by SoftBank once it raised the acquisition price following the appearance of a rival bidder. The leading shareholder of Beam acquired by Suntory was also a financial investor, Pershing Square Capital Management. Although Beam was a part of Fortune Brands Inc., it was spun off in 2010. The Beam acquisition price was 16 billion dollars (1.65 trillion yen), but the market capitalization of Fortune Brands prior to the spin-off was no more than 7 billion dollars. On the sale to Suntory, Beam Chairman David Mackay said, "We were able to provide [Beam] shareholders with an attractive price. The return to shareholders since the standalone listing of Beam in October 2011 is 106%."[5] Thus, Western financial investors have obtained major returns from these sales to Japanese companies.

These one-trillion-yen acquisitions are deals in which the speculations of the buyers, the lenders, and the sellers overlapped in the same way (refer to Table 1.2).

One-Trillion-Yen Acquisitions and Their Respective Likelihoods of Success

While these three acquisitions had points in common in their backgrounds, after the acquisitions, the acquiring companies took different paths in their strategies and management.

In acquiring Nycomed, Takeda Pharmaceuticals aimed to catch up in the markets of Europe and emerging countries, which it had entered late. Takeda obtained sales channels in these regions and it expected to generate a synergy of 30 billion yen. However, Takeda failed to restructure

Table 1.2 Comparison of the one-trillion-yen acquisitions

	Takeda Pharmaceuticals	*SoftBank*	*Suntory*
Target company	Nycomed	Sprint Nextel	Beam
Business	Pharmaceuticals	Mobile phones	Spirits and liquors
Acquisition year	2011	2013	2014
Acquisition price	1.1 trillion yen	1.8 trillion yen	1.65 trillion yen
Bank loan amount	600 billion yen	1.5 trillion yen	1.4 trillion yen
Lenders	Sumitomo Mitsui Bank and others	Mizuho Corporate Bank and others	Tokyo-Mitsubishi UFJ Bank and others
Sellers' leading shareholder	Private equity fund	Hedge fund	Investment management company
Revenue of the target company at the time of acquisition	3.1 billion euros	35.3 billion dollars	2.5 billion dollars
Operating profit or loss of the target company at the time of acquisition	Loss of 44 million euros	Loss of 1.8 billion dollars	600 million dollars
Most recent major acquisitions	Millennium Pharmaceuticals, 2008 (US, new cancer treatments)	eAccess, 2012 (Japan, mobile phones)	Orangina, 2009 (France, beverages)

Prepared by the author from the companies' press releases and Nihon Keizai Shimbun

Nycomed's unprofitable business after the acquisition, and Takeda's profits declined significantly in its consolidated financial results. Takeda President Yasuchika Hasegawa said, "Our efforts were not enough," and the company appointed its first foreign president in the 230 years since its establishment.

With its acquisition of Sprint, SoftBank aimed to enter the US mobile phone market and reproduce through acquisition of its successful Japanese model. SoftBank acquired Vodafone's Japan business in 2006 and it became a major player in the mobile sector in its home market. SoftBank did not expect synergy effects between Sprint and its domestic business. As Sprint's business was not profitable, SoftBank's first tasks after the acquisition were reducing employees and closing stores and call centers.

SoftBank President Masayoshi Son said, "Up until now, I had thought that it was best to leave the running of American companies to Americans, and I said nothing. But now it is different. We shall not hold back …." In addition, he himself appealed to the authorities and to consumers that SoftBank's entry into the United States would promote competition.

With the acquisition of Beam, Suntory emphasized the significance of adding a strong product portfolio in the spirits sector. As Beam was highly profitable, Suntory placed importance on generating synergy in sales and product development. Suntory's domestic spirits business was transferred to the acquired company, now known as Beam Suntory, and the two companies' liquor businesses were integrated. In addition, the Beam CEO was retained even after the acquisition. Suntory President Nobutada Saji said, "This acquisition accelerates the globalization of our spirits business and heralds a new dawn in the history of Suntory."

Can Takeda Pharmaceuticals, SoftBank, and Suntory succeed with their one-trillion-yen acquisitions? (Refer to Table 1.3.) With its acquisition, Takeda Pharmaceuticals bought itself the time required to enter markets in emerging countries through this acquisition. Attention will focus on whether the new foreign president will be able to improve Nycomed's loss-making operation and steer a course to realize the synergy that the company expected.

Table 1.3 The likelihood of success and issues after one-trillion-yen acquisitions

	Strategic intention at the time of acquisition	*Management challenges after acquisition*
Acquisition of Nycomed by Takeda Pharmaceuticals	Sales in Europe double and quintuple in emerging countries by acquiring sales channels	Restructure Nycomed's business
	Generate synergy of 30 billion yen a year	Appointed first foreign president since its foundation
Acquisition of Sprint by SoftBank	Reproduce in the United States its success in the home market (Japan)	Restructure Sprint business and increase scale by merger with T-Mobile in US
	Become big three with Verizon and AT&T through additional acquisition	President Son himself directed the restructuring in the United States
Acquisition of Beam by Suntory	Become a world leader in spirits and liquors	Complete organizational integration of Beam Suntory
	Open up the spirits markets in emerging countries with a powerful portfolio	Beam CEO was retained

Prepared by the author from company press releases

SoftBank wanted to quickly establish itself within a structure of three major players with Verizon and AT&T. To this end, it began to approach US-based T-Mobile for acquisition to increase the scale of its mobile business in the United States, but the US authorities did not approve of the proposed acquisition, so the negotiations were put on hold. SoftBank then decided to first complete the restructuring of Sprint. In 2018, Sprint and T-Mobile agreed on the merger and they wait for the approval from Federal Communications Commission and Department of Justice.

Suntory wanted the acquisition of Beam to improve the efficiency of its spirits and liquors business as a whole. At the time of the acquisition, Beam's net profit was 360 million dollars, which would only pay the interest on the borrowed 1.4 trillion yen; thus, Beam Suntory is expected to create significant synergy by integrating the two operations. It is too early to determine whether those one-trillion-yen acquisitions have been successful or not since they are still working on their post-acquisition management to reach sustainable profit growth. The results of the acquisition will not become clear until a much later stage.

What about their respective competitors' outbound acquisitions?

In the pharmaceutical sector, other companies have also conducted deals targeting markets in emerging countries. In 2008, Daiichi Sankyo invested 500 billion yen to acquire Ranbaxy Laboratories of India, a manufacturer of generic pharmaceuticals. Daiichi Sankyo's objectives were to "Establish a presence in emerging countries and to dramatically expand the Daiichi Sankyo Group's global reach." However, Ranbaxy's results worsened due to the embargo on exports to the United States stemming from quality problems in India. As a result, Daiichi Sankyo recorded an extraordinary loss, and six years after the acquisition, it had no choice but to sell its shares in Ranbaxy.

In the mobile phone sector, NTT DoCoMo invested in AT&T Wireless in the United States, KPN Mobiel in the Netherlands, and Hutchinson 3G UK in the United Kingdom in 2000. At that time, NTT was trying to develop its i-mode service overseas, but its minority investments failed to achieve that objective. Instead, NTT recorded a huge impairment loss on the valuation of shares, and it had to sell all the shareholdings. In 2009, NTT invested in Tata Teleservices (TTSL) to enter the Indian market, but it could not win in the price competition with the local companies. In 2014, NTT decided to withdraw from India. NTT spent 266.7 billion yen to acquire TTSL shares but again it repeatedly recorded an impairment loss. At the time of the withdrawal, the book value of its holding in TTSL had already fallen to 44.8 billion yen.[6]

Kirin, which at one point had considered a merger with Suntory, went ahead with acquisitions in countries such as Australia and Brazil. However, currently, the company's priorities are strengthening its domestic businesses and improving the profitability of its existing overseas subsidiaries. In fact, Kirin exited Brazil in 2017 by selling Kirin Brazil (Schincariol), the company it acquired six years ago. Kirin recognized more than a 1-billion-dollar loss on this transaction. Kirin's total operating profit remains around 211 billion yen and its operating profit margin is 11.3% in 2017. Whereas, Anheuser-Busch InBev has grown in scale through M&A, its operating profit has exceeded one trillion yen and its operating profit margin has exceeded 30%.

Thus, the domestic competitors of these companies have not yet been able to succeed in outbound acquisitions.

The true value of the one-trillion-yen acquisitions will become apparent in time. Each of these three companies, Takeda, SoftBank, and Suntory has a strong management team and good track record of M&A. However, while there is the potential to generate synergies and achieve sustainable growth in the future, there are still many obstacles that must be cleared. It seems that it will be necessary for the acquiring companies to look at their businesses over the next 10 years to evaluate whether or not their acquisitions have been a success.

1.3 Analogy Between Outbound Acquisition and Professional Baseball

The ultimate goal for the team is not the acquisition of a major league player itself, but winning the pennant.

In the first place, what are the objectives of companies conducting outbound acquisitions, and what is important to ensuring their success?

When an acquirer is in the process of completing a transaction, the company tends to be busy with the negotiations at hand and with internal coordination. The company only pays attention to the process up to the completion of the acquisition. In addition, professional advisors also tend to focus on the technical aspects relating to the terms and condition of transactions.

Here, however, I want to take a small step back from these sorts of frontline scenes and clarify what roles outbound acquisition should play in a company's operations. For ease of understanding, I use the acquisition of foreign talent by Japanese professional baseball teams as an analogy (refer to Fig. 1.2).

There are many similarities between outbound M&A and the acquisition of foreign talent by professional baseball teams. The teams thoroughly investigate the abilities of the players currently on their roster, envisage strategies for the coming season, and think about the aspects that need to be strengthened. The baseball team executives and the team manager in charge of the frontline of the team repeatedly hold meetings about additions and discuss whether they should target foreign players, and if so which ones. They discuss if they should acquire a pitcher or a fielder, and if a pitcher, whether a starter or a relief pitcher, and if a fielder, whether to acquire a player who is a long-distance hitter or an all-rounder who is good at batting, fielding, and running. Foreign players are expensive purchases whose success or failure can impact the outcome of the pennant race, so every team makes its best effort to select and approach players while keeping a close watch on their budgets. When scouts look

Baseball team's acquisitions of players		Companies' overseas M&A
Enhancing pitching or batting capabilities	**Objective**	Horizontal or vertical integration and diversification
Player	**Target**	Companies and business
Scouting activities	**Investigation**	Due diligence
FA market and player's current salary	**Valuation**	DCF and multiples
Player's agent	**Negotiation**	Seller's advisor (investment banks)
Terms and incentives	**Contract**	Acquisition price and earnout
Manager	**Management**	CEO
Incorporating player into batting and rotation	**Focus**	Creating synergies by integrating target business
Improvement in ERA and RBI	**Indication of effects**	Improvement of profitability
Winning championship	**Success**	Sustainable profit growth
Returning home owing slumping results	**Failure**	Withdrawal and exit

Fig. 1.2 Analogy between acquiring foreign players and overseas M&A

for foreign players to improve their teams' rosters, they investigate the player's performance and personality (whether they would feel at home on a team in Japan and in Japanese baseball), their injury history, and the possibility of being a free agent (FA). They take videos of the pitching and batting of the players being considered, which are sent to Japan for evaluation. This process corresponds to the due diligence conducted for a company acquisition.

Normally, major league players have an agent. As Japanese players also use an agent when they join a major league team in the United States, the role played by agents is known even in Japan.

The agent's work is to conduct contract negotiations with the team on the player's behalf, such as on annual salary, incentives, and the contract's duration. When acquiring a player, the team indicates the contract conditions to the agent and conducts the negotiations. In the case of a company acquisition, the investment bank mandated by the seller company corresponds with the agent and plays the role of extracting favorable acquisition conditions from the buyer.

The player and the agent, and the selling company and the investment bank, negotiate the contract conditions so that their interests align. The player's annual salary will be that player's "price" to the team with reference to his performance up to that time and considering his activities after entering the team in addition to the market price of other players. This salary corresponds to the valuation and the negotiations on conditions in a company acquisition.

When negotiations are held with several teams to acquire a player, the team with the most funds has the advantage. Similarly, when several companies compete for an acquisition, the buyer with the greatest financial strength is in the best position to advance the negotiations.

However, it cannot be said that the team will have achieved its objectives for the future simply by acquiring a powerful player. The team must not merely strengthen its roster of players, it must convert this player acquisition into improved "team fighting strength" by focusing on how to incorporate him into the rotation and relief pitching, if he is a pitcher, and into the batting order, if he is a batter.

As the team's objective is to win and to keep on winning, the general manager and the manager will consider a strategy and the weapons (players) at their disposal for a long season. It is essential that they consider a long-term strategy to build a stable team.

A baseball team's objective of continuing to win games can be replaced with a company's objective of achieving sustainable profit growth. If a team keeps on winning, it will increase spectator numbers and its exposure in the media. As a result, the value of the team goes up. Enhancing the roster of players is an investment in order to win.

Therefore, there are cases that can be described as failures, such as when a player's performance is poor causing him to return to his home country (or when he must return home for other reasons), or even when the player himself has performed well, but he cannot function as part of the team and the team ends up in a low position in the league table. These cases are the same as a company acquisition that failed to generate the anticipated synergy after an acquisition and in which the buyer ultimately withdraws from the acquired business.

A case in which the team is strengthened by an expensive powerful batter, but still does not function is similar to the failure of a large-scale acquisition and the recording of an extraordinary loss soon after.

However, on the other hand, if the acquired foreign player contributes to his team's pennant race and to victories by playing a key role as a relief pitcher or clean-up hitter that raises the team's scoring ability, the acquisition of foreign talent can be said to have been a success. In the same way, if through the outbound acquisition the target company complements the acquiring company's existing businesses, increases its competitiveness, and results in profit growth, the acquisition will have been a success for that acquiring company.

Two things can be said from this comparison of M&A with the acquisition of players by baseball teams. The first is that the success or failure in strengthening the team is not determined at the time the player is acquired, but when the team finishes the season. It is more important to look at how the team performs after the acquisition. To say this in terms of a company acquisition, the success or failure of an acquisition is not determined at the time the transaction is completed, but by the resulting operating performance after the acquisition. The second is that rather than the scout-focused player acquisition process and related expertise, what is most important is a team building strategy with strengthening as a prerequisite as well as leadership after the team has added players.

In outbound acquisitions, rather than the negotiations and the valuation techniques at the time of the acquisition, what is most important is a strategy that depicts how the target business will complement the acquiring company's operations and grow profits together with integration management expertise after the acquisition. Company management and baseball teams are the same in that an acquisition is meaningless unless the whole operation can function and continue to win after players have been added.

Financial or legal expertise to complete a transaction is important, but it does not secure the success of an acquisition. A successful acquisition involves a strategy leading to profit growth and integration management after the acquisition. Therefore, in this book, I want to advance the discussions focusing on strategies of acquiring companies and their management after acquisition.

1.4 The 30 Years Since Japanese Outbound Acquisitions Became Full-Fledged

Considering the essential factors behind success and failure.

Japanese overseas acquisitions became full-fledged upon the appreciation of the yen due to the 1985 Plaza Accord and trade friction with the United States and Europe. It was necessary for Japanese companies to start production overseas instead of exporting from home in order to minimize the impact of trade friction on currency and duties. In the second half of the 1980s, there were a series of large-scale Japanese outbound acquisitions, with Sony acquiring US Columbia Pictures, Bridgestone acquiring the major US tire manufacturer Firestone, and Seibu Saison acquiring InterContinental Hotels. I think many people still remember these acquisitions as they were widely reported at that time.

As there had also been speculative investments in hotels and buildings overseas during Japan's bubble period, we tend to think all the acquisitions at that time were the same. However, even at that time, companies were conducting acquisitions in order to accelerate their overseas business development. This objective has hardly changed for Japanese companies, even today.

The management environment in the late 1980s was very similar to that of today. Japanese companies held ample cash reserves, and Japanese banks had a strong willingness to lend. The yen was strong, and companies reported record high profits from their domestic businesses during the bubble period, therefore, many managers sought growth overseas. Conversely, on the other side of the Pacific in the United States, conglomerate corporations were reconsidering their strategies of diversification, while the government was advancing deregulation in fields such as communications and the banking sector. These efforts coincided with a rapid increase in the import of goods manufactured overseas and businesses for sale alongside industry restructuring. Therefore, there were lots of acquisition opportunities in United States for Japanese companies.

Compared to that time, Japanese companies today have become more familiar with the M&A process, and they are able to prudently use experts like bankers, accountants, and attorneys for due diligence and negotiations to complete transactions. Some companies even have their own in-house M&A team. Despite this, however, there has been an endless stream of companies whose outbound acquisitions ended in failure, and more than several cases in which they incurred significant losses. It would seem that Japanese companies are repeating the same mistakes.

"Why did the acquisition end in failure?" Further, "What can be done to make an outbound acquisition a success?" In this book, we will seek the answers to these fundamental questions on a dimension different from that of the techniques in the acquisition process. The history of overseas M&A is still short at 30 years, but despite this short history, company managers today can learn many things from the outcomes of the overseas acquisitions conducted thus far. I want us to find lessons for success, not from M&A technical expertise, but rather from the strategy and management of Japanese companies that took on the challenge after past acquisitions.

Notes

1. Takeda Pharmaceuticals press release, May 19, 2011.
2. SoftBank press release, June 26, 2013.
3. Suntory Holdings press release, January 13, 2014.
4. After conducting the acquisition, refinancing was carried out, including a subordinate loan.
5. Suntory Holdings press release, January 13, 2014.
6. NTT DoCoMo press release, April 25, 2014.

PART I

The Nature of Failure

CHAPTER 2

The Five Pitfalls

Revisiting Conventional Wisdom on Outbound Acquisition

2.1 The Five Benefits of Acquisition Sought by Managers

Buying time, capturing market share, generating synergies, acquiring local talent, and taking advantage of the strong yen

When announcing the acquisition of an overseas business, Japanese companies often talk about obtaining the following benefits:

1. Buying time
2. Capturing global market share
3. Generating synergies
4. Acquiring competent local managers and engineers
5. Taking advantage of the strong yen

These benefits and rationales are frequently introduced in M&A textbooks, and investment bankers often mention them when they propose an acquisition to clients. The specific objectives of each rationale are as follows.

Buying time means that, compared to a green field advance into a market (through the company's own investment), an acquisition enables the acquiring company to build a beachhead into the local market in a short period of time. It takes time for a company on its own to develop sales networks, establish production bases, and have its brand take root

S. Matsumoto, *Japanese Outbound Acquisitions*,
https://doi.org/10.1007/978-981-13-1364-6_2

locally. While it is possible to estimate the time and funds required to build production bases, it is difficult to predict the time required to develop sales channels locally and whether or not those efforts will be successful. Thus, it is considered preferable to "buy time" by acquiring a company that includes brands and sales channels that are already known locally.

Many managers cite capturing global market share as a benefit of an overseas acquisition based on the scenario that they will not only become more influential in the industry, but also improve profitability through utilizing economies of scale. There have been many cases where mid-ranked companies, in terms of global market share, rose into the upper ranks through an acquisition. Moreover, the media's reporting of an acquisition often illustrates the global market share with a pie chart after the acquisition is announced.

Synergy is the advantage managers most frequently refer to when they explain how the acquisition will benefit their company. There are companies who even announce potential synergy amounts in dollars to justify how promising their deals are. They argue that they can generate synergy by increasing sales of their products through the use of the target company's distribution networks, reducing cost through the consolidation of duplicate sales and production bases, and combining purchasing efforts. The greater the anticipated synergy effects the more attractive the deal seems to managers.

Many managers also see the value of an acquisition from being able to acquire competent local managers and engineers. A company may not have the appropriate manager to develop the market and undertake management in their targeted regions. Thus, if it can welcome into its group managers from the target company who are fully familiar with the local market environment and who have a good track record in that industry, business development becomes more promising. Rather than sending managers from headquarters in Japan with different cultures and customs, it may make more sense to have reliable local managers run the business.

During phases in which the yen is strong, the impression spreads among managers in Japan that overseas companies targeted for acquisition are undervalued, and during these phases the number of overseas acquisitions increases (refer to Fig. 2.1). Against the backdrop of the historically strong yen, the number of overseas acquisitions (IN-OUT, Japanese acquisitions outside of Japan) reached a record high of 515 in 2012. This figure

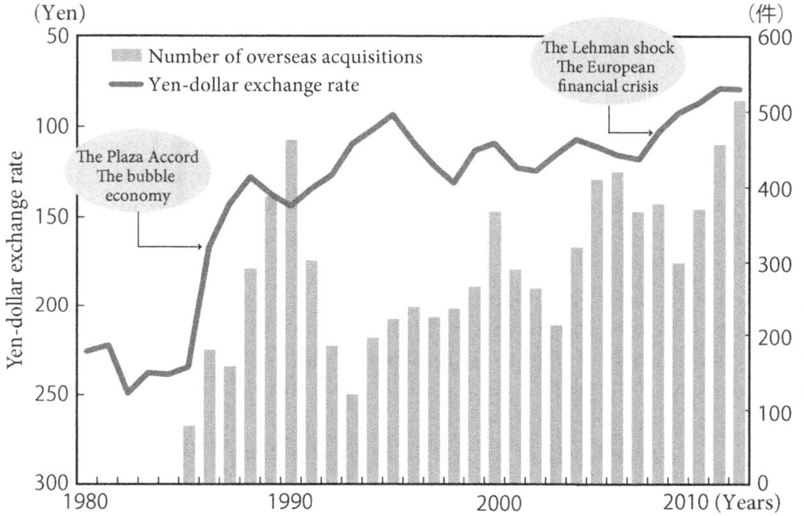

Fig. 2.1 Trends in the exchange rate and the number of overseas acquisitions. (Bank of Japan exchange rate statistical data and Thomson Reuters data)

exceeded the previous high of 463 in 1990, 22 years earlier, when the yen was strong due to the Plaza Accord, and the economic bubble was at its peak. Both figures were a result of the strong yen pushing managers to take action.

These five rationales are often the decisive factors when managers conduct an outbound acquisition. When a company plans to expand its business overseas, an acquisition target can appear as a once-in-a-lifetime opportunity. However, these benefits can cause them to lose their perspective, and with the time constraints of a deal process, they plunge forward.

However, there had been many cases where, after the acquisition was conducted based on those expected benefits, the target company's business slumped to the extent that it had an adverse impact on the acquiring company's results, and even prompting the acquiring company to withdraw from or sell that business. There are pitfalls hidden behind the benefits of outbound acquisitions. In this chapter, we start to carefully describe the benefits of outbound acquisitions as well as the traps lying in wait within them.

2.2 Three Case Studies Illustrating the Pitfalls Within the Potential Benefits

Bridgestone, Nippon Sheet Glass, and Furukawa Electric

There are cases of overseas acquisitions in which leading Japanese companies, despite the clear appearance of benefits at the time of the acquisition, found themselves in predicaments after the acquisition. Below, I introduce three deals, their benefits, and the traps they fell into.

1. Acquisition of Firestone by Bridgestone
2. Acquisition of Pilkington by Nippon Sheet Glass
3. Acquisition of Lucent Technologies' fiber-optic cable business by Furukawa Electric

Acquisition of Firestone by Bridgestone (1988)

Bridgestone is the world's largest tire company today. It is also one of the most successful Japanese companies in the United States, and its founder, Mr. Shojiro Ishibashi, was inducted into the United States Automotive Hall of Fame in 2006.

Bridgestone began local production in the United States following its acquisition of the Nashville factory producing truck and bus radial (TBR) tires from major the US tire manufacturer Firestone in 1982. Then, alongside the strong yen after the Plaza Accord in 1985 and Japan-US trade friction, Japan's major auto manufacturers, including Toyota and Honda, began full-fledged local production in the United States. In this context, Bridgestone acquired Firestone through a tender offer. At that time, the US tire industry was undergoing a restructuring, and Bridgestone attempted the tender offer in competition with the Italian tire manufacturer Pirelli, which was also aiming to acquire Firestone.

Other Japanese tire companies also acquired tire companies in the United States in the 1980s, Sumitomo Rubber acquired Dunlop in 1986 and Yokohama Rubber purchased Mohawk Rubber in 1989.

Through its acquisition of Firestone, Bridgestone obtained 21 tire factories, a customer base including Ford and GM, the Smart Care network of 1500 direct sales tire stores, and 1000 affiliated dealerships. In an instant, through this acquisition, its tire sales leaped to a level comparable with those of the global leaders Michelin and Goodyear. Bridgestone

President Akira Yeiri, who decided on the acquisition, said, "We considered it would take too long to expand our sales network by ourselves, and also if Firestone was acquired by Pirelli, the opportunity to develop business in the United States would be lost forever, so I decided to buy time with this acquisition."[1]

In the deal to acquire Firestone, Bridgestone was aiming for some of the major benefits from an outbound acquisition, in particular buying time in order to quickly expand its US business and capturing market share to join Michelin and Goodyear in forming the "Big Three" in the global tire market (refer to Fig. 2.2). After the acquisition, it maintained Firestone as a corporate entity and the management was entrusted to Firestone Chairman and President John Nevin. Thus, Bridgestone planned to make use of the local management.

However, Bridgestone was forced to tread a thorny path in the management of Firestone immediately after its acquisition. First, as Firestone had become a subsidiary of Bridgestone, GM notified Firestone that it was terminating its tire supply contract. This event pertained to the Japan-US trade friction at that time, and in particular, the severity of the friction in the automotive industry. The termination of this supply contract cost Firestone around 100 million dollars in sales. As Bridgestone suddenly found itself with excess production capacity in the United States, it was forced to start its post-acquisition management of Firestone with an operating loss.

Further, around 500, or one-third, of the stores in the Firestone's Smart Care retail network were also operating at a loss and the situation was worsening. Bridgestone announced that it would invest 1.5 billion dollars in restructuring Firestone over three years, and that in addition to this capital investment, it would actively provide technical support from Japan. However, despite these efforts, Firestone's results did not improve, and in 1990, two years after the acquisition, Firestone's after-tax loss reached 350 million dollars.

Because of this situation, Bridgestone President Yeiri announced a policy change. Bridgestone was originally saying that "in principle, management is to be carried out by the current Firestone management team." However, in 1991, Bridgestone Vice President Yoichiro Kaizaki was appointed CEO of Firestone to replace the Firestone management, which had failed to put the brakes on its deteriorating results. At that time, the cost of restructuring Firestone was soaring, and Bridgestone's balance of interest-bearing debt had risen to 700 billion yen, while the group's

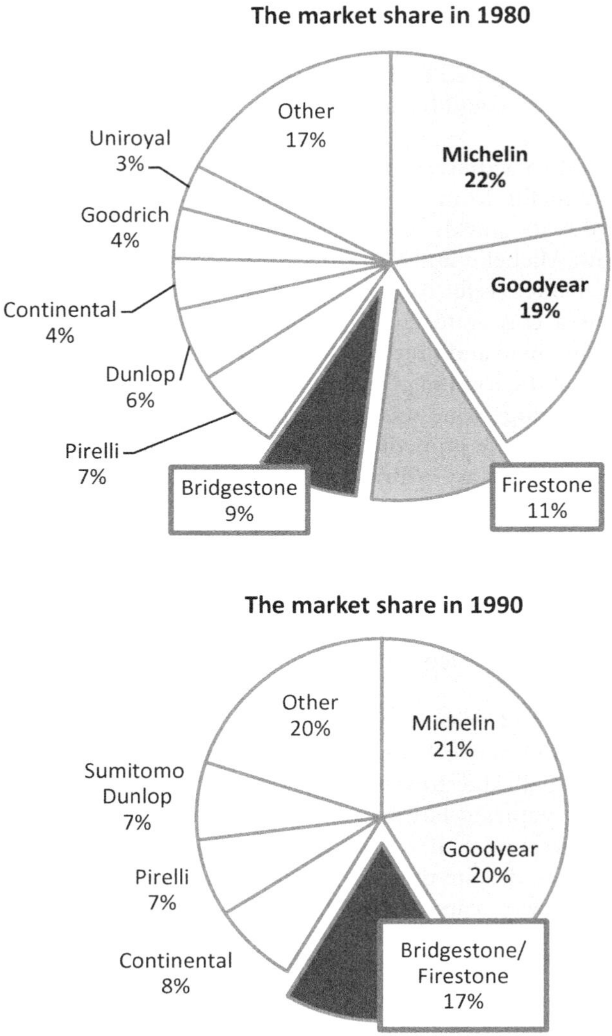

Fig. 2.2 Global tire market share. (The Japan Rubber Yearbook)

operating profit had also fallen. With its acquisition of Firestone, Bridgestone had succeeded in becoming one of the Big Three in terms of scale, but the results continued to deteriorate after the acquisition, and it found itself with its back to the wall to the extent that it was uncertain whether its business in the United States, which was the world's largest automotive market, could even survive. In 1992, Bridgestone relocated the Firestone headquarters from Akron, Ohio, to Nashville, Tennessee; reduced employee numbers by 2500 people; and changed its name to Bridgestone Firestone (BFS), with the intention of making a fresh start with management. It overcame a long labor strike lasting 270 days from 1994 to 1995, which paved the way to addressing the pressing labor union issue. The restructuring initiated by the Bridgestone management finally began to produce results, and in the second half of the 1990s, Firestone started to record an operating profit on a single fiscal year basis.

Although Bridgestone's US business seemed to be back on track, it faced another problem with the frequent rollover accidents involving the Ford Explorer, which was equipped with Firestone tires. In 2000, it announced a voluntary recall of 14.4 million tires. In addition to the recall of tires, Bridgestone's results were severely impacted by the dispute with Ford over the cause of the accidents. In 2001, it reached a settlement with the US legal authorities, but the business relationship with Ford that had lasted nearly 100 years ended, and it recorded an operating loss of 33.5 billion yen in its US segment.

Can we say that Bridgestone realized the benefits from its outbound acquisition of Firestone? Today, 30 years after the acquisition, we understand that the acquisition of Firestone to a certain extent played a role in the success of Bridgestone's North American business.

However, upon looking at the trends in the operating profit margin and the balance of interest-bearing debt after the acquisition, we can see that Bridgestone did not realize its originally envisaged benefit of "buying time" for its North American business expansion because it became caught up in the restructuring of Firestone (refer to Fig. 2.3). Further, although it increased its global market share on par with those of Michelin and Goodyear that time, far from improving profits, the move actually resulted in a huge loss.

In addition, immediately after the acquisition, Bridgestone targeted synergy effects between its tire production business in Japan and Firestone's production sites, such as through a sister factory system, but this move also did not immediately lead to improved results. Further, a few years

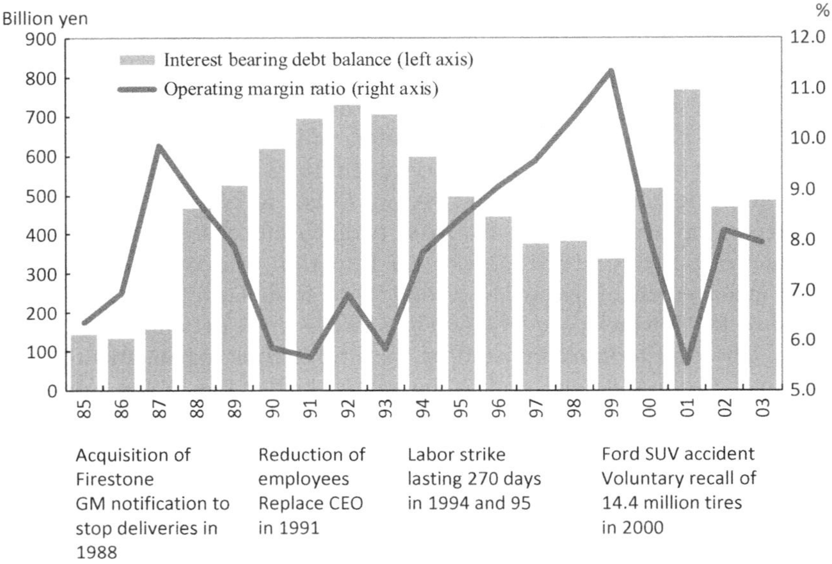

Fig. 2.3 Trends in Bridgestone's operating profit margin and balance of interest-bearing debt (1987–2003). (Prepared by the author from the Bridgestone annual reports (1987–2003) and company information)

after the acquisition, it had to replace the local US management team to which it had entrusted management after the acquisition.

This case study of the acquisition of Firestone by Bridgestone shows that it is not easy to realize the benefits of outbound acquisition and that various traps lay in wait within these benefits.

The Acquisition of Pilkington by Nippon Sheet Glass (2006)

The acquisition of Pilkington by Nippon Sheet Glass in 2006 is another case study that shows that the benefits from an overseas M&A will not necessarily be realized in the short term.

The deal in which Nippon Sheet Glass acquired Pilkington has been described as a touchstone for the global business expansion of Japanese companies, as an acquisition in which David beats Goliath, as Pilkington's sales at that time were more than twice those of Nippon Sheet Glass. In

2000, Nippon Sheet Glass had invested in 10% of Pilkington, and raised its ownership stake to 20% in 2001. Thus, by the time of the acquisition in 2006, the two companies already had a partnership, and to a certain extent, Nippon Sheet Glass is considered to have already understood Pilkington's operations.

At the time of the acquisition, the rationale for Nippon Sheet Glass to conduct this transaction was to become a global flat glass supplier and to take advantage of economies of scale by integrating the two operations. It explained that the objectives of the acquisition were to become "a company with a global presence," and moreover, to maximize the synergy effects with Pilkington in fields in which they have accumulated high-level development and technological capabilities.[2]

In the deal to acquire Pilkington, Nippon Sheet Glass aimed for the benefit of "buying time" to become a global flat glass supplier by capturing the global market share. It also announced that both companies would reduce costs by 4.4 billion yen a year, as a specific numerical goal to help achieve synergy effects. After the acquisition, it actively appointed members of the former Pilkington management team and aimed to utilize those competent local managers.

However, management after the acquisition did not proceed as planned. While in 2007, the year immediately after the acquisition, Nippon Sheet Glass achieved increases in both sales and profits in its financial results, it recorded a net loss for the next two consecutive years. Further, the production facilities and personnel it was saddled with in the Pilkington acquisition became a heavy burden in the operations following the decline in demand due to the European financial crisis, and it recorded a loss for five consecutive fiscal periods from fiscal year 2011 (refer to Fig. 2.4). Also, because of the continued poor performance, Nippon Sheet Glass has struggled to pay back its heavy debt that it borrowed for the acquisition and has not recovered its capital structure (refer to Fig. 2.5). During this time, the global financial crisis, especially in Europe, undoubtedly had an adverse impact on Pilkington's business. However, the fact that Nippon Sheet Glass recorded losses five times in the seven years after the acquisition cannot be explained by the global financial crisis alone, because other major glass suppliers, like Asahi Glass, recovered their performance immediately after the crisis. So, where did it stumble after the acquisition?

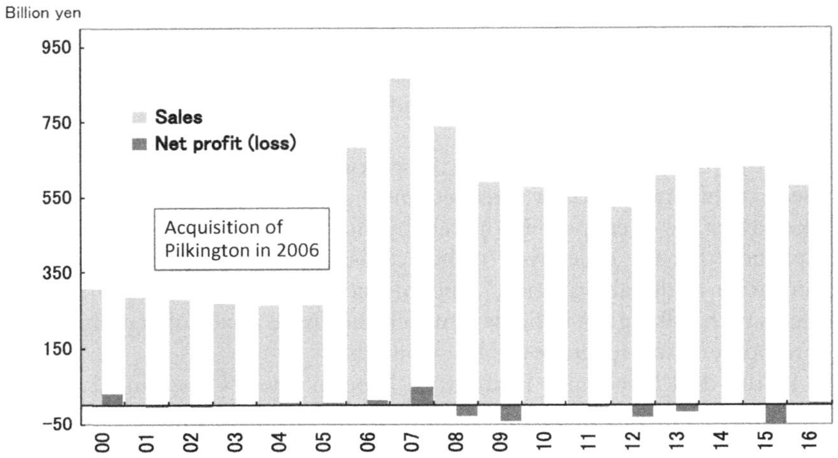

Fig. 2.4 Nippon Sheet Glass sales and net profit (2000–2016). (Nippon Sheet Glass annual securities report 2000–2016)

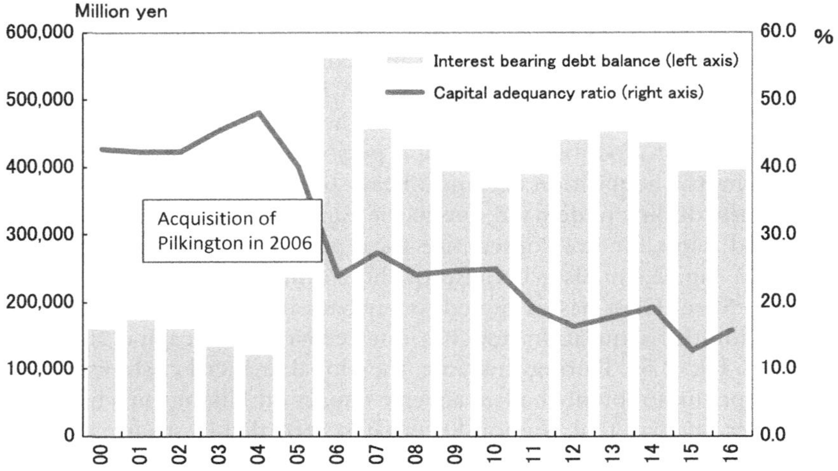

Fig. 2.5 Trends in Nippon Sheet Glass interest-bearing debt balance and capital adequacy ratio (2000–2016). (Nippon Sheet Glass annual securities report 2000–2016)

Reference materials: Nippon Sheet Glass press release

NSG to proceed with recommended cash acquisition of Pilkington plc. February 27, 2006

Nippon Sheet Glass Co., Ltd. ("NSG") announces that its board of directors has today resolved to proceed with a recommended cash acquisition of the entire issued share capital of the major British glass maker, Pilkington plc. (Head Office: St Helens, United Kingdom; CEO: Stuart Chambers) ("Pilkington") to make it a wholly owned subsidiary of NSG (the "Transaction").

Pilkington is a 20% owned affiliated company and global business partner of NSG. The formal announcement of the Transaction will be made today in London in compliance with local rules and regulations.

Following the completion of this Transaction, the combination of NSG and Pilkington will be a global leader in the flat glass industry with the largest market share in the world (NSG estimates) and approximately 760 billion yen of sales. NSG will be further strengthened with increased competitiveness in costs, quality, and service and able to take full advantage of enhanced economies of scale and combined technologies. Given these expected achievements, NSG believes that this Transaction will significantly enhance shareholder value.

The Transaction is a friendly acquisition and is being recommended by Pilkington's board. Pilkington's CEO and other key management members have agreed to continue their commitment to Pilkington and NSG group management post-Transaction.

Post-Transaction, Pilkington will be maintained as an NSG consolidated subsidiary and at the appropriate time, there will be a transition to a group management structure to maximize the benefit of synergies between the two companies.

(Omission)

Post-Transaction group management structure and synergies between the two companies

Post-Transaction, Pilkington will be maintained as an NSG consolidated subsidiary and at the appropriate time, there will be a transition to a group management structure to maximize the benefit of synergies between the two companies. In terms of the expected synergies, approximately 4.4 billion yen per year of short-term pre-tax synergies are expected within three years of closing. This will include integration of engineering and development functions to eliminate surplus resources, combined purchasing power, improvement of facility utilization through optimized production allocation, cooperative float glass productions between the two companies, integration of marketing offices, [and] improvement of performance at plants through exchange of existing technologies.

In the longer term, the following is expected: innovation and improvement of manufacturing processes, development of new and value-added products, and improvement of quality levels and cost competitiveness.

With the acquisition, Nippon Sheet Glass captured the global market share and became second only to Asahi Glass in the field of automotive and architectural flat glass. At the same time, in terms of the sales by region of Nippon Sheet Glass, before the acquisition, the Japanese market accounted for more than 80% of its sales, but after the acquisition, Europe accounted for 40% and Japan only 30%. Refer to Fig. 2.6. In other words, rather than capturing a share of the global market, it can be said to have purchased a share of the European market. Increasing market share in a specific region makes a company's entire operation very susceptible to changes in that region's business environment.

In the economic recession that followed the European financial crisis, the European production bases and personnel that Nippon Sheet Glass obtained in the acquisition instantly became excess capacities, and its European sales were cut in half. In this situation, it was forced to concentrate its management resources to restructuring Pilkington. It announced personnel reductions of 5800 people in 2009 and 3500 people in 2012, and its equity ratio fell to as low as 15%. The synergy effects from the cost reductions, initially estimated at 4.4 billion yen, were also lost, and the benefit of "buying time" became hard to see as Nippon Sheet Glass became caught up in the management restructuring of the company it had acquired.

Nippon Sheet Glass attempted to actively utilize the Pilkington personnel it had acquired. In 2008, two years after the acquisition, Pilkington President Stewart Chambers was appointed Nippon Sheet Glass President and CEO, and he was entrusted with achieving the goal of steering the company on a course to become the global leading company in terms of scale, profits, and financial performance. At the same time, Nippon Sheet Glass welcomed four out of the eight directors from Pilkington, excluding outside directors. The president at that time, Katsuji Fujimoto, explained the background for this decision, saying, "Nippon Sheet Glass is no longer a company focused on Japan."[3]

However, this appointment also failed to achieve the results that were hoped for. After his appointment, President Chambers replaced many of the Nippon Sheet Glass Japanese executives with foreigners and decided to reduce production capacity and personnel numbers, but he then resigned one year after his appointment to "put family first and company second." Mr. Chambers had joined Pilkington in 1996, and from 2002 to 2006, had served as its Group Chief Executive. Despite this impressive track record, he did not prove to possess any loyalty to Nippon

Fig. 2.6 Regional percentages of Nippon Sheet Glass sales. (The Nippon Sheet Glass annual securities report)

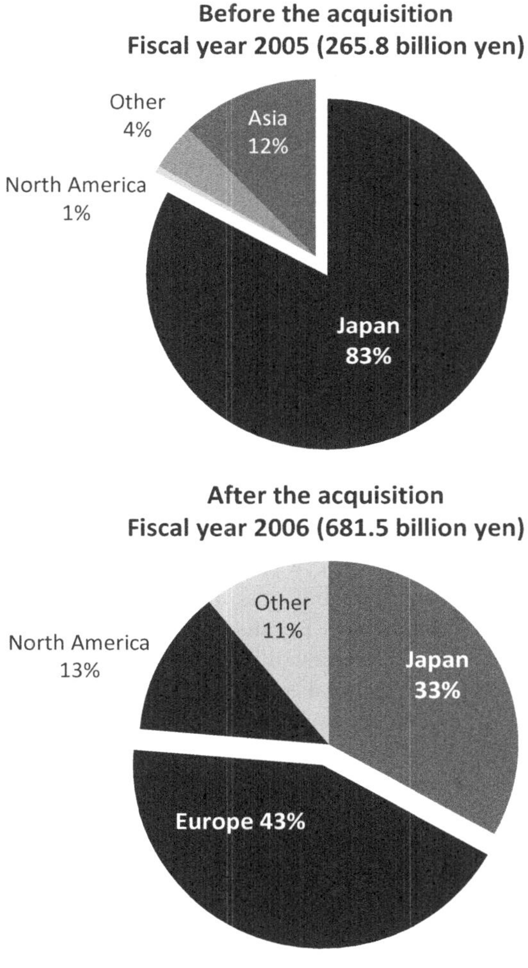

Sheet Glass. Subsequently, a vice president of the US chemical manufacturer DuPont was appointed as the second foreign president, but he also resigned after two years. In 2012, a Nippon Sheet Glass career company man, Keiji Yoshikawa, was appointed as its president, and with regard to the slumping management performance after the acquisition of Pilkington, he said, "We lacked the competence to control a company larger than ourselves."[4]

Ten years have passed since Nippon Sheet Glass acquired Pilkington. Nippon Sheet Glass still struggles to improve its financial performance, but it is still too early to tell if the acquisition has been a success or failure. As previously described, even in the tenth year after the acquisition, Bridgestone was still restructuring Firestone. Nippon Sheet Glass possesses technological capabilities and a powerful customer base, including Japanese major automakers, so it is considered fully able to recover from the losses up to the present time, and it would be premature to label the acquisition a failure based on the current situation.

However, if we look at the post-acquisition management of Nippon Sheet Glass, we once again can understand that it is not easy to realize the benefits that conventional wisdom says an outbound acquisition will provide: the benefits of "buying time," increasing global market share, generating synergy, and acquiring a competent local management team.

The Acquisition of Lucent Technologies' Fiber-Optic Cable Business by Furukawa Electric (2001)

Furukawa Electric was focusing on its wavelength division multiplexing (WDM) devices business, in which multiple optical signals are sent over fiber-optic cables. Because the fiber optics market was growing rapidly in the 1990s, Furukawa Electric was shifting its management resources away from the electrical wiring business to concentrate on its optics-related business. Then, Furukawa Electric was sounded out by Lucent for the sale of its fiber-optic cables business due to their poor financial performance. Lucent has been reducing capital investment in fiber optics because of the slump of the US telecommunications sector in 2000. When Furukawa Electric completed its transaction, President Junnosuke Furukawa summarized the negotiations for the acquisition, saying, "We cannot afford to miss this once-in-a-lifetime opportunity with great potential for the future."[5] Many of the patents for fiber-optic technologies, such as large-capacity seabed cables, were owned by Corning and Lucent, both of which had a contract for the mutual use of the other's cables. This meant that there were limitations placed on Japanese companies, including Furukawa Electric, for new product development and sales. In fact, Corning and Lucent together held close to a 50% share of the global market for fiber optics-related products (refer to Fig. 2.7).

Through its acquisition of Lucent, Furukawa Electric would obtain its patents and technologies and become able to manufacture and sell fiber-optic products throughout the world. In other words, its fiber-optic cable business had been limited up to that time to Japan and part of Asia, so it was aiming for the benefit of "buying time" to develop its business globally, including in the United States. Also, Furukawa Electric sought economies of scale by increasing its global market share in fiber-optic products; leaving behind its domestic competitors Sumitomo Electric Industries and Fujikura to become second only to Corning globally. President Furukawa said that "Japanese manufacturers have only been able to produce general purpose fibers, called single mode, but with the acquisition of the patents, we will be able to manufacture and sell globally high-value-added products, such as fibers for WDM systems. We can generate synergy from the fiber-optic cable and the WDM parts business."[6] On the other hand, with regard to management after the acquisition, he commented that "There remain concerns about whether Furukawa can conduct a global fiber-optic business by itself."[7] It established a joint venture with the major US cable company CommScope, to which it transferred the business after the acquisition and to which it outsourced sales. Through the acquisition, Furukawa Electric inherited a business with 10 production bases and 4200 employees around the world.

However, Furukawa Electric faced problems managing Lucent's fiber-optic cable business just six months after the acquisition. The recession in the communications sector, centered in North America, caused a freeze in

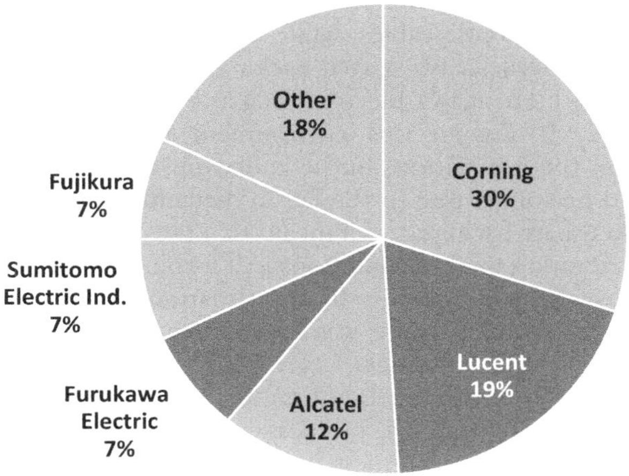

Fig. 2.7 Fiber optics-related products global market share (2000). (Nihon Keizai Shimbun 2001)

global demand for fiber optics, and the utilization rate of the 10 factories it acquired fell to around 20%. In its financial results announcement for fiscal year 2001, then Managing Director Wada explained the sudden deterioration in the market conditions as "An eventuality that occurs once every 100 years." Subsequently, the decline in demand for fiber optics continued, and sales of the Lucent business, which had exceeded 200 billion yen at the time of the acquisition, had fallen dramatically to 30 billion yen by fiscal year 2002. As a result, Furukawa Electric's information and communications business segment reported an operating loss of over 60 billion yen.

Furukawa Electric began to consolidate the factories and reduce employees, but it could not keep up with the decline in the fiber-optic cable business, and in fiscal year 2003, it had to downwardly revise its forecasts four times. It finally recorded a consolidated loss of 141.9 billion yen and failed to pay a dividend for the first time in 54 years, and it recorded an extraordinary loss of 162.5 billion yen as an impairment loss in the fiber-optic cable business (refer to Fig. 2.8).

By acquiring Lucent business with its patents and technologies, Furukawa Electric took on the challenge of developing its business globally, but it fundamentally misread the global market demand. In 2001, the year of the acquisition negotiations, it was apparent that one part of the market had already entered an adjustment phase. For example, Corning, the largest company in the industry, had suspended its production of fiber-optic cables, while CommScope, which was reliant on its fiber optics sales, also started backing out at the beginning of the cooperation with Furukawa Electric, such as by lowering its stake in the joint venture. It was in this environment that Furukawa Electric embarked on the acquisition, but it ended up with excess production facilities and personnel due to the fall in demand. The expansion of its global market share backfired, as it meant that the company was impacted by the deteriorating market conditions in a form many times larger than it would have been previously. In the situation of a rapid decline in demand for fiber optics, there was little prospect to generate synergy with the existing WDM business.

It was four years after the acquisition, in 2005, that Furukawa's information and communications business segment, which includes the acquired fiber-optic cable business, became profitable again for a single fiscal year, and since then, it has been able to stably record profits, if only

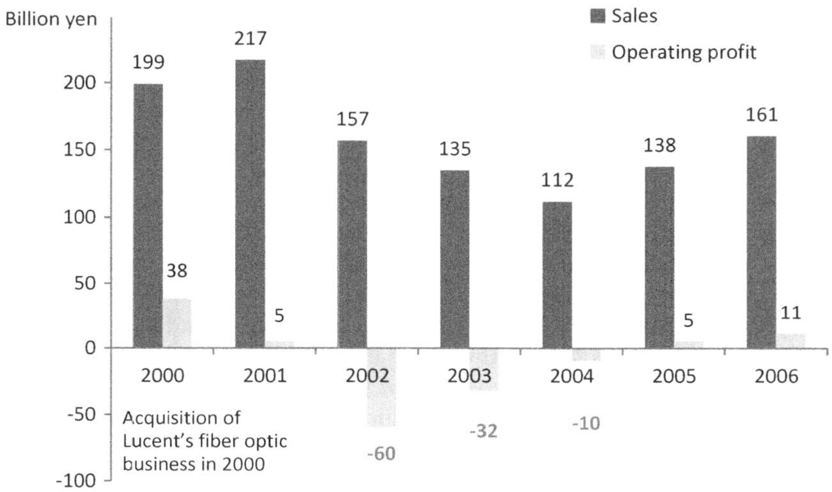

Fig. 2.8 Trends in Furukawa Electric information communications business segment, 2000–2006. (The Furukawa Electric annual report 2000–2006)

on a small scale. Indeed, the situation in the information and communications business has improved in recent years. However, this outbound acquisition shows that the benefit of increasing global market share that Furukawa Electric aimed for might, on the contrary, cause the acquiring company to find itself in a predicament if the market conditions suddenly change for the worse after the acquisition.

2.3 Is an Acquisition a Good Deal When the Yen Is Strong?

Managers' judgment can be clouded when the target appears to be a bargain

As we can see from Fig. 2.1, Japanese acquisitions increase when the yen is strong. In general, Japanese companies have ample funds, and Japanese banks are also willing to provide the financing to fund acquisitions. When the yen strengthens, the seller, shareholders of target companies, and investment banks come to expect that Japanese companies will acquire at high prices. In addition, when the yen is strong, the media in Japan tends to advocate the merits of overseas acquisitions, which is no different today than it was during the economic bubble period in the second half of the 1980s. Many companies have cited outbound acquisitions in their management plans as a means of realizing a growth strategy. During the phase of a historically strong yen, the atmosphere becomes one in which even managers with no experience conducting overseas acquisitions think that now might be a good time to start.

So, does an outbound acquisition conducted when the yen is strong take advantage of the opportunity provided by a "bargain" target company? Since little time has passed for the acquisitions conducted after the global financial crisis during the phase in which the yen was strong, it is still too early to evaluate whether or not those transactions have been successful. Therefore, I investigated the current conditions of Japanese outbound acquisitions that were conducted when the yen was strong in the second half of the 1980s.

Between 1985 and 1990, there were 71 acquisitions in which the purchase price was 10 billion yen or more (excluding financial institutions, real estate, and natural resource sectors). In 35, or nearly half, of these cases, the acquiring company has already withdrawn from or sold the acquired business.

Moreover, of these cases, there were even those in which the acquiring company went bankrupt after the acquisition, and many in which an acquisition that appeared to be a bargain resulted in a major loss for the acquiring company.

Up to the present time, the year with the highest number of overseas acquisitions was 1990, during which there were 19 acquisitions worth 10 billion yen or more. However, in 12 of these cases, the acquiring company has already withdrawn from or sold the business or had gone bankrupt (refer to Table 2.1).

Acquisitions in the United States included National Steel by NKK and Dataproducts by Hitachi Koki. National Steel subsequently went bankrupt and was sold to US Steel, while Hitachi Koki withdrew from the printer business. In Europe, Mitsubishi Electric acquired the computer business of the UK computer manufacturer Apricot and made an additional investment after the acquisition, but subsequently, it withdrew from the business. Renown acquired the prestigious UK men's apparel company Aquascutum and held on to it for a long period, over 20 years, after the acquisition, but its results did not improve, and it finally sold the business.

Table 2.1 Japanese outbound acquisitions in 1990 (acquisitions of 10 billion yen or more, excluding real estate, financial institutions, and natural resource sectors)

Acquiring company	*Target*	*Result*
Fujitsu	ICL	Continued holding
Kyocera	AVX	Continued holding
Panasonic	MCA	Sold
Hitachi Koki	Dataproducts	Sold
Anritsu	Wiltron	Continued holding
Nissei Electric	Arcotronics	Bankrupt
Mitsubishi Electric	Apricot	Withdrawal
Fuji Xerox	Rank Xerox	Continued holding
Ishihara Sangyo	SDS Enterprises	Sold
Mitsubishi Co	Aristech Chemical	Sold
Mitsubishi Kasei	Verbatim	Withdrawal
Onoda Cement	California Portland Cement	Continued holding
Seven & i	Southland (Seven Eleven Inc.)	Continued holding
Kyotaru	Restaurant Associates Paragon Steakhouse	Bankrupt
Renown	Aquascutum	Sold
NKK (JFE)	National Steal	Sold
NSK	UPI	Sold
CSK	Micro gnosis	Unknown

Prepared by the author from Thomson Reuters, company press releases

In each of these cases, the acquiring company recorded major losses from the withdrawal or sale. There are even cases in which the acquiring company itself was forced into bankruptcy after the acquisition, such as Kyotaru and NISSEI Electric.

I investigated overseas acquisitions worth 10 billion yen or more conducted between 1985 and 2001, but I did not find any differences in the percentages of cases that ended in a withdrawal or sale after the acquisition during this entire period and the period when the yen was strong, from 1985 to 1990. Acquisitions made during a phase when the yen was strong that appeared to be a bargain in many cases conversely turned out to be costly.

A strong yen can be the trigger for managers to conduct an overseas M&A. However, many acquisitions conducted when the yen is strong end in failure, and it is not the case that the probability of success is any higher at such a time than at other times. Thus, when conducting an overseas acquisition, it is not a good idea to focus on the exchange rate at the time of the acquisition. As the percentage of the total business accounted by the overseas business increases after the acquisition, the consolidated results will become even more sensitive to changes in exchange rates. Thus, it is necessary to be aware of the unexpected pitfalls that lay in wait when conducting an acquisition solely because a target company appears to be a bargain owing to the exchange rate.

2.4 Correcting Illusions Surrounding Overseas Acquisitions

Preparing for the potential pitfalls

Up to this point, we have considered the validity of the benefits of outbound acquisitions based on actual cases by leading companies, such as Bridgestone.

By quickly launching an overseas business through acquisition, a company can increase global market share and expand its influence in the industry, improve its profit margin through synergy effects, and obtain management and engineering teams well versed in local conditions. These benefits accelerate business globalization and push managers in this direction. Further, when the yen is strong, the tendency is to view targets as a bargain and consider the time to be right for an acquisition.

Of course, it is without question that each of these is a benefit, but it is also necessary to be aware that what at first glance seems like a benefit of an overseas M&A may be a benefit that also contains a pitfall.

Company managers must be on the lookout for the pitfalls that lay in wait within the benefits of overseas acquisition and fully assess the feasibility of the benefits. Below, I explain the five benefits and their pitfalls as a summary of this chapter.

Time You Can "Buy" by an Acquisition and Time You Cannot Buy by Acquisition

The time that can be bought with an acquisition is the time up until business entry; an acquiring company cannot "buy time" up until the point that profit growth is achieved

The time that can be bought with an acquisition is that time up to the entry into a business, such as "the time required to build overseas production bases and a sales network," but it cannot buy "time as far as realizing profit growth overseas." Building business bases is not the same as achieving sustainable profit growth in the region the company entered.

In many cases, the business after the acquisition does not proceed as initially envisaged. There are cases when the target company's brand, sales network, and customer base were damaged after the acquisition. There are also cases in which the acquiring company gets caught up with quality problems at the production bases they acquired and in labor disputes with local employees. Consequently, the results of the acquired company may deteriorate, and if it has to restructure the acquired company, it may end up spending an enormous amount of time and management resources to do so.

Thus, even though the acquiring company intended to "buy time" with the acquisition, when it has to spend time restructuring the acquired company in order to get it on the right track, there are cases in which the company had to conversely detour onto a different track compared to if it had developed the business itself independently. In addition, while the possibility of a course correction is not an issue, there are examples of acquiring companies failing in the restructure and being forced to withdraw from the business. For example, when viewed from a long-term perspective, there is no doubt that for Bridgestone, the acquisition of Firestone became a solid foundation on which to build its business in the United States. However, in terms of whether it was able to "buy time" with the acquisition, it actually seems closer to reality that rather than "buying time," it actually "bought hardships" that ultimately led to its business development in the United States.

Through an outbound acquisition, the acquiring company can obtain local production bases and a sales network immediately. The time that is actually bought through the acquisition is the time up to the business entry, but what is more important for managers is the time up to achieve profit growth based on the assets they have acquired. This is time that cannot be bought simply by conducting an acquisition.

As a company spends enormous funds on an acquisition, it is required to deliver rapid profit growth compared with organic growth.

However, managers in the acquiring company need to carefully consider the time that can be bought through the acquisition and the time required until the objective of the acquisition is achieved. Even in a case in which a major local company becomes available for purchase, it is better not to think that it will be possible to easily "buy time" through the acquisition if the target is not profitable. If the company cannot restructure the target and improve its profitability, rather than buying time, the acquiring company may have to withdraw from the market or sell the business. A successful restructuring in cross-border acquisition, such as of Firestone by Bridgestone, is in fact quite an achievement.

Pitfall of Increasing Global Market Share

Expansion of market share can create excess capacity when market conditions deteriorate

A company can buy the global market share with an acquisition. When conducting an overseas acquisition, the spotlight is placed on the global market share of the target business, and in many cases, much is made of the fact that it ranks first or second in the world. Further, upon examining its own business portfolio, there are company managers who prioritize market share and consider it unacceptable if their company is not ranked first or second in the world.

However, even if it is enjoyable for managers to sit at their desks and see their company ascend to the upper ranks in industry, this achievement in itself will not lead to profit growth. Conversely, once the acquiring company comes to have large-scale production facilities and employees from the acquisition, if market conditions change after the acquisition, it will face bigger waves than it would have before the acquisition.

If we think in terms of the speculation of the seller, in the cases of a withdrawal from a business with a high market share, in many cases, the target company's ability to generate profits was inferior to those of its competitors. In cases of withdrawals from businesses in the middle or low rankings for market share, they were often a result of reading the changes in the market environment and industry structure. A divestiture or a withdrawal can become the trigger for a restructuring of the entire industry, but even if a company made an acquisition and increased its market share, it is not easy to improve profitability soon after the acquisition.

Conversely, there are buyers who are too preoccupied with market share and who underestimate the changes to the business environment in which the target company is located.

When market conditions become adverse, the portion by which market share has increased becomes the portion by which loss increases. When Furukawa Electric acquired the fiber-optic cable business, its competitor, Corning, had already suspended production due to the rapid decrease in demand, while Lucent itself had frozen its capital investment in information communications. Thus, the alarm bells should have been sounding for Furukawa Electric, but it embarked on the acquisition while observing these changes to the market conditions in North America. When the IT bubble collapsed immediately after the acquisition, the sales of the acquired business fell to one-fifth of their previous level. Compared to the operational bases developed by Furukawa Electric itself, it was difficult to restructure the organization, including production and distribution bases, it acquired from Lucent, so they were vulnerable to tremors such as deteriorating marketing conditions.

In research conducted in the United States, it has been noted that in the background of acquisitions there have been unexpected structural changes in specific industries (Andrade et al. 2001). Deregulation and the rapid increase in imports in the 1980s and 1990s caused changes to the business environment for the oil and gas, textile, rubber product, steel, banking, and media industries in the United States. As a result, the number of M&As increased, and consolidations were carried out. At that time, Japanese companies conducted a series of acquisitions of tire, steel, banking, and entertainment companies in the United States, but in the background to these acquisitions were the changes in the business environment due to deregulation.

When buying market share, it is necessary to be sensitive to changes in market conditions and seller speculation. While a market share situation close to oligopoly can be a source of competitive advantages, it is also necessary to be aware of the risks associated with increasing market share through acquisitions.

Pitfall of Cross-Border Synergy

An acquiring company can generate synergy by investing financial and human resources after the acquisition. The acquisition itself does not create synergy

Many managers expect to generate synergy when they decide to conduct overseas acquisitions. However, these synergies are not generated simply through an acquisition. Acquiring companies tend to overestimate the possibility of generating synergy effects and to underestimate the management resources that are required after the acquisition to realize these effects.

It is not easy to generate synergy owing to the differences in the management environments in a company acquired overseas and the existing domestic business in Japan. It is better to think that, at least in the short term, after an acquisition, synergy effects will not be generated in cross-border transactions. Often, the first place in which Japanese companies attempt to generate synergy after an acquisition is production sites where they excel. This goal takes the form of introducing their superior production bases into the target company with the aim of increasing its production efficiency and improving quality.

However, even if the two companies share only one part in common, if the country is different, the specifications and quality level required will also be different, so it will not be possible to adopt a newly introduced aspect immediately at work sites. Further, even if the latest production equipment is introduced, it will take time for this to translate into improved profits. For example, in the case of Bridgestone, it initially established a cooperative relationship system of sister factories between Firestone's main factories in the United States and its own factories in Japan and attempted to generate synergy effects. However, the results were limited because of the major differences in their corporate cultures and labor unions.[8]

Further, many companies attempt to generate synergy effects through using the acquired company's local distribution networks to sell their own products. They think that because their product is popular domestically in Japan, it will also undoubtedly sell well overseas if only they can acquire local sales channels through an acquisition. However, if they do not actually invest in marketing to ensure the product meets local preferences, it will not sell so easily.

This point can be understood if we consider the sales of the foreign products acquired overseas in Japan. For example, Suntory Beverage & Food Limited is currently attempting to generate synergy from the introduction of Orangina, the "national carbonated beverage" of France, which it acquired in 2009 in its home market. Awareness of this brand is excellent in Europe, and Suntory has a strong nationwide distribution network in Japan. Therefore, from desktop analysis, Suntory would sell Orangina in Japan even without marketing if it utilized its sales network. However, in actuality, sales began to grow only after it developed a large-scale domestic marketing campaign, including high profile commercials starring Richard Gere. Cross-border synergy cannot be generated after the acquisition without investing management resources in the target business over a long period.

Further, outbound acquisitions, aimed for diversification of the business, have more challenges to create synergies. In the examples of Japanese companies, when Matsushita Electric Industrial (Panasonic) acquired US entertainment giant Music Corporation of America (MCA), it advocated the "fusion of hardware and software," while when Yamanouchi Pharmaceuticals (Astellas Pharma) acquired US health foods manufacturer Shaklee, it stated that it was aiming for synergy effects "by using the food business as a foothold to accelerate the advance of our U.S. pharmaceuticals business."

For those transactions, these were "double" cross-border, between two countries and between two businesses. As both Matsushita and Yamanouchi failed to create the synergies they expected from the acquisitions, they sold their respective businesses at a loss.

Trap of Overconfidence in Local Managers

The acquiring company, not local managers, will be responsible for management after the acquisition

There is the tendency for a Japanese company in the acquisition negotiations to assume that there is a competent management team in the target company to which it will be able to confidently entrust local management after the acquisition.

As the target company's managers are well versed in the local business environment and have the strong trust of the target company's employees and customers, in many cases, the management after the acquisition remains with the current management team if no appropriate human resources can be found within the acquiring company to whom the management overseas can be entrusted.

Of course, up to the present time, there have been successful cases where the acquiring company was fortunate enough to have competent local managers to whom it was able to entrust the management after the acquisition in the long term, and who, based on their excellent performance, went on to become executive officers or directors in the acquiring company. However, these ideal cases are rare, and in several cases, entrusting management to local managers after the acquisition ended in failure.

In my experience, there are few talented Western managers who like to stay on after a company is taken over, especially by a foreign acquirer. In many cases, the more talented the manager, the more likely they are to move to a new company as soon as possible once the residual period imposed as a condition by the Japanese company has passed. This tendency is due to the higher liquidity that exists in the job market for managers outside of Japan. In fact, even in Japan, it is difficult to imagine a situation in which the managers in the acquired company are highly motivated to work for the acquiring company after the acquisition. Caution is especially required when the target company is owned by financial investors, as the managers entrusted with the management by private equities are often "professionals." The mission given by the financial investors to these professionals is to improve the performance of the target company and increase the value, and the professionals are ultimately rewarded handsomely if they succeed in helping private equity to sell the company at a gain. Thus, while these professionals are competent managers, they disappear after the acquisition and go on to the next assignment.

On the other hand, caution is also required in the case of local managers who are happy to remain. They see the Japanese companies, who are not knowledgeable of local conditions, as good sponsors from whom to demand, for example, additional acquisitions and capital investment. However, often in these cases these local managers do not allow the parent company to be involved in the operation. This situation would not be a problem if the target company's management continues smoothly, but after entrusting the management to the local managers, it is not unusual for them to repeatedly request additional investment even as performances noticeably deteriorate. Sony's acquisition of Columbia Pictures is frequently used in US business schools as the "Sony Goes to Hollywood" case study of a cross-border M&A. At the time, Sony conducted the acquisition without understanding the special industry that is Hollywood, and as a result, it recorded a major loss because it tolerated the lax management of famous Hollywood movie producers and it was unable to realize synergies between the hardware and software business aspects that it had envisaged at the time of the acquisition. This is not a problem unique to Japanese companies. Even in the friendly acquisition of Chrysler of the United States by Daimler of Germany, Daimler initially gave consideration to Chrysler and announced the acquisition to be a "merger of equals," and entrusted the management to Chrysler's management team. However, after the acquisition, one after another, Chrysler's senior managers left the company, and Daimler was unable to stop the deterioration of its results. Consequently, it dispensed with the sugar-coated merger of equals approach and dispatched a large number of German managers to Chrysler and worked to restructure it. However, even these efforts did not produce results.

Today, Japanese companies still attempt to entrust the management of a company acquired overseas to local management, an approach that has not changed since the 1980s. However, the reality is that in many cases, the more competent the manager, the more likely they are to leave after the acquisition. Moreover, even when local management remains, there are examples of results deteriorating even though they repeatedly demand additional investment from the parent company in Japan. In this situation, the Japanese company eventually gives up on the local managers and dispatches Japanese managers from its head office. The restructuring of a company for which the results have deteriorated becomes a difficult enough task domestically, and it becomes even more challenging when an overseas company is being reconstructed, placing a heavy burden on the head office. Thus, it would not be wise to assume that operation after the acquisition can be left to local managers simply because the acquired company is overseas.

A Strong Yen Does Not Necessarily Increase the Probability of Success

The impact of the exchange rate is neutral, including on the business after the acquisition

During a phase when the yen is strong, there is a danger of management deciding to acquire an overseas company because they perceive it to be a bargain.

Whether or not an overseas acquisition goes well is in large part due to the timing of the acquisition. At a time in which the industry in question is undergoing major changes to its management environment, expanding market share may result in a major loss, such as with Furukawa Electric's acquisition of a fiber-optic cable business. In addition, as was touched upon in the previous section, in fact, an acquisition when the yen is strong has not been shown to produce a good outcome compared to an acquisition at other times, and conversely, there are cases that ended with a withdrawal or sale at a significant loss after the acquisition. Thus, it would seem appropriate to consider exchange rate trends separately from the timing of the acquisition.

While the yen may further strengthen after the acquisition, it also may weaken. If the yen weakens after an acquisition, what happens when a loss is recorded in the results of the acquired company overseas and the loss increases when it is converted to yen? At that time, the exchange rate will have an adverse impact on the acquiring company's consolidated results, and the sense of a bargain and the related benefits envisaged at the time of the acquisition will disappear.

Caution is also required when utilizing leverage at the time of the acquisition. This is not a problem if the target company's results trend positively and the debt can be repaid from the operating cash flow in the local currency. However, if the acquired company's financial performance slumps after the acquisition and the repayment of the debt must come from Japan, this situation will place a major burden on the head office during a phase when the yen becomes weak. Alternatively, should the yen further strengthen after the acquisition, the target company's consolidated profits will be reduced when converted into yen. In short, it is better to consider the impact of the exchange rate to be neutral, including for the business after the acquisition.

According to conventional wisdom, the benefits from outbound acquisition include generating synergy, increasing global market shares, and buying time, but there are also pitfalls lying in wait with these benefits. Thus, managers should be aware that conventional wisdom does not always apply when conducting an acquisition.

In addition, when we evaluate overseas acquisitions only from a short-term viewpoint, we may misjudge their essential benefits. If, as an example, we look at five years after the acquisition of Firestone by Bridgestone, we cannot say the acquisition was a success at all. However, upon evaluating the acquisition in the long term, that is, over the past 30 years, Firestone can be described as the foundation on which Bridgestone has developed its North American business today.

Only ten years have passed since Nippon Sheet Glass' acquisition of Pilkington, while 15 years have passed since Furukawa Electric acquired Lucent's fiber-optic cable business. Comparing these acquisitions with that of Bridgestone, there were periods when Bridgestone incurred a major loss during the first 10 years from a strike lasting 270 days, and during the first 15 years from the voluntary recall of tires because of accidents involving Ford vehicles. Neither Nippon Sheet Glass nor Furukawa Electric has been able to realize, in the short term, the benefits that they initially aimed for through their outbound acquisitions. After the acquisition, their management fell into the pitfalls that were lying in wait within the benefits. However, it is possible that the businesses they acquired will be on track for profit growth in next 10 years like Bridgestone and Firestone. Thus, when considering the benefits of outbound acquisition, it is essential to take a long-term perspective.

The acquiring company has limited access to information about the target company before the transaction; it will learn more good and bad things about the operation after the acquisition. The acquiring company should fully consider the benefits of outbound acquisition and not overestimate them, nor should it underestimate the pitfalls that lie in wait.

Notes

1. Bridgestone company information, "The Bridgestone Story."
2. Nippon Sheet Glass press release, February 27, 2006.
3. Nikkei Business, April 28, 2008.
4. Nihon Keizai Shimbun, October 5, 2012.
5. Nihon Keizai Shimbun, November 17, 2001.
6. Nihon Keizai Shimbun, November 17, 2001.
7. Nihon Keizai Shimbun, July 29, 2001.
8. Bridgestone company information "The Bridgestone Story."

Reference

Andrade, G, M. Mitchell, and E. Stafford. 2001. "New Evidence and Perspectives on Mergers." *Journal of Economic Perspectives* (15) 2:103–120.

CHAPTER 3

Measuring Performance of Japanese Outbound Acquisitions

Determining the Success or Failure of 116 Outbound Acquisitions

3.1 How Do You Measure the Success or Failure of Acquisitions?

Rather than looking at the immediate impact on share price, look for sustainable profit growth after the transaction

In Chap. 2, we reviewed the conventional wisdom on the benefits of outbound acquisitions and noted that it may not be as easy as expected for the acquiring company to "buy time" and generate synergies with its existing business, and also that increasing global market share can actually become a burden rather than a benefit if the external business environment changes after the acquisition. The acquiring company must spend an enormous amount of resources to complete transaction, and if it falls into this common trap, it will need to invest even more to rebuild its business overseas. Thus, can an outbound acquisition really create value?

Barney states that "It is clear that company acquisitions are an important corporate strategy. What is not clear is whether or not conducting an acquisition will generate profit above the company's standard." (Barney 2001, 178). Even for acquisitions that are praised by the media and for which the stock market's response is positive enough for a limit-high, or the maximum allowable single-day gain for a stock, if you do not look at

S. Matsumoto, *Japanese Outbound Acquisitions*,
https://doi.org/10.1007/978-981-13-1364-6_3

the performance after the transaction, you will not know whether or not it is a good acquisition.

Please look at Fig. 3.1. It shows the trends in the share price of Furukawa Electric before and after the announcement of its acquisition of Lucent's fiber-optic cable business that was discussed in the Chap. 2. After the announcement of the acquisition on July 24, 2001, Furukawa Electric's share price reached a limit-high due to the market's positive reaction to its dramatic leap forward in adding the world's second largest fiber-optic cable business through acquisition in the United States.

Before the acquisition was announced, Furukawa Electric's share price followed a trend similar to the TOPIX (Tokyo Price Index, Capitalization weighted index that measures stock prices on Tokyo Stock Exchange), but after the announcement, it rose and greatly diverged from the TOPIX. This is considered to be due to the effects of the acquisition announcement, which created short-term gains for Furukawa Electric's shareholders.

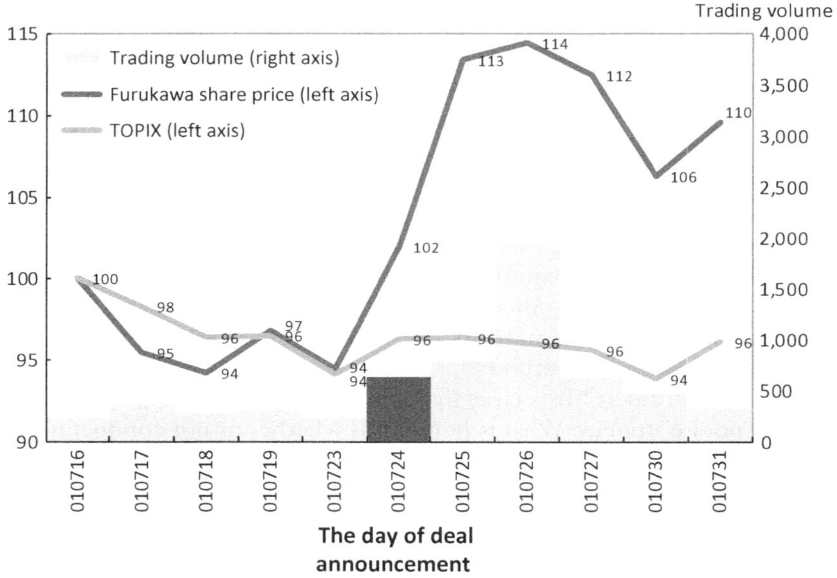

Fig. 3.1 Trends in the share price of Furukawa Electric before and after its acquisition announcement (July 16 share price = 100) (SPEEDA)

Next, please look at Fig. 3.2. It shows the trend in Furukawa Electric's share price in the years after the acquisition (July 2001–July 2004). Immediately after the acquisition, the IT bubble collapsed and global demand for fiber optics declined dramatically, and Furukawa Electric ended up recording a major impairment loss.

After the acquisition, Furukawa Electric's share price diverged significantly from the TOPIX again, in a negative direction this time. In the context of a greater-than-forecasted decline in global demand for fiber optics, Furukawa Electric had to repeatedly downwardly revise its financial forecast and recorded a significant loss, failing to pay a dividend for the first time in 54 years. The fall in its share price can be said to have been from the effects of the deterioration of the results from the acquired business.

Did this acquisition create value for Furukawa Electric's shareholders? Please look at both Figs. 3.1 and 3.2. Would you, readers, not evaluate the acquisition as creating short-term gain for Furukawa Electric shareholders before the acquisition, who sold their shares after the time limit imposed immediately after the announcement?

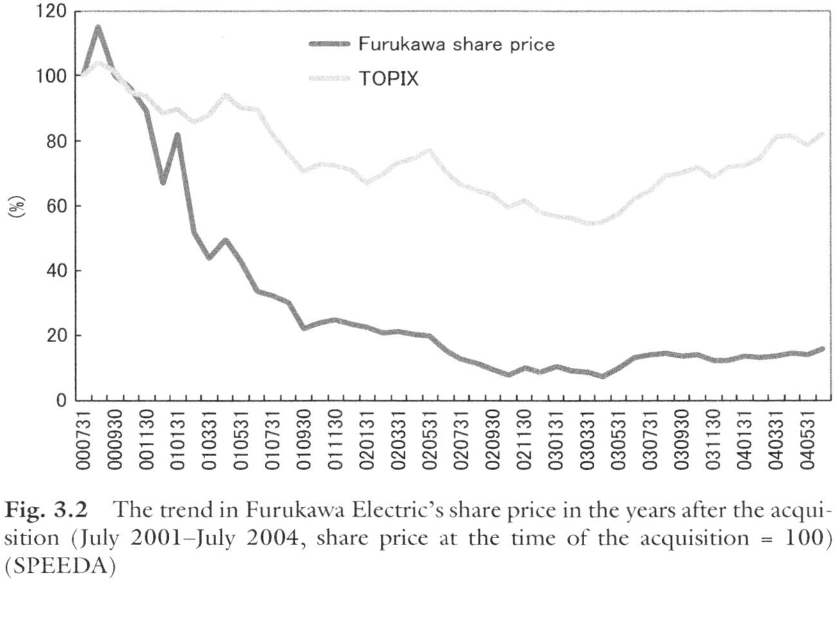

Fig. 3.2 The trend in Furukawa Electric's share price in the years after the acquisition (July 2001–July 2004, share price at the time of the acquisition = 100) (SPEEDA)

On the other hand, do you think, readers, that it did not at all create value for those shareholders who bought Furukawa Electric's shares after the announcement based on its talk of the synergistic effects it expected after the acquisition, and who held onto their shares for a number of years but were ultimately disappointed because the results of the acquisition were wide of the market? To say even further, the outcome of the acquisition differed from expectations when viewed from the different positions of the various stakeholders, such as the customers and employees.

From the example of Furukawa Electric, we understand that the expectations of the stock market at the time of the acquisition do not necessarily match the actual outcome after the acquisition. Short-term share price effects from the acquisition announcement can be evaluated as creating profits for the target company's shareholders, or in other words, the sellers, but these effects are not useful for the evaluation of the acquirer. Regardless of whether we are considering the short term or the long term, there are limits to using share price performance to evaluate the success or failure of an acquisition. This is because short-term share price effects at the time of the acquisition are not necessarily reflected in future results, and long-term share price effects tend to be absorbed in the noise from other events after the acquisition.

Judging the success or failure of an acquisition requires a long-term evaluation method different from the share price performance.

So, how should we define a successful outbound acquisition?

The purpose of a corporate strategy is to realize sustainable profit growth. Therefore, as one method of conducting this strategy, the success or failure of an M&A should be judged by the extent to which profit growth was achieved after the acquisition.

Normally, an acquisition often involves the payment of a premium based on the forecast for the target company's cash flow, so first, success can be said to be realizing accelerated rather than sustainable growth.

The most common method used up to the present time has been to evaluate the M&A based on the share price effects, mainly at the time of acquisition announcement, as individual and independent cases. However, the results of an acquisition do not appear soon after the announcement, so it is not appropriate to judge its success or failure over the short term. In this book, we consider overseas acquisition to be long-term corporate activity and evaluate based on whether the acquiring company achieved profit growth after the acquisition. To say this in another way, the question that should be answered in order to clarify whether or not an M&A was a success is not whether the acquisition itself was a success, but whether the long-term business resulting from the acquisition was a success.

3.2 The Three Criteria for Determining Success or Failure

A company's survival, continuous ownership, and profit growth

The criteria to judge the success or failure of an overseas M&A were set as shown in Fig. 3.3. Profit growth after the acquisition was evaluated from the criteria set from the first stage to the third stage. I think the fact that a method to evaluate the success or failure of an acquisition has not been established up to the present time is actually one of the reasons for the repeated failures of M&As. While a complete evaluation method does not exist, here, I explain the criteria set and the thinking behind them.

The First Stage: Company Survival Condition

The company survival condition, or the continued survival of the acquiring company, was set for the first stage of determining an acquisition's success or failure. There have been cases when the debt acquisition finance proved a heavy burden and the slump in the performance of the acquired business affected the core business to the extent that the acquiring company went bankrupt. It defeats the purpose if companies squander their fortunes and, far from profiting, lose everything that they invested as a result of investment overseas that exceeded their reach. Acquiring companies that in the first stage filed an application for the Corporation Rehabilitation Act and went bankrupt after the acquisition are determined to be failures. There are examples of an acquiring company changing its name due to a merger with another company after the acquisition, but these are determined to correspond to the company's survival, so are not considered failures.

Second Stage: The Continuous Ownership Condition

The continuous ownership condition, or whether the acquiring company still owns the acquired business today, was set for the second stage of determining an acquisition's success or failure. Rather than for speculative investment aiming at short-term capital gain, the assumption is that the objective of the strategic outbound acquisition is to deliver profit growth by adding business over the long term.

There are a number of reasons for the acquiring company to withdraw from or sell a business after acquisition, including the deterioration of the

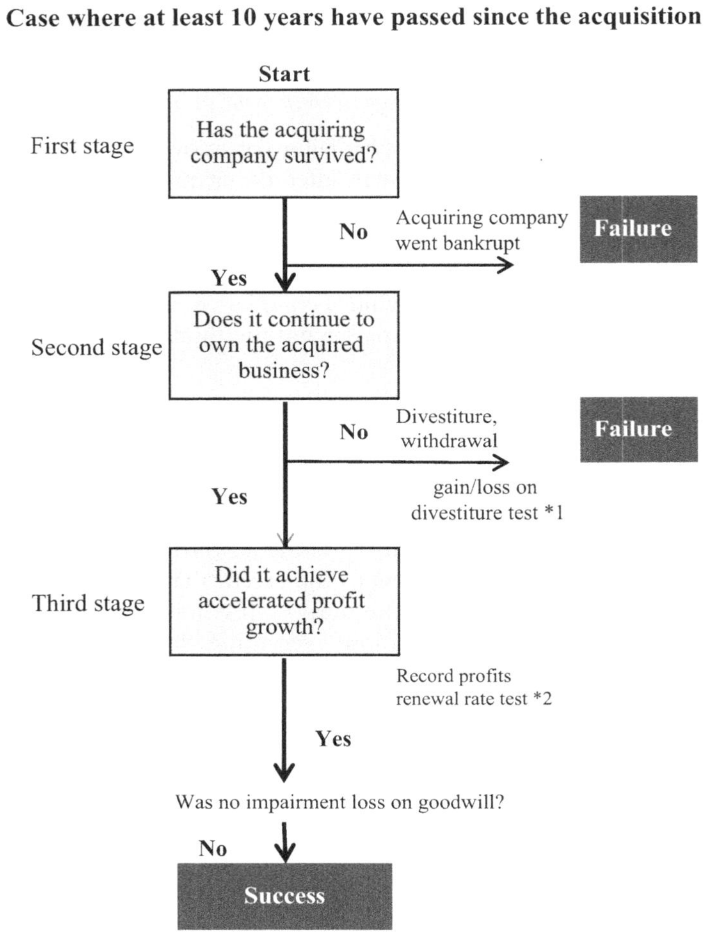

Fig. 3.3 Criteria to determine the success or failure of an overseas acquisition;[*1] Cases in which a gain upon the sale of the acquired company was recorded at the time of the sale are not determined to be failures;[*2] Achieved record operating profit renewal rate at least 50% in both the relevant regional/overseas and business segments, with the starting point of the fourth year after the acquisition

target company's performance, a change in strategy for the targeted business or region, a slump in the domestic business's financial results, a review of the business portfolios ahead of a merger with another company, or simply because the company needs cash to improve its balance sheet. However, whatever the reason, the fact that they occurred because the results deviated from those initially targeted does not change.

Therefore, if the acquiring company has already sold or withdrawn from the acquired business in the second stage, the acquisition is determined to have been a failure.

If a gain was recorded at the time of the sale, the acquisition is not judged a failure. However, considering that the company's objective for the acquisition was not to obtain a gain on sale, and that it invested significant management resources up to the time of the sale, these cases are not judged to be successes either, even if a gain is obtained from the sale transaction.

Third Stage: The Profit Growth Condition

Cases that satisfied the conditions in the first and second stages are those in which the acquiring company still survives today and continues to own the acquired business. However, simply owning the business over the long term cannot be termed success. The aims of an overseas M&A include expanding the overseas market through horizontal integration, forward and backward vertical integration, and diversification from taking on the challenge of a business in a new field. The acquiring companies' specific motivations are also various, such as entering a new market, acquiring a local brand, incorporating a local customer base, supplementing production and sales bases, avoiding price competition through forming an oligopoly, acquiring competent engineers, and acquiring the equity of a joint venture partner or rescuing a partner company.

However, the final objective shared by all deals is profit growth, and rather than starting to pursue this goal with green field investment, they aim to achieve it faster and over a longer term through an outbound acquisition. In the third stage, the profit growth condition is set and success is determined by using the record profits renewal rate to measure the sustainability of profit growth after the acquisition. Here, the record profits renewal rate involves counting the number of years for the operating profit to achieve a new record high and is shown as a percentage of the whole period. The higher the percentage, the greater the achievement of sustainable profit growth. We take this profit growth approach which is similar to a practical sense of success or failure in business.

Adopting long-term financial performance means that noise will be tolerated, but the following three points should be noted with regard to setting a method of determining success or failure that uses the record profits renewal rate.

- Measurement of profit growth—targeted regional and business segment operating profit

First, regarding the selection of values used for the determination of success or failure, profit growth from the overseas acquisition is considered to be reflected in the results of the regional segment in which the acquired business is located and of its business segment. To generate synergy with the existing business after the acquisition, in many cases, restructuring is carried out not only at the target company, but also for the existing business. As a result, there are cases where profit at the acquired business improves but worsens in the existing business, or vice versa. Therefore, compared to tracing the standalone results of the acquired business, evaluating the results of the region where the acquiring company is located and of its business segment is more appropriate in order to see the performance of the acquisition. Thus, success or failure is determined by asking whether profit growth was achieved in those targeted segments.

When considering the acquisition, the valuation method often used is the discounted cash flow method based upon the target company's future profit and cash flow forecast. It is meaningless for only the target company to achieve profits on a standalone basis as planned because the acquiring company has already paid for that at the time of the transaction. It would seem that the actual value for an acquirer can be said to have been created starting from the appearance of the acquisition's effects in the regional and business segment they targeted. Therefore, we use the operating profit for the relevant business segment and the acquired company's region/overseas segment to determine success or failure of acquisitions.

- Period used for the determination—from the fourth year after the acquisition

Next, what point in time should be used as the starting point to measure the record profits renewal rate? The target company's results in the first few years after the acquisition, whether good or bad, will not be a result of the abilities of the acquiring company. In addition, it is not appropriate to use this time period to determine profit growth owing to the possible deviation in the results after the acquisition that occurs alongside the integration with the existing business and the restructuring. In fact, after outbound acquisition, in many cases, Japanese companies prefer to achieve a smooth transfer and retain the target company's management team. Around the third year is generally the time when acquiring companies aim to stabilize the organization after eliminating duplicate production and sales force with the existing business and preparing to generate operational synergies.

In a study that investigated 1483 acquisitions from 1981 to 2000, which included 12,893 factories in the US manufacturing industry, it was reported that in the three years after the acquisition, 27% of the factories had been sold and 19% closed (Maksimovic et al. 2011, 317). Thus, it can be considered that around three years is required for the review of operations and restructuring after the acquisition, so the starting point to measure the record profits renewal rate was set as the fourth year after the acquisition.[1]

- Profit growth determination criteria—record profits renewal rate of at least 50%

Finally, where should the criteria to determine profit growth after the acquisition be set? Within the research of Professor Kazuhiro Mishina of Kobe University (Mishina 2007, 56), he argues that "With regards to the sustainability of a company's profit growth, if it achieves, at least once, record-high profits during the period of the medium-term management plan—in other words, a three-year period—it would be reasonable to view this outcome as evidence that the company's strategy was functioning." The objective of an outbound acquisition is to achieve profit growth much faster than if starting from a green field investment especially because acquisition costs much more. Thus, the determination criterion was set as the company achieving new record profits at a faster pace, at least once in two years.

With regards to the acquiring company's profit growth in the third stage, the values used for the determination of success or failure are the operating profit of both the relevant business and the regional segments. The time period starts from the fourth year after the acquisition, and cases acquiring company achieved record profits renewal rate of at least 50%, or once in two years, are determined to be successes. It seems fair to say an acquisition is a success if it is clear that the profit growth after the acquisition exceeded the standard expectation for it on a sustainable basis. Below is a summary of the above points.

- Criteria for determining the success or failure of an overseas M&A
  - With the starting point of the fourth year after the acquisition, successes are those that achieve a record profit renewal rate of at least 50% for operating profit in both the relevant business segment and the regional/overseas segment.
  - Failures are those cases in which the acquiring company goes bankrupt after the acquisition or it sells or withdraws from the acquired business.

3.3 Only 9 Deals Were Successes, While 51, or Nearly Half, Were Failures

What we learn from evaluating all 116 cases

Results of the Determination

So, have Japanese companies achieved profit growth after their acquisitions?

With regard to all 116 cases of overseas acquisitions (IN-OUT)[2] with a value of 10 billion yen or more,[3] for which at least 10 years have passed since the acquisition,[4] and for which the company[5] acquired a controlling stake,[6] the criteria described in the previous section were used to determine whether they were a success or failure. The subjects of the research are the 116 overseas acquisitions that satisfied the conditions shown in Table 3.1. Incidentally, of the 116 acquisitions, in 91 cases, the acquiring company still owned the acquired business at least 10 years after the acquisition (Fig. 3.4). This situation shows that Japanese companies manage the companies they acquired overseas over the long term, and it justifies this long-term approach to evaluating acquisitions.

The determination shows that 51, or nearly half, were failures, while only 9, as far as the profit growth condition is concerned, were determined to be successes (Fig. 3.5).

Table 3.1 Attributes of the cases researched

	Attribute	*Application*
Acquiring company	Japanese companies	
Target company	Overseas companies and businesses	Specifically, outbound acquisitions
Sectors	All sectors, excluding resources, finance, and real estate	Excluding sectors that may include a speculative objective
Value	10 billion yen or more	With reference to previous research
Period	Acquisitions from 1985 to 2001	A searchable period going back to cases for which at least 10 years have passed since the acquisition
Ownership after acquisition	Over 50%	Specifically, cases in which the controlling stakes were acquired

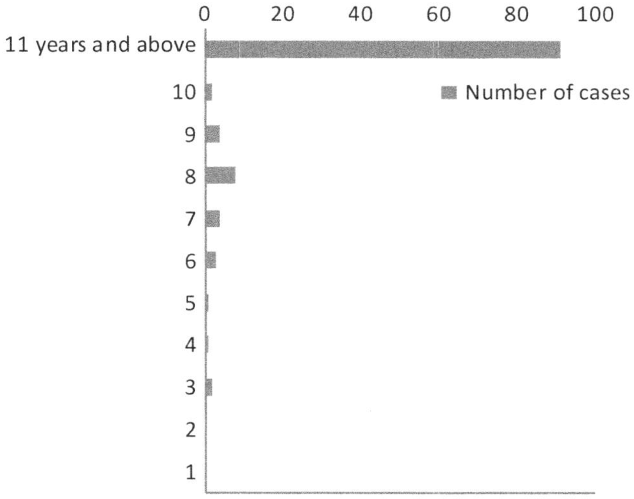

Fig. 3.4 Number of years of ownership after outbound acquisitions

To a certain extent, the fact that many Japanese outbound acquisitions ended in failure was foreseeable, but even so, the record of Japanese companies can be said to be less than stellar.

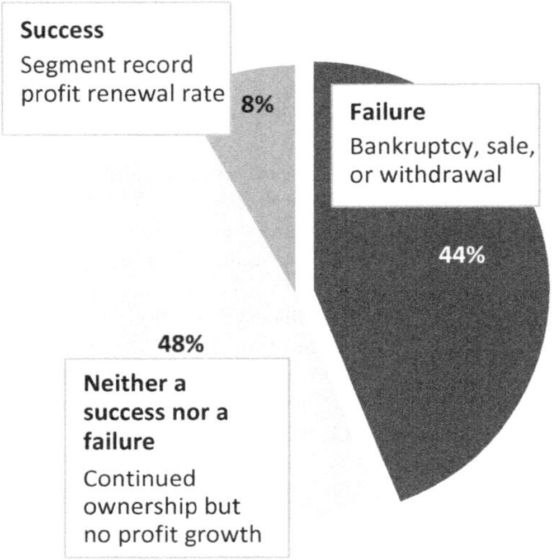

Fig. 3.5 Results of the determination of success or failure for the 116 overseas M&As

Looking at their performance corresponding to each of the respective determination criteria, from the acquiring company's survival condition in the first stage, we see that many overseas M&As ended in failure, with six companies and seven acquisitions going bankrupt, including filing an application for the Company Rehabilitation Act (Fig. 3.6). There are a number of cases in which, despite conducting an acquisition overseas, the acquiring company itself ran into difficulties after the acquisition, such as Kyotaru, Sogo, and NISSEI Electric. There are also cases when the acquiring company actively invested during the period of the bubble economy in Japan and the acquired business performed well, but later, the former was forced to sell the latter to repay its debts. There are also failures in which the dispersion of management resources proved fatal.

In the determination of success or failure from the continuous ownership condition in the second stage, there were 44 cases in which the acquiring company has already sold or withdrawn from the acquired business. Unlike acquisitions targeting capital gains by financial investors, strategic investors assume the long-term ownership of the acquisition with the objective of the acquired business becoming a source of profits. In many cases, the acquiring company recorded a significant loss on the sale of the acquisition, including of NedCar (Netherlands Car) by Mitsubishi

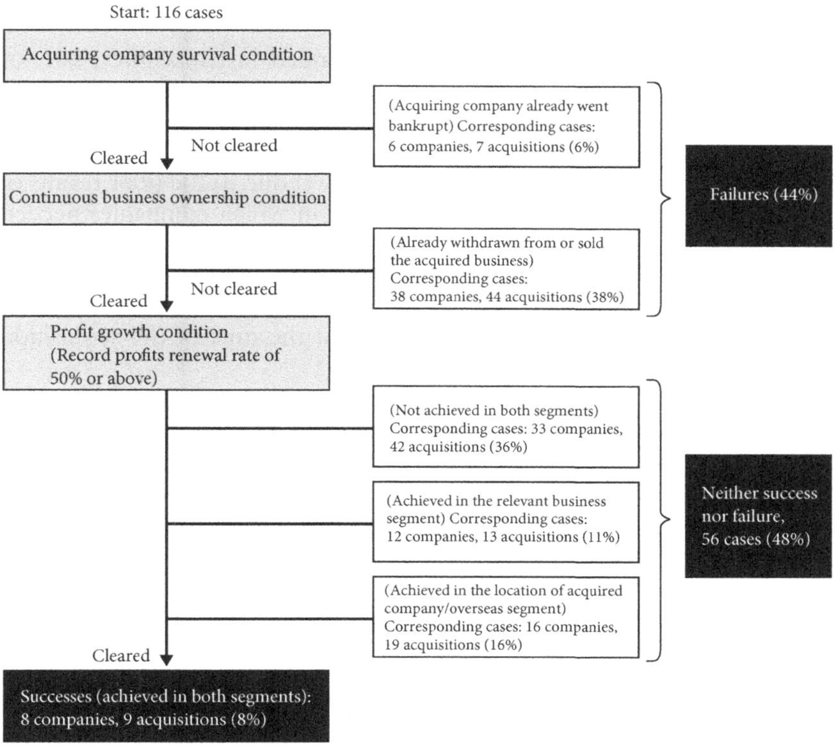

Fig. 3.6 The results of the determination of success or failure

Motors, of Shaklee by Yamanouchi Pharmaceuticals, and of National Steel by NKK (Nihon Kokan). There are a number of examples where profit growth was not achieved through the overseas M&A.

The 51 cases that did not satisfy the first or second stage conditions were determined to be failures.

There were 65 cases in which the acquiring company still owned the acquired business 10 years after the acquisition. Of these, eight companies and nine acquisitions satisfied the third stage profit growth condition of a record profits renewal rate of at least 50% in the relevant business segment and the regional (the location of the acquired company)/overseas segment.

Cases Determined to Be Failures

Out of the 116 cases, 51, or nearly half, ended in bankruptcy, sale, or withdrawal after the acquisition, which, once again indicates that succeeding in an overseas M&A is not easy. Upon investigating the reasons for the sale of or withdrawal from the business within the 51 cases, the most common reason, in 21 cases, was sale or withdrawal due to the poor results of the acquired business, followed by 12 cases in which companies needed cash (including cases of bankruptcy of the acquiring company), and finally in 10 cases, as a result of a review of the business portfolio in advance of a merger with other companies. In each case, the acquiring company could not achieve the profit growth it envisaged at the time of the acquisition and it itself fell into a predicament.

On totaling the acquisition amount of the cases determined to be failures, we find that it exceeds 2.8 trillion yen. When adding to this the management resources invested over the long term, it is clear that these failed acquisitions came at a tremendous cost to the companies. The resources for the acquisition are mainly the profits from the domestic business, so these failures can also be described as an overseas transfer of domestic wealth.

Further, within the 51 cases of failure, there were 28 cases of companies owning the acquired business for 10 years or more, so we can see traces of the long-term efforts made by the Japanese companies to improve results.

NTT Communications and Furukawa Electric each recorded extraordinary losses on the impairment of goodwill from their respective acquisitions of a US IP systems business and a fiber-optic cable business, but they continue to own these businesses. Thus, as the opportunity remains for such cases to achieve profit growth, they were determined not to be failures.

Cases Determined to Be Successes

There were eight companies that achieved accelerated profit growth from outbound acquisitions—Kuraray, Shin-Etsu Chemical, Seven & i, Japan Tobacco, Terumo, Sumitomo Electric Industries, Ricoh, and TORAY (of these, Seven & i had two successes). Each of these companies used an overseas M&A to expand its targeted business on a global scale and developed these businesses into revenue pillars, showing it is possible for acquisition to be an effective corporate strategy.

These success stories will be considered in more detail in Chap. 5, "The eight successful deals that achieved profit growth."

Notes

1. For example, in the case of an acquisition in 2000, the starting point is the operating profit of the acquiring company in fiscal year 2004.
2. Overseas acquisitions conducted in the researchable period of 1985–2001.
3. Acquisitions for industries that include acquisitions for speculative purposes (real estate, resources, and finance) are excluded from the analysis.
4. Excluding cases where more than 50% of the shares were acquired after the acquisition, minority ownerships, and joint ventures.
5. Singh and Montgomery (1987) and Kaplan and Weisbach (1992).
6. Extracted from the data of Thomson Reuters.

References

Barney, J. 2001. *Gaining and Sustaining Competitive Advantage.* Second Edition Pearson Education.

Kaplan, S, and M. Weisbach. 1992. "The Success of Acquisitions: Evidence from Divestitures." *The Journal of Finance* (47) 1. https://doi.org/10.1111/j.1540-6261.1992.tb03980.x

Maksimovic, V, G. Phillips, and N.R. Prabhala. 2011. "Post-merger restructuring and the boundaries of the firm." abstract, *Journal of Financial Economics.* (102) 2:317–343.

Mishina, K. 2007. *The causes of strategy failure*, Toyo: Keizai, Inc. (in Japanese)

Singh, H, and C. Montgomery. 1987. "Corporate acquisition strategies and economic performance." Strategic Management Journal 8 (4), https://doi.org/10.1002/smj.4250080407

CHAPTER 4

The Causes of Failure: Case Studies of Eight Failed Acquisitions Ending in a Sale or Withdrawal at a Loss

In the previous chapter, we determined which overseas M&A deals ended in failure, or in other words, which cases failed to realize profit growth. The cases determined to be failures were those in which the acquiring company withdrew from or sold the acquired business, or in which the acquiring company itself was subsequently forced into bankruptcy. In each of these cases, the strategy envisaged at the time of the acquisition did not work due to the subsequent management.

In this chapter, 8 of the 51 cases determined to be failures will be presented as case studies. We will aim to capture the overall consequence of these failures by considering not just the conditions at the time of the acquisition, but also the management after the acquisition. Specifically, we will consider them from four angles, the objective at the time of the acquisition, the managers, the post-acquisition management and its challenges, and the consequences.

1. Acquisition of MCA by Matsushita Electric Industrial (Panasonic)
2. Acquisition of Shaklee by Yamanouchi Pharmaceutical (Astellas Pharma)
3. Acquisition of NedCar by Mitsubishi Motors Corporation
4. Acquisition of Aquascutum by Renown
5. Acquisition of National Steel by NKK (JFE)
6. Acquisition of Talbots by JUSCO (AEON)

S. Matsumoto, *Japanese Outbound Acquisitions*,
https://doi.org/10.1007/978-981-13-1364-6_4

7. Acquisition of Reichhold Chemicals by Dainippon Ink and Chemicals
8. Acquisition of Hankuk Electric Glass by Asahi Glass

As much as possible, I have attempted to allow readers to superimpose their experiences from their own deals onto these case studies. At the end of the chapter, I have listed all 51 cases determined to be failures.

1. The objective at the time of the acquisition

What are the objectives when conducting a large-scale acquisition overseas? The investment of considerable management resources in order to acquire an overseas company represents companies' strategies. In this section, I summarize the acquiring company's idea extrapolated from the management issues at the time of the acquisition, the management environment of the targeted business, and the strategic direction of the deal.

2. The managers

What kinds of managers are conducting the deal? The true colors of managers will appear most vividly when conducting large-scale acquisitions, while their subsequent responsibilities will also be heavy. In Japanese companies, as well as in Western companies, we have frequently seen cases of managers being forced to resign in order to take responsibility for the fact that, despite investing enormous sums of money, the results of the acquired business were poor, and even those of the acquiring company deteriorated. In this section, I summarize the thoughts of the managers about the acquisition and their relationships with the targeted business, including from media interviews conducted at that time.

3. The post-acquisition management and its challenges

The management that was placed under the spotlight at the time of the acquisition may also remain the focus of attention after the acquisition, but for the wrong reasons, such as when their company records an extraordinary loss or when the extent of its predicament becomes clear. How should the acquiring company conduct management after the acquisition? In addition, how can the management overcome the challenges that it will face after the acquisition? In this section, I summarize the measures taken by the management after the acquisitions.

4. The consequences

What were the final outcomes of the acquisitions? In this section, we will finally consider the consequences of the deals.

4.1 Case Study 1: Matsushita Electric Industrial (Panasonic)

Acquiring company: Matsushita Electric Industrial (currently, Panasonic)
Target company: MCA (United States)
Shareholders: Tender offer (United States)
Targeted business: Entertainment
Acquisition year: 1990
Sales year: 1995

The Objective at the Time of the Acquisition

In 1990, Matsushita Electric Industrial acquired MCA, the parent company of Universal Pictures, a major US movie production company. At the time of the acquisition, then company president Mr. Akio Tanii spoke of the expected synergy effects, saying, "In the (AV) audio-visual industry, the relationship between software or contents and hardware can be described as like the wheels of a car. We agreed with the opinion of MCA, on seeking the ideal integration of the soft and hard aspects, which led to the current agreement."[1] At that time, ahead of the full-fledged sales of high-definition (HD) TVs, the ruling idea within Matsushita Electric Industrial was that the contents, such as movies, would be the decisive factor behind the sales of the hardware and AV equipment, including its mainstay TVs and videos. It is thought that Sony's management decision to acquire the major US movie company Columbia Pictures Entertainment in the previous year, 1989, also affected Matsushita's management decision.

Another factor in the background to this deal was the deterioration of the profitability of Matsushita Electric Industrial's exports because of the yen appreciation due to the 1985 Plaza Accord, and the stagnation of its profit growth in the long term. In 1985, it recorded an operating profit of 561.1 billion yen, but in 1987, this figure fell to 74 billion yen. In 1988, it merged with Matsushita Electric Trade Company, and in 1990, it spun off four businesses from its headquarters, including its TV business, and carried out restructuring. However, despite these efforts, the results did not recover as expected.

On the acquisition of MCA, there were voices both inside and outside of Matsushita Electric Industrial that expressed concerns about whether it could manage a US movie company. However, because it had reached a transition period for profit growth from its exports of consumer electronics products, it decided to diversify its businesses through the large-scale acquisition in the United States.

It was one year after the company founder Konosuke Matsushita passed away, and in the same year, 1990, Matsushita Electric Industrial set "Break Through" as its management slogan.

The Managers

Mr. Tanii served as president from 1986 to 1993. As previously mentioned, this was a period in which the company faced the major management issue of responding to the decline in the profitability of exports due to the appreciation of the yen. President Tanii said that through the acquisition of MCA, they would attempt to escape from a business that overemphasized hardware and "to form a corporate culture in Matsushita through coming into contact with a different culture."[2] However, after the collapse of the bubble economy, a bad debt problem at its subsidiary National Lease coincided with a quality problem with its refrigerators, and the president resigned in 1993, only three years after the acquisition of MCA. Further, in the periods before and after the president was replaced, other members of the board who had been involved in the acquisition, such as a vice president, also resigned.

The Post-acquisition Management and Its Challenges

For the management after the acquisition, discussions were held in the executive committee established by the leaders of Matsushita Electric Industrial and MCA, and it was decided that the remaining MCA management team would run the business in accordance with the committee's policies. The participation of Matsushita Electric Industrial's management, which had no experience in movie production in Hollywood, was to be kept to a minimum, but MCA's results improved thanks to big movie hits like *Jurassic Park*, and in fiscal year 1994, it contributed approximately 9% of Matsushita Electric Industrial's total operating profit.

However, the synergy effects initially envisaged by Matsushita Electric Industrial for its business proved to be limited. Direct cooperation was only limited to the game software field with the establishment of a joint venture in the United States. Also, after the acquisition, sales of AV equipment like TV and video, which had been expected to increase, remained sluggish. President Tanii's idea for the acquisition, that "We want to actively utilize the MCA acquisition, so it positively affects the group companies too,"[3] had not been realized.

On the other hand, MCA's management team proposed to Matsushita Electric Industrial the additional acquisitions of US TV stations and music companies, from a "Hollywood" viewpoint. These proposals made sense from a local viewpoint in the extremely competitive US media and entertainment industry, but Matsushita Electric Industrial did not like the idea of taking on new financial burdens and thus, did not approve these proposed acquisitions.

MCA was also wide of the mark in assuming that Matsushita Electric Industrial would be an ideal cash rich sponsor. Neither company's expectations at the time of the acquisition were met—the synergy effects with its hardware business that were expected by Matsushita Electric Industrial, nor the business expansion in Hollywood through the supply of funds by Matsushita Electric Industrial that was expected by MCA (refer to Fig. 4.1).

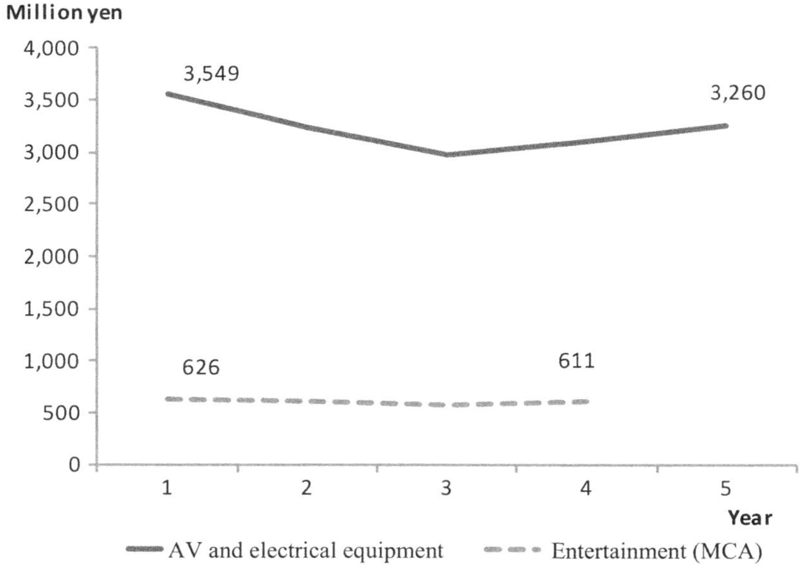

Fig. 4.1 Trends in revenues of AV and electrical products and the entertainment segment during the period Matsushita Electric Industrial owned MCA. (Entertainment indicates the revenues of MCA. It was sold in 1995.) (Matsushita Electric Industrial's annual securities report)

The Consequences

After the resignation of President Tanii in 1993, Mr. Yoichi Morishita was appointed president, and then in 1995, Matsushita Electric Industrial sold 80% of its shares in MCA to Seagram, a major Canadian beverage company. At the time it announced the sale, President Morishita said that "Matsushita's core business is electronics. Through this sale, we can allocate management resources to growth fields such as multimedia, to important parts technologies, and to the overseas business." Thus, on the occasion of appointing a new president, five years after the acquisition, Matsushita completely revised its diversification strategy.

At the time it sold its MCA shares, the yen had strengthened even further compared to at the time of the acquisition, and in fiscal year 1995, Matsushita Electric Industrial recorded an exchange rate loss in excess of 100 billion yen.[4]

4.2 Case Study 2: Yamanouchi Pharmaceuticals (Astellas Pharma)

Acquiring company: Yamanouchi Pharmaceutical (currently, Astellas Pharma)
Target company: Shaklee Corporation (United States)
Shareholders: Tender offer (United States)
Targeted business: Health foods
Acquisition year: 1989
Sale year: 2004

The Objective at the Time of the Acquisition

Yamanouchi Pharmaceutical acquired the major US health foods company Shaklee Corporation in 1989. Before acquiring the Shaklee parent company, it had already acquired Shaklee Japan; subsequently, however, a US financial investor attempted a hostile acquisition of the Shaklee parent company, and Yamanouchi Pharmaceutical made the company into a subsidiary following the company's request to be rescued from this hostile takeover. This acquisition is said to be the first time that a Japanese company had acted as a white knight in the acquisition of a US company.

In terms of the objectives of the acquisition, the president at that time, Mr. Shigeo Morioka, said, "When we had explored a wide range of methods of advancing into the United States without specifying a business, we were approached by Shaklee of the United States to discuss the acquisition. Our main business is pharmaceuticals but increasing sales of pharmaceuticals overseas will take an enormous amount of time and effort. We wanted to build a foothold for the full-fledged advance of our pharmaceuticals business by first making the Yamanouchi brand known through the foods route."[5]

Shaklee had grown through the direct sales of products such as protein supplements and vitamins using a contracted sales force organization, and at the time of the acquisition, its sales were on a scale of 627 million dollars. Mr. Hisakazu Iizuka, the Yamanouchi managing director at that time, evaluated the Shaklee sales network as follows: "It has the wonderful asset of a sales network of 1.4 million users. Anything is possible through this route, and we think it is appropriate for the Shaklee brand. We will be able to jointly develop new products with Shaklee in the United States and to conduct sales using its global sales network," adding that, "For a long time, we have been aiming to advance into fields adjacent to pharmaceuticals."[6]

The Managers

Mr. Morioka served as president until 1999 and was involved in the management of Shaklee for a long period of over 10 years. Speaking of the acquisition, he said that "A merit of Shaklee is the strength of its sales force. Even as a low estimate, we can expect it to grow by more than 5% a year. We have deemed the acquisition cost of 100 billion yen to be financing from the Shaklee Group that will result in our major growth in the long run."

When discussing the rapid increase in acquisitions of US companies by Japanese companies at that time in 1989 against the backdrop of the strong yen, he said that, "Looking at the recent developments by the U.S. government, we see it is strengthening the regulations imposed on Japanese companies. Thus, for this reason, it is necessary to directly enter the U.S. market as quickly as possible and to grow the business to reach a certain scale. There is no doubt that M&A are one effective method to achieve this."

The Post-acquisition Management and Its Challenges

After the acquisition, Yamanouchi Pharmaceutical kept Shaklee US and Shaklee Japan unchanged as corporate entities. Directly after the acquisition, Yamanouchi Pharmaceutical established the Consumer Business Development Department in-house and began to piggyback its Japanese products onto Shaklee's mail order business, which was centered on the

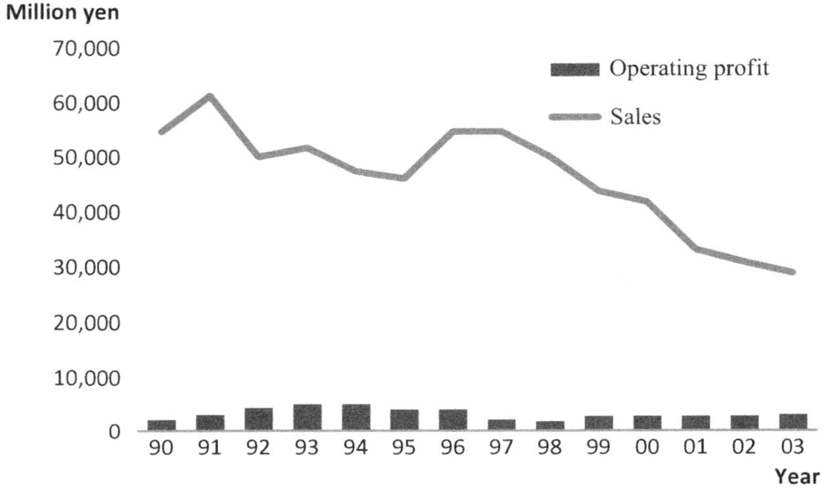

Fig. 4.2 Trends in revenues and operating profits for Yamanouchi Pharmaceutical's nutritional supplement, foods, and personal care product segments. (Yamanouchi Pharmaceutical's annual securities report)

nutritional supplements that accounted for 30% of Shaklee's sales. Further, it established Yamanouchi Consumer Inc. in 2000 in the United States, with the aim of propping up the business of Shaklee in the United States.

However, it was unable to achieve the growth in sales and profits that it expected from diversifying into the nonmedical pharmaceuticals business, particularly from Shaklee's business (refer to Fig. 4.2). Nor was it able to generate the synergy effects initially expected between its pharmaceuticals business and Shaklee's powerful door-to-door sales network. Thus, Yamanouchi Pharmaceutical's management, which was unable to grow its profit margin even in its mainstay pharmaceuticals business, found itself being asked by its foreign shareholders, "How long do you intend to keep Shaklee, as its consumer business is not contributing to profits?"[7]

The Consequences

Yamanouchi Pharmaceutical owned Shaklee over a long period of 16 years, but in 2004, it sold Shaklee to a US investment fund to prepare for its merger with Fujisawa Pharmaceutical in 2005. It took time to persuade the president at the time of the sale, Mr. Toichi Takenaka, who had been involved in the acquisition and had a soft spot for Shaklee, to go ahead with the sale, and it seems that the Yamanouchi management team from the time of the acquisition held a fondness for Shaklee.

Yamanouchi Pharmaceutical explained its reasons for the sale in a press release as follows:

> The four companies of Shaklee Japan, Shaklee Corporation of the United States, Inobis, and Bear Creek Corporation, under the umbrella of the wholly owned subsidiary Yamanouchi Consumer Inc. (hereafter, YCI), operate in the consumer business (nutritional supplement and personal health care products business, food business, and flower business).
>
> In the context of the intensifying competition in the consumer business environment, we have reached a final agreement to transfer this business in order to establish a system to concentrate management resources into our core business, the medical pharmaceuticals business, and also in order to further strengthen our business foundations so that we can be successful in global competition.[8]

In 2001, Yamanouchi Pharmaceutical recorded a loss on the sale of Shaklee's shares of 30.1 billion yen.[9] Although after the acquisition, it continuously managed Shaklee over the long term, this did not lead to diversification, synergy with the pharmaceuticals business, nor the expansion of its US business.

4.3 Case Study 3: Mitsubishi Motors

Acquiring company: Mitsubishi Motors Corporation (MMC)
Target company: Netherlands Car (NedCar) (Netherlands)
Shareholders: Volvo (Sweden)
Targeted business: Automotive
Acquisition year: 2001
Sale year: 2012

The Objective at the Time of the Acquisition

In 2001, Mitsubishi Motors purchased its joint venture partner Volvo's stake in NedCar, a Dutch automotive manufacturing and sales company, and made it a wholly owned subsidiary. The capital relationship between Mitsubishi Motors and NedCar can be traced back to 1991. At that time, Mitsubishi Motors invested in Holland Volvo Car, which was managed by the Dutch government and Volvo, and the three parties launched NedCar as a joint venture. Subsequently in 1999, it acquired the Dutch government's stake in the joint venture and switched to an equal-ownership joint venture with Volvo.

As Mitsubishi Motors did not have any production bases in Europe, it was aiming to share a platform with Volvo and to produce compact cars to expand its sales in Europe. One of the reasons cited by Mitsubishi Motors at that time for embarking on the joint venture was that its ideas on manufacturing vehicles and on quality were consistent with those of Volvo.[10]

In the subsequent consolidation of the automotive industry, Volvo Car Corporation became a part of the Ford Group of the United States and came to share a platform with Ford, so it no longer needed NedCar.

Conversely, Mitsubishi Motors acquired from Volvo its stake in NedCar, made it a wholly owned subsidiary, and aimed to switch to a joint venture with Daimler, based on the fact that it formed a capital tie-up with Daimler Chrysler in 2000. At the time of the acquisition, NedCar's production capacity was 200,000 units and it had in excess of 6000 employees. Mitsubishi Motors explained its objective in making NedCar a wholly owned subsidiary in a press release[11] as follows:

- Reason for the acquisition of NedCar shares

  Mitsubishi Motors Corporation (MMC) and Daimler Chrysler shall jointly manage Netherlands Car BV as part of a series of measures in their business alliances. In accordance with this, MMC has acquired all of the shares in Netherlands Car BV held by the Volvo Car Corporation.

- Future outlook

  Currently, Netherlands Car BV produces the Mitsubishi Carisma/Space Star, and the Volvo S40/V40, but from 2004 onwards, it is scheduled to newly produce the Z car, a small global strategic vehicle that will be the pillar of the alliance between Mitsubishi Motors and Daimler Chrysler, for both the Mitsubishi brand and for the Smart brand.

The Managers

At the time of the acquisition, Mitsubishi Motors' president was Mr. Takashi Sonobe. After serving as the head of the North American passenger vehicle head office, he was appointed president in November 2000 following the "defects cover-up" recall scandal that led to the resignation of President Katsuhiko Kawasoe. In 2000, after accepting investment from Daimler Chrysler, both companies considered how to deepen their cooperation and Mitsubishi Motors decided to make NedCar a subsidiary premised on its joint production with Daimler in the future.

In June 2002, President Sonobe relinquished his position to former Daimler executive Mr. Rolf Eckrodt and became chairman of the board of directors, but he died soon after in 2003.

The Post-acquisition Management and Its Challenges

At the time that Mitsubishi Motors made NedCar into a wholly owned subsidiary, the majority of the units it produced were Volvo vehicles. As its outsourcing of production from Volvo had ended, the utilization rates at NedCar's factories had fallen greatly. The production of the Smart Forfour small passenger car was expected to replace this, but it was not until 2004, three years after it was made a subsidiary, that the production of this vehicle began. Further, there continued to be little progress in the negotiations between Mitsubishi Motors and Daimler for the transfer of NedCar shares and the establishment of a joint venture, and Daimler ended its capital tie-up with Mitsubishi Motors in 2005. This event was compounded with a slump in sales of the Smart Forfour in 2006; Daimler ended the agreement to outsource its production to NedCar after two years, and once again, the utilization rates at its factories in the Netherlands fell.

In 2008, in addition to its Colt small passenger vehicle, Mitsubishi Motors outsourced to NedCar one part of the production of its Outlander sports utilities vehicles (SUV), for which exports to Europe had been strong, and it worked to improve the operating rates at NedCar's factories. However, in contrast to NedCar's production capacity of 200,000 units, it was only producing in the range of 50,000 units.

Due to the subsequent major decline in sales in Europe following the Global financial crisis, it suspended the production of the Colt and Outlander in 2012.

Mitsubishi Motors had made NedCar a subsidiary through the acquisition premised on the plan for joint production, but this also came to nothing. Subsequently, it attempted to utilize NedCar as its own production base in Europe, but due to its aging facilities and the limitations on procuring parts in the Netherlands, its business continued to record a loss (refer to Fig. 4.3).

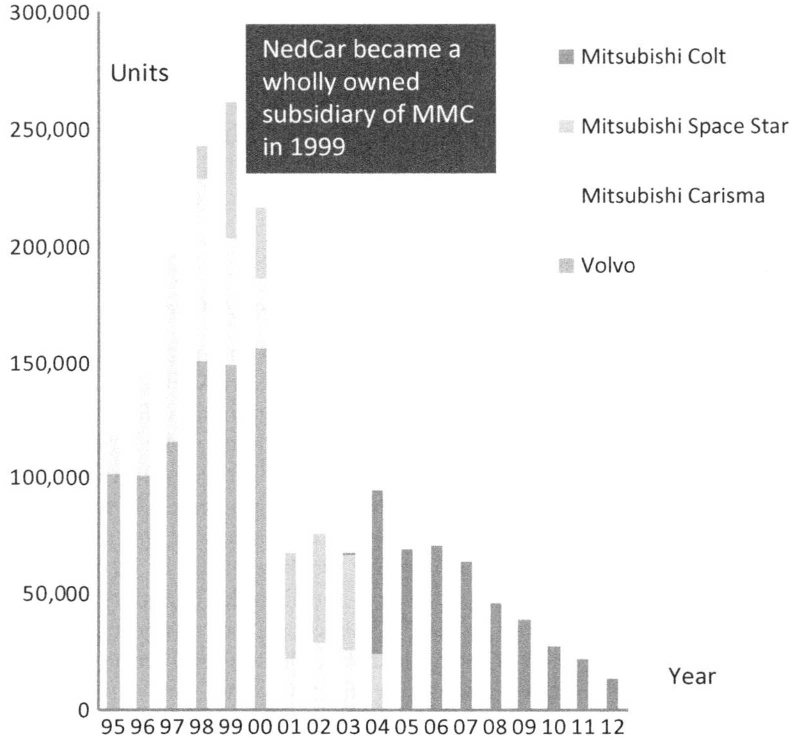

Fig. 4.3 Trends in the number of units produced by NedCar (1995–2012). From 2001 to 2004, NedCar produced the Volvo V40, and for two years from 2004, it produced Daimler's Smart Forfour, but the number of units produced of these vehicles is unknown. The Outlander is not included in the definition of the Automobile Association due its semi knocked-down (SKD) production method. (The Mitsubishi Motors Corporation Fact Book 2001)

The Consequences

In 2012, Mitsubishi Motors decided to sell its shares in NedCar to the VDL Group for one euro and announced its withdrawal from production in Europe. Due to the slumping results of NedCar, Mitsubishi Motors recorded a loss of 15.6 billion yen in its Europe region segment in 2011. Mr. Osamu Masuko, the president at the time the sale was announced, said that "It was a tough decision for management, but when thinking about the future, it was a path we had no choice but to take."[12] In conjunction with the sale of NedCar, in 2012, Mitsubishi Motors recorded an extraordinary loss of 25.1 billion yen.[13]

Mitsubishi Motors owned NedCar over a long period of 21 years from the capital participation in the joint venture and 11 years after making it a wholly owned subsidiary. However, it found itself at the mercy of the global consolidation in the automotive industry and finally withdrew from this heavy burden it had carried for many years. Subsequently, Mitsubishi Motors advanced an alliance with the French auto manufacturer Peugeot-Citroën (PSA), established a joint venture in Russia, and in 2012, began production there of the Outlander, as its sales were strong in that country. In 2016, Mitsubishi Motors entered into the alliance with Nissan and Renault.

4.4 Case Study 4: Renown

Acquiring company: Renown
Target company: Aquascutum (UK)
Shareholders: Tender offer (UK)
Targeted business: Apparel
Acquisition year: 1990
Sale year: 2009

The Objective at the Time of the Acquisition

Renown acquired the long-established UK apparel manufacturer Aquascutum in 1990 through a tender offer. At the time of the acquisition, its rivals Sanyo Shokai had acquired a production license for the prestigious UK brand Burberry, while Onward Kashiyama was increasing revenue through a partnership with an Italian designer and apparel manufacturer. In contrast, in 1989, the year before the acquisition, Renown, which was centered on casualwear and underwear, had recorded a major fall in profits of 45%, and it was said in the apparel industry that the sale of luxury brand apparel was a decisive factor in the overall results of companies.

In addition to acquiring the luxury Aquascutum brand, a member of the Renown management team at the time of the acquisition described the objectives of the acquisition in terms of the following two benefits. The first was to supplement its product mix by acquiring men's suits and coats. Renown's lineup was centered on casualwear, and it had already spun off the D'Urban men's apparel business, so it had little presence in this field. The second was the fact that Aquascutum had 12 production and sales bases in seven countries in Europe. Renown thought it would be able to use these sales channels for its own products. At that time, companies such as Onward Kashiyama had gone ahead of Renown in terms of establishing overseas businesses, and Renown desperately wanted to build sales and production bases in Europe, which was "the home of fashion."[14]

On the other hand, the situation in Aquascutum at that time was that a group of UK financial investors had acquired 25% of its shares, and these investors judged that "The company has no prospect of developing in the future with the current management team," and it was receiving proposals for a hostile takeover.

Aquascutum's sales in the Japanese market were growing at that time, and it requested that Renown, a major Japanese apparel manufacturer, rescue it from a hostile takeover. This situation became the starting point for the acquisition.

The Managers

The Renown president at the time of the acquisition was Mr. Yasuo Kaneda. Around that time, President Kaneda said, "We have lagged behind our rivals such as Onward Kashiyama in terms of overseas development, but we believe that we can catch up with them in an instant with this acquisition."[15] In fact, before the acquisition, he inspected Aquascutum's Europe and US sales networks and evaluated them highly. He said that it could take up ten years to develop similar routes, but they could be established almost immediately if the acquisition were successful.[16] Thus, his idea was to use this sales network to increase the overseas sales of Renown's products.

In the 1980s, Renown had some of the most popular brands in its markets, such as Simple Life, and its results had grown mainly from department store sales, so the acquisition of Aquascutum was a turning point.

However, in the end, President Kaneda, who had himself envisaged the sales of Renown's products in Aquascutum's Europe and US sales networks, retired as president in 1997, eight years after the acquisition, without the expected synergy effects ever having been realized.

The Post-acquisition Management and Its Challenges

After the acquisition, Renown announced that it would intervene in the management of Aquascutum as little as possible. The Aquascutum management team, which had invited Renown to act as a white knight in order to avoid a crisis, also did not want to transfer management to Renown after the acquisition.

The annual sales of the Aquascutum brand in the Japanese market at the time of the acquisition were 30 billion yen, and Renown continued to focus its energies on the Japanese market after the acquisition, and its business performed well. However, in contrast, Aquascutum's business outside Japan performed disappointingly.

Renown continued to support Aquascutum's business expansion in the United States and elsewhere, such as through underwriting a third-party allocation of shares. However, its US business continued to underperform, and ultimately, Aquascutum's results did not recover.

Upon entering the second half of the 1990s, the results at the Renown parent company also declined significantly, due to the slump in department store sales and the rise of inexpensive clothing brands in Japan. Thus, Renown embarked on a restructuring, including by reducing personnel numbers, and in 2003, it aimed to rebuild itself through a merger with the D'Urban business that it had previously spun off. Despite these efforts, it continued to record losses. However, Renown managed to maintain its ownership of Aquascutum despite a situation in which it was forced to use stopgap emergency measures to do so, such as an allocation of new shares to financial investors.

The Consequences

Renown ended up owning Aquascutum for 20 years, but ultimately, it did not produce the expected results. Aquascutum's Japanese business performed strongly thanks to the efforts of Renown's local sales force, but its overseas business underperformed, and it recorded losses for five consecutive fiscal years, from 2004 to 2008.

Renown had expected to generate synergy by utilizing Aquascutum's production bases and sales network in Europe and the United States. Instead, however, after the acquisition, those businesses outside Japan continued to slump and became a heavy burden for Renown. This situation coincided with its own restructuring due to the recession in the apparel industry in Japan from the second half of the 1990s, and Renown was unable to implement its long-term management strategy of growing its overseas business.

In 2009, Renown sold its shares in Aquascutum and its trademark rights, with the exception of those for Asia, to a UK financial investor, and in Asia, it sold its trademark rights to YGM, a Hong Kong apparel company, thereby withdrawing from its overseas business. However, it concluded a licensing agreement with YGM for Aquascutum's business in Japan. Subsequently, Renown itself was forced to change its management by its major shareholder, an investment fund, and ironically in 2010, the Chinese clothing company Shandong Ruyi made Renown a member of its group with the objective of utilizing the Renown brand. Following its sale, Aquascutum went into bankruptcy in 2012.

4.5 Case Study 5: NKK (JFE)

Acquiring company: NKK (currently, JFE)
Target company: National Steel (United States)
Shareholders: National Intergroup (NII) (United States)
Targeted business: Steel
Acquisition year: 1990
Sale year: 2002

The Objective at the Time of the Acquisition

NKK purchased its joint venture partner NII's stake in National Steel and made it a subsidiary in 1990.

Going back further, the first time that NKK invested in National Steel was in 1984. It acquired from NII 50% of National Steel shares for a joint venture. After the acquisition, NKK introduced facilities, such as electric galvanizing lines and continuous casting equipment, and made National Steel's facilities state of the art, and in 1987, National Steel, which had previously recorded a loss, achieved profitability.

On the other hand, the joint venture partner, NII, wanted to withdraw from the steel business and sounded out NKK for the sale of its stake. In order to offset the amount borne by NII for the National Steel employees' pension obligations, NKK underwrote its 20% stake and raised its own stake to 70%.[17] Although joint venture businesses in the United States by

Japanese steel manufacturers had increased in the second half of the 1980s due to the Japan-US trade friction at that time, NKK was the first Japanese company to acquire the controlling stake of a local US steel manufacturer.

At the time it acquired National Steel, then Vice President Yukio Hatori explained the reasons for the acquisition as follows:

> We responded to our partner NII's wish to withdraw from the steel business. However, in order for it to continue to be a United States company into the future, we avoided making it a wholly owned subsidiary. Going forward, we wish to actively work to build a structure that will be highly competitive.

From this comment, we understand that rather than NKK wanting to acquire the controlling stake in National Steel, it somewhat reluctantly acquired that due to the withdrawal of its joint venture partner.

It is considered that NKK understood that National Steel's blast furnace facilities were aging and that it would have to undertake a significant financial burden to upgrade them, and also that based on the downward path of the US economy at that time, in 1990, the outlook for its results was abysmal.

The Managers

The president of NKK at the time it acquired the management rights of National Steel was Mr. Yoshinari Yamashiro. He was appointed NKK president in 1985 and held this position until 1992, being appointed the company chairman in the same year.

In the second half of the 1980s, President Yamashiro considered there to be little prospect for profits from conventional exports to the United States due to the yen appreciation following the 1980 Plaza Accord and the steel-related trade friction between Japan and the United States, so he decided on the acquisition of National Steel. At the time of the acquisition, President Yamashiro gave three reasons for the high costs in the US steel industry—first, that companies owned their own mines, second, that facilities were aging, and third, that companies kept excess workers—and said that National Steel's management would work on improving the situations relating to facilities and workers.[18]

The Post-acquisition Management and Its Challenges

After acquiring National Steel in 1990, the economic recession in the United States also had an impact and National Steel recorded losses. However, NKK considered this deterioration in results to be transient due to the economic cycle and continued to invest in National Steel.

However, the economic recession in the United States became prolonged, continuing into the 1990s, and the US steel industry suffered a major recession due to the increase in imports of steel products into the country. The so-called "legacy costs", of pensions for retirees and medical expenses, also became a burden, while the blast furnace facilities continued to age, and the industry lagged behind in terms of technological innovation. Responding to these conditions in the steel industry, from 1998 onward, the US government imposed an anti-dumping tax on steel imports and invoked emergency import restriction methods (safeguards) in an attempt to protect US steel manufacturers. However, in the end, 30 US steel manufacturers, including major companies like LTV and Bethlehem Steel, filed for bankruptcy.

National Steel had steel plants in Michigan, Indiana, and Illinois, and NKK positioned them as strategic bases within its medium-term target of a global steel production system of 20 million tons. In 2000, on a standalone basis, NKK produced 13.46 million tons of crude steel, but in contrast, National Steel produced only 5.57 million tons. Further, while NKK's standalone sales were 678.9 billion yen, National Steel's sales were on a smaller scale of 321.2 billion yen.

In 2001 NKK sent its managing director from headquarter to serve as the CEO of National Steel, and he worked on various measures to improve the situation, such as to reduce labor and purchasing costs, and to suspend operations of some of the blast furnaces. However, despite these efforts, National Steel recorded operating losses of 12.2 billion yen in fiscal year 2000 and 57.1 billion yen in fiscal year 2001. Moreover, due to the impact of these losses on its consolidated operating profit, NKK itself recorded an operating loss of 32.2 billion yen.

The Consequences

National Steel could not halt the deterioration of its results, and NKK judged it would be difficult to continue to support it, so in 2002, it decided to transfer ownership of National Steel to US Steel. In the same year, National Steel filed with the United States Federal Bankruptcy Court for the application of Article 11 (Chapter 11) of the US Bankruptcy Code.

NKK owned National Steel for 13 years after making it a subsidiary and managed it as a strategic base of the NKK Group, but despite its efforts, it was unable to improve its results. In conjunction with the bankruptcy of National Steel, NKK recorded an extraordinary loss of 26 billion yen (refer to the following NKK press release).

Reference material: NKK press release

On March 6, 2002, NKK's US subsidiary National Steel (NKK's shareholding ratio, 53.5%) filed for reorganization proceedings with the US Federal Bankruptcy Court based on the application of Article 11 (Chapter 11) of the US Bankruptcy Code. This was a decision taken by NKK's management and Board of Directors based on the current severe conditions in the US steel industry and with the objectives of securing the liquidity of National Steel and advancing its reconstruction.

In accordance with this filing, on a consolidated basis NKK expects net profit to decline in the region of 18 billion yen (an extraordinary loss of around 26 billion yen). In addition, on a non-consolidated basis, it expects net profit to decline in the region of 11 billion yen (an extraordinary loss of around 19 billion yen). Up to the present fiscal year, National Steel's results have been reflected in NKK's consolidated financial statements, but from the end of the current fiscal period it will be removed from the scope of consolidated and its assets, liabilities, and results will no longer be reflected in NKK's consolidated financial statements.

The effects on this on NKK results will be basically the same as in the event of realizing the management integration of National Steel and US Steel as a result of the previously concluded agreement for the conditional transfer of shares.

Going forward, National Steel, in accordance with the procedures set forth in Chapter 11, shall be placed under the fair supervision of the Bankruptcy Court and undergo restructuring. With regard to debtor-in-possession (DIP) financing also, a basic agreement with financial institutions is already in place and the necessary working capital has been secured. Therefore, NKK's corporate activities, including production and sales, are expected to continue as usual.

National Steel's current management structure will continue for the time being, and NKK, while intending to keep a watch on the efforts of National Steel described above, does not intend to invest new funds or capital.

With regard to the integration of National Steel and US Steel, consultations will be held with US Steel based on the status of the filing for Chapter

11, while NKK expects the plan to integrate the two companies to continue to progress, and it also hopes that the discussions between NKK and US Steel on a business alliance will continue.

4.6 Case Study 6: JUSCO (AEON)

Acquiring company: JUSCO (currently, AEON)
Target company: Talbots (United States)
Shareholders: General Mills, Inc. (United States)
Targeted business: Luxury women's apparel specialty stores
Acquisition year: 1988
Sale year: 2010

The Objective at the Time of the Acquisition

JUSCO acquired Talbots, a US chain of women's apparel specialty stores, in 1988, which was the period when JUSCO had started to focus on its international business. In 1985, it opened the first JUSCO overseas store in Malaysia and established a local subsidiary in Hong Kong. In 1986, it established Laura Ashley Japan jointly with Laura Ashley of the United Kingdom and began developing a chain of stores in Japan.[19]

JUSCO ranked fourth in sales in the retail industry at that time, but it did not intend to stop at its supermarket business. Based on its philosophies of "business specific federal management" and "community-based management," it was expanding its business as a developer and service provider in areas such as leisure. The acquisition of Talbots, was one part of this business expansion.

Talbots had recorded a loss at the time of the acquisition, but JUSCO's main objective was to develop the Talbots brand in the Japanese market.

The Managers

The company chairman at the time of the acquisition was its founder, Mr. Takuya Okada. In addition, the current AEON Group CEO Mr. Motoya Okada was appointed president of Talbots Japan, which was established the year after the acquisition.

Mr. Takuya Okada, who changed the name of the group of 151 companies from JUSCO to AEON, conducted management in Japan that respected the autonomy of each respective business, and even following the acquisition of Talbots, kept its local management team in place and entrusted the management to them.

Rather than the acquisition of Talbots corresponding to AEON, by acquiring the controlling stake and reconstructing the company itself, the situation was closer to extending an invitation to a luxury women's apparel specialty stores business, which the group did not possess, to become a member of the group. The Talbots president at that time, Mr. Arnold Zetcher, stressed that it was a friendly acquisition, saying that it was "A relationship facilitated by extremely smooth communication with President Okada," and he explained the merits of receiving the backing of AEON, saying that "By having the AEON Group as a stable partner, we can advance our long-term vision for management while avoiding the risk of an Leveraged buyout (LBO) and related issues that recently have been sweeping the United States retail industry."[20]

The Post-acquisition Management and Its Challenges

After the acquisition, Talbots' business trended smoothly. While it had recorded a loss at the time of the acquisition, it returned to profitability in the following year of 1989, was listed on the New York Stock Exchange in 1993, and achieved a record-high profit of 15.6 billion yen in 2000. In the five-year period from the acquisition to its listing on the NYSE, the number of Talbots stores had risen from 126 to 338, and its sales had grown from 340 million dollars to 700 million dollars. The Talbots' local management team was entrusted with steering the course for the United States, while AEON focused on developing Talbots stores in the Japanese market.

At the start of the 2000s, profits fell in AEON's core business of domestic general merchandise stores (GMS), but Talbots' business contributed to profits to the extent that the president at the time, Mr. Motoya Okada, described it as "The greatest success among acquisitions by Japanese companies." In addition to women's apparel, Talbots was newly developing a children's apparel business at Talbots Kids stores in the United States and also planned to advance into the United Kingdom and Canada.

However, by the second half of the 2000s, sales in Talbots' mainstay women's apparel business had stopped growing, the results of its children's apparel business had also started to deteriorate, and it continued to be unprofitable. Seeing that its existing businesses had reached an impasse, to break out of this situation, Talbots decided to conduct a large-scale acquisition. In 2006, Talbots acquired the J. Jill Group, which was listed on the US NASDAQ for 60 billion yen, for AEON; this was an additional acquisition of a US specialty stores business.

While Talbots was a luxury women's apparel brand, J. Jill was a casual-wear brand that conducted sales of not only apparel, but also other items such as accessories and shoes at its 200 stores nationwide. Through this acquisition, Talbots changed from being a single brand to a multi-brand company and thereby, aimed to improve its profits.

However, this additional acquisition would end in failure after only three years. J. Jill's results worsened significantly, and in 2007, Talbots recorded a final loss of 22 billion yen. AEON, unable to hold back from intervening any longer, resolved on a policy to sell J. Jill even though it had only recently acquired it.

At the same time, Talbots announced that it was withdrawing from its unprofitable UK and Canada businesses and its men's apparel and children's apparel businesses and that it would be focusing its management resources on the core Talbots' brand.[21]

Nonetheless, Talbots' results continued to worsen, and in 2008, it recorded a loss of 57.1 billion yen. Moreover, the AEON Group recorded a loss in its consolidated results, so for AEON, restructuring Talbots became its most pressing issue (refer to Fig. 4.4).

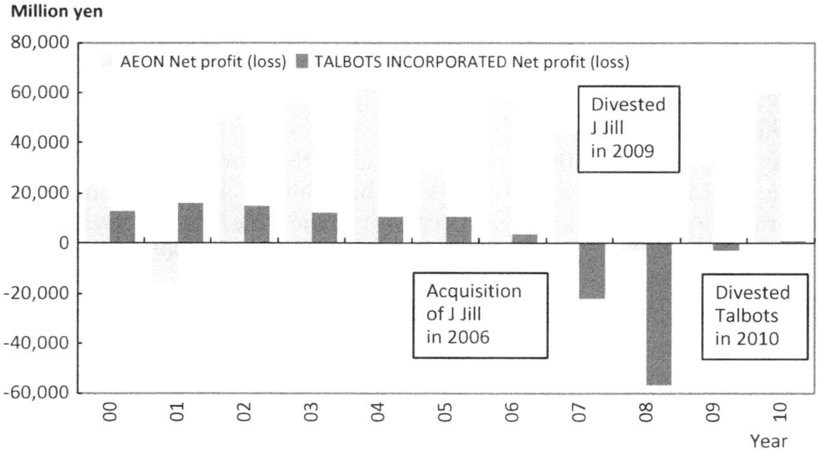

Fig. 4.4 Trends in AEON and Talbots net profits (2000–2010). (Prepared by the author from AEON's annual securities report 2000–2010)

Subsequently, AEON provided 200 million dollars of financing to Talbots, and further, asked the major Hong Kong apparel company Li & Fung for advice on Talbots' business. In such ways, it implemented bold and aggressive support measures and tried to stop the bleeding at Talbots.

The Consequences

AEON was forced to record an impairment loss of 50 billion yen relating to the sale of J. Jill, which had been acquired by Talbots.[22] Subsequently, once Talbots had returned to profitability, AEON announced that it was transferring Talbots to a US financial investor, and it sold its shares in Talbots in 2010.[23]

AEON's policy of "federal management," of entrusting the business to the local management team, worked well at the stage when Talbots' business was progressing smoothly after the acquisition. However, this policy backfired when Talbots' results were slumping, and it tried to recover through an additional acquisition, which ultimately resulted in AEON withdrawing from its North American specialty stores business.

AEON did not intervene when Talbots was performing well, but when it sales slumped, it was unable to appropriately intervene and lend a hand. When we see that AEON recorded enormous losses and was forced to acquire J. Jill, which ended up being sold after 3 years, and then embarked on the reconstruction of Talbots, and even requested advice from a major Hong Kong apparel company on inventory reduction and product development, unfortunately, we have no choice but to conclude that even after the passage of 20 years from the acquisition, AEON had still not acquired the skills to manage a specialty store business in the United States.

4.7 Case Study 7: Dainippon Ink and Chemicals

Acquiring company: Dainippon Ink and Chemicals (currently, DIC)
Target company: Reichhold Chemicals (United States)
Shareholders: Tender offer (United States)
Targeted business: Synthetic resins
Acquisition year: 1987
Sale year: 2005

The Objective at the Time of the Acquisition

Dainippon Ink and Chemicals (DIC) acquired the US resin manufacturer Reichhold Chemicals (hereafter, Reichhold) in 1987 through a tender offer.

Even in 1986 before this acquisition, DIC had acquired the Graphic Arts Department of Sun Chemicals, a US ink manufacturer. With the acquisition of Reichhold, it had built in the United States a complete production and sales structure, from raw resin through to ink.

The relationship between Reichhold and DIC can be traced back to the 1950s. Reichhold was a manufacturer of thermosetting resins, and in 1952 in Japan through a joint venture with Reichhold, DIC launched a resin business, which it subsequently made into a wholly owned subsidiary. Before the acquisition, Reichhold's results had been poor, and in fiscal year 1985 it recorded a loss of 28.4 million dollars. Moreover, it had around 20–30% in reserve in terms of its production capacity utilization rate. With regard to how it would improve profits at Reichhold, DIC said that "We will transfer to it our own technologies, such as urethane resin for synthetic leather, and we are aiming for it to return to profitability at the earliest by the third year and at the latest by the fifth year."[24]

The president at the time of the acquisition was Mr. Shigekuni Kawamura, who said that "20 years after our 100th anniversary, we want to become a company on the same scale as the world's big chemical companies, such as DuPont of the United States and Hoechst of Germany."[25] Through a series of overseas acquisitions, Dainippon Ink and Chemicals' overseas sales had grown to almost 250 billion yen, while domestically, its sales were close to 400 billion yen. In addition, speaking of the overseas acquisitions that it had carried out in rapid succession, President Kawamura explained that,

> The reason why we selected M&A rather than advancing by building factories is simple. Even when looking at the industry globally, the feeling is that the ink industry is mature and there is an excess of facilities. So, we determined that even if we built new factories, this would only make the competition for market share even more severe, so a better approach would be to utilize existing facilities. Therefore, we embarked on an M&A strategy.[26]

The Managers

Dainippon Ink and Chemicals' M&A-focused global expansion strategy at that time was said to be basically planned and executed by President

Kawamura alone; at that time, he was one of the managers most actively conducting acquisitions of overseas companies.

In 1958, Mr. Kawamura married the eldest daughter of Dainippon Printing Ink Manufacturing President Katsumi Kawamura, and in 1959, he transferred to DIC (then called Dainippon Printing Ink Manufacturing) from the Long-Term Credit Bank of Japan and was appointed finance director. At the time of Mr. Kawamura's transfer, it was still only a relatively small company with a capital of 600 million yen and sales of 5 billion yen.

He was subsequently appointed president in 1978, serving in the position 17 years, until his retirement in 1994.

At the time of the acquisition, Mr. Kawamura said,

> Presently, there are great opportunities for overseas M&A now that the exchange rate is at around 125 yen to the dollar. The strengthening of the yen is making tangible Japan's transformation from an exporting nation to an investing nation. These two years are the biggest opportunity for both Japanese companies and the government to realize this transformation. It is useless to spend money and energy on competition for shares and prices domestically. If a company has surplus capacity, it is the responsibility of its top management to first turn their eyes overseas. I would like to request that the government review the corporate tax system to make it easier for profits acquired through overseas investment to flow back into Japan.

He made these comments 30 years ago in 1987, but they are hardly different to the comments we hear from managers today.

Directly after the acquisition, the top management of the acquired overseas subsidiaries gathered in Tokyo to hold the DIC Group's International Conference, and they worked to "create a family" from the group companies. They considered appointing a foreigner as a director of the DIC parent company, and, aiming to leap forward to become a comprehensive chemicals manufacturer, they embarked on international management, which was pioneering for Japanese companies at that time.

The Post-acquisition Management and Its Challenges

After the acquisition of Reichhold, DIC entrusted the business to the local management team and worked actively on additional acquisitions.

Mr. Kawamura said, "In order to stand shoulder-to-shoulder with big chemical companies, the companies that have joined our group must expand their businesses through additional acquisitions."

In 1988, the year after the acquisition, it acquired Koppers, the US-based unsaturated polyester business, and in 1989, it acquired the US resin coating manufacturer Spencer Kellogg, both via Reichhold. In each case, the acquisition was planned and proposed to DIC by Reichhold's local management team. A Reichhold employee at that time said, "For employees of Reichhold, Dainippon Ink and Chemicals is like a good brother who supports Reichhold's business."

Reichhold was placed under the jurisdiction of Dainippon Ink and Chemicals' polymer-related business head office, but as the expansion of the resin business in the United States was left to the local management and as the scale of Reichhold's resin business was larger, synergy effects were not generated with its existing businesses in Japan and the management integration did not progress easily.

In 1992, Reichhold recorded a loss of 6.7 billion yen, and for the first time, DIC also recorded a consolidated loss. In the five years since the acquisition in 1987, Reichhold had not achieved profitability even once. At that time, DIC considered that it would take another four to five years for Reichhold to become profitable.

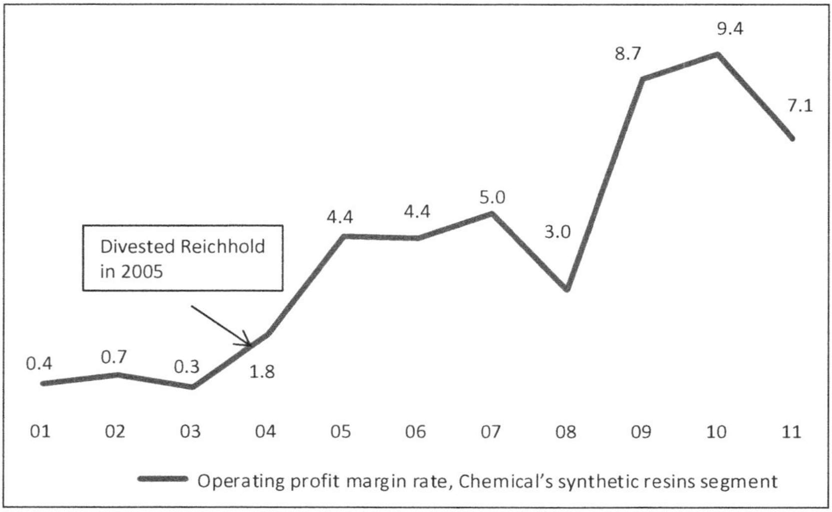

Fig. 4.5 Trends in the operating profit margin of Dainippon Ink and Chemicals' synthetic resins segment (2001–2012). (Dainippon Ink and Chemicals' annual securities report 2001–2012)

Consequences

DIC continued to own Reichhold over a long period of 19 years, but in 2005, it sold its shares to the local management team through a management buyout (MBO). In the year prior to the sale, Reichhold had recorded a loss of 23.6 billion yen.[27]

In terms of its reasons for selling Reichhold, DIC cited factors such as that Reichhold's main products were generalized and becoming obsolete, that the technologies transferred from Japan had not produced sufficient results due to Reichhold's unwillingness to accept them, and that the synergy effects generated with the ink manufacturer Sun Chemicals acquired in the United States had been limited.[28] In fact, after the sale of Reichhold, the operating profit margin of Dainippon Ink and Chemicals' synthetic resins segment greatly improved (refer to Fig. 4.5).

Alongside the sale of Reichhold, in fiscal year 2005, DIC recorded an extraordinary loss of 54.2 billion yen from the combination of a loss on the sale of shares and a debt waiver. This outcome was in contrast to that of the ink business of Sun Chemicals acquired during the same period, which had continued to record a profit.

4.8 Case Study 8: Asahi Glass

Acquiring company: Asahi Glass
Target company: Hankuk Electric Glass (South Korea)
Shareholders: Daewoo Group (South Korea)
Targeted business: Cathode ray tube (CRT) glass
Acquisition year: 1999
Withdrawal year: 2010

The Objective at the Time of the Acquisition

In 1999, Asahi Glass acquired cathode ray tube (CRT) glass manufacturer Hankuk Electric Glass from the Daewoo Group of South Korea.

At that time, Asahi Glass' CRT glass sales were approximately 180 billion yen. It also had production bases in seven other countries, including the United States and Singapore, while its customers were mainly Japanese electrical machinery manufacturers. Conversely, Hankuk Electric Glass' customers were South Korean electrical machinery manufacturers such as LG Electronics, and it had a global market share of around 10%. Daewoo Group's interest-bearing debt had swelled due to the economic slump

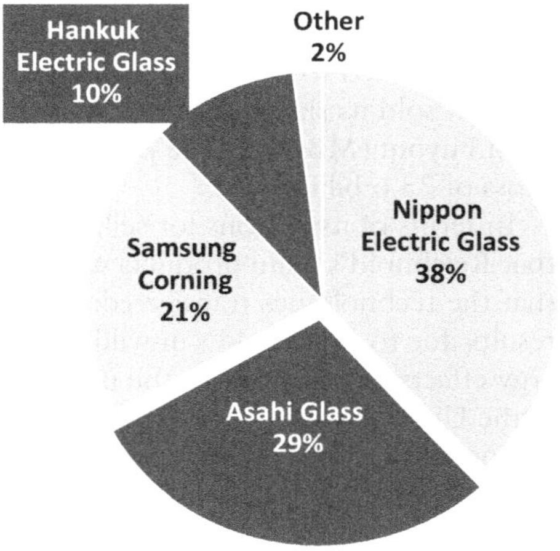

Fig. 4.6 Global share of the CRT glass market in 1998 at the time of the acquisition. ("Asahi Glass purchased Hankuk Electric Glass" 1999)

caused by the Asian currency crisis, and its group was being dismantled, initiated by the South Korean government.

Through this acquisition, Asahi Glass would surpass its competitor Nippon Electric Glass and acquire the leading global market share for CRT glass (refer to Fig. 4.6).

The president at the time of the acquisition, Mr. Shinya Ishizu, said, "We are aiming to be the global number one or number two for all our products."[29] Moreover, it was reported that another of Nippon Electric Glass' objectives for the acquisition was to stabilize market conditions by incorporating Hankuk Electric Glass, which tended to compete through low prices. The scale of the CRT glass market at that time was stable at approximately 600 billion yen, and it was an acquisition aiming for an oligopoly, which in terms of strategy is a powerful method for a mature market. In Asahi Glass' medium-term plan at that time for its CRT glass business, domestically, it was specializing in highly functional products, such as wide and flat products, and was reducing its scale, while overseas, it was strengthening facilities for general-purpose goods.

The Managers

Mr. Ishizu, the president at the time of the acquisition, was appointed to the position in 1998 and served as the head of Asahi Glass for a long period until 2008, when he retired as the Chairman of the Board of Directors. Soon after his appointment as president, Mr. Ishizu set out his management strategy of "shrink to grow,"[30] aiming for selection and concentration for the company's own businesses.

In February in the year after his appointment, he announced emergency measures to reduce 28 billion yen of fixed costs, then in June, suspended the operations of the glass kilns at the Keihin Factory, which was the birthplace of Asahi Glass' glass manufacturing. In September, he decided to withdraw from the liquid crystal display (LCD) business with Mitsubishi Electric, thereby executing the "shrink" part of the strategy.

At the same time, Asahi Glass acquired the fluorinated resin business of UK chemicals manufacturer Imperial Chemical Industries (ICI) in October, and in November, announced the acquisition of Hankuk Electric Glass, thereby embarking on the "grow" part of the strategy.

At that point in time, Asahi Glass already had a track record of overseas acquisitions, having acquired automotive glass manufacturers in Europe and the United States, and it had established a three-pillar system of Japan, the United States, and Europe.

The Post-acquisition Management and Its Challenges

After the acquisition, Asahi Glass dispatched a president and executives to Hankuk Electric Glass and embarked on its management as the South Korean base for its own CRT glass business, but market conditions rapidly deteriorated.

In 2001, it was working hard to secure CRT glass orders each month, and a flustered Asahi Glass reduced its 51% stake in Hankuk Electric Glass, which it had only just acquired, by selling 20% of its shares to the major South Korean consumer electronics company LG Electronics. LG Electronics was a major customer of Hankuk Electric Glass, accounting for half of the latter's product deliveries, and its aim was to secure a stable supply through cross-shareholding.

Subsequently in 2003, Asahi Glass acquired Nippon Electric Glass' shares in Hankuk Electric Glass and raised its stake to 42%. In 2004, it built a new factory in Hunan Province in China and provided investment support to Hankuk Electric Glass with the aim of capturing the increasing demand for CRT TVs in China.

However, around the middle of the 2000s, flat-screen TVs, such as LCD and plasma TVs, gained momentum, exceeding expectations and expanding their markets. As a result, demand for CRT TVs shrank rapidly. On the one hand, Asahi Glass responded to this development and expanded its liquid crystal panel glass business, but on the other hand, it reduced its production of CRT glass. In 2006, it stopped all production of CRT glass domestically, also withdrawing from production in countries such as Indonesia and Taiwan. By 2007, only Asahi Glass' subsidiary, Hankuk Electric Glass, was producing CRT glass. In order to accelerate the restructuring of Hankuk Electric Glass, in 2007, Asahi Glass planned to delist it through a tender offer. It conducted a tender offer for all shares excluding the 20% owned by LG Electronics, but was only able to acquire 8.71% as a result of this tender offer.

While Asahi Glass had increased its stake to 51.47%, this was not sufficient for it to delist Hankuk Electric Glass, so the latter continued to produce CRT glass.

The Consequences

In 2010, Asahi Glass decided to completely withdraw from the CRT glass business. It once again conducted a tender offer for Hankuk Electric Glass and raised its stake to 95.87%,[31] after which it delisted it and decided to permanently stop the operations of the CRT glass kilns. In conjunction with the ending of operations at Hankuk Electric Glass, Asahi Glass recorded an extraordinary loss of 9.5 billion yen.[32]

The flat-screen TV market expanded at a rate exceeding expectations, and Asahi Glass had no choice but to rationalize its CRT glass business and eventually withdraw from it. However, as the acquisition of Hankuk Electric Glass increased its market share and the acquisition target was a South Korean listed company with complex labor management relations, Asahi Glass ended up worrying over the CRT glass business for the long term.

There were clear differences between this acquisition and the acquisitions of Glaverbel (Belgium) and AFG Industries (United States) that enabled them to leap forward in the plate glass business.

4.9 Summary of All of the Failed Deals

Electrical Machinery

- Matsushita Electric Industrial

In 1990, it acquired MCA of the United States, including the movie production company Universal Pictures. It attempted to integrate the electronics and contents business but changed its strategy when it replaced the management team. It sold MCA to the Canadian beverage company Seagram in 1995 in order to concentrate on the electronics business.

- TDK

In 1989, it acquired Silicon Systems, a major US semiconductor company, through a tender offer. It invested 10 billion yen a year in manufacturing bases in the United States and Singapore, aiming for synergy effects with its electronic components business.[33] However, due to the decline of profits and a review of its policy of diversification, it sold Silicon Systems in 1996 to Texas Instruments of the United States.

- Mitsubishi Electric

In 1990, it acquired the personal computer (PC) division and other hardware business divisions of Apricot Computers of the United Kingdom. In advance of the market integration in Europe, it strengthened the UK production capacity threefold, but the results deteriorated due to the falling prices of PCs and a decline in demand, forcing it to close factories. In 1999, it recorded an allowance for a loss on overseas investments of 45.8 billion yen.[34]

- NEC

In 1998, it acquired the US PC manufacturer Packard Bell, having previously acquired a 19.99% stake in this company. However, its results worsened, including due to the fall in sales prices in the US PC market, and in 2000, it withdrew from production in the United States. In 1999, it recorded an extraordinary loss of 189.2 billion yen, which is the amount of its cumulative investment in Packard Bell.[35]

In 1999, it acquired its subsidiary, Packard Bell Europe, with the objective of supporting Packard Bell. However, the losses did not improve, and in 2006, it sold Packard Bell to Gateway.

- Fujitsu

It received a request to be acquired by the US computer manufacturer Amdahl, in which it had capital participation, and acquired it through a tender offer in 1997. It made Amdahl a subsidiary and attempted to rebuild it, but in 2003, Fujitsu recorded a 201-billion-yen loss on valuation of the shares on the assumption of Amdahl's liquidation.[36]

- Hitachi Koki

In 1990, it acquired the US printer manufacturer Dataproducts through a tender offer as a white knight. However, due to slumping results, in

2002, it sold Dataproducts together with its Japanese printer business to Hitachi. Hitachi subsequently sold the printers business to Ricoh.

- Toshiba

In 1999, it made the US semiconductor memory joint venture business Dominion Semiconductor into a wholly owned subsidiary, following the withdrawal of its joint venture partner IBM. However, alongside the deterioration of the conditions in the dynamic random access memory (DRAM) market, in 2002, it sold Dominion to Micron Technology of the United States.

- Matsushita Kotobuki Electronics Industries

In 1997, it acquired the controlling stake of the magnetic head business of the US hard disk drive (HDD) manufacturer Quantum. Matsushita Kotobuki outsourced the HDD manufacturing to Quantum and aimed to achieve synergy effects, but due to its slumping results, in 1999, it withdrew from the magnetic head business, recording a loss on the valuation of shares of 11.2 billion yen in the same year.[37]

- Akai Denki

In 1995, it obtained the capital participation of the Hong Kong Semitec Group and acquired the Konwa Group, a Hong Kong AV equipment manufacturer. It advanced overseas production using Konwa's factories in South-East Asia and China, but by 2000, it had accumulated excessive debts, filed for the application of the Civil Rehabilitation Law, and went bankrupt.

- Yuasa Battery

In 1991, it acquired the industrial battery division of Exide of the United States. It established Yuasa-Exide, which acquired Exide's three factories and 70 sales offices in the United States. It attempted to make industrial batteries its second business pillar after car batteries, but it sold the company to the local management team through an MBO in 2000 and withdrew from the US industrial battery market.

- NISSEI Electric

In 1990, NISSEI acquired from Black & Decker of the United States the European subsidiary capacitor manufacturer Arcotronics. However, due to the deterioration of the results in its domestic business, in 2000, it sold Arcotronics to KEMET of the United States. NISSEI itself went bankrupt in 2010.

Chemicals

- Mitsubishi Kasei

In 1990, it acquired the floppy disk (FD) manufacturer Verbatim Corporation of the United States from Kodak, also of the United States. However, due to the rapid decrease in demand for FDs, in 1998, Verbatim recorded a cumulative loss of 150 million dollars,[38] and it closed the FD factory, sold the magnetic tape factory to the Taiwanese company CMC Magnetics, and withdrew from production in the United States.

- Mitsubishi Corporation

In 1990, it conducted an LBO and acquired Aristech Chemicals, a major US polypropylene resin company and the chemicals business division of USX of the United States. It became Mitsubishi Corporation's largest subsidiary, but its results were sluggish, and in 2000, it was sold to SUNOCO, a major US petroleum chemical company. It recorded a loss of 38 billion yen on the sale.[39]

- Settsu

In 1988, it acquired Uarco, a US printing company with products such as paper for official documents, and it attempted to expand its business in the United States. However, in 1998, ahead of the merger with Rengo, it sold Uarco to Standard Register of the United States.

- Dainippon Ink and Chemicals

In 1987, it acquired the US synthetic resins manufacturer Reichhold through a tender offer. In 1988, it additionally acquired the unsaturated polyester business of the US company Koppers, and in 1989, the US paint-use resin manufacturer Spencer Kellogg, both through Reichhold. In 1997, it also acquired the polyester company Jotun Polymer. However, due to slumping results, in 2005, it sold Reichhold to the Reichhold management team through an MBO, recording an extraordinary loss of 54.2 billion yen in the same year.[40]

- Nippon Sanso

In 1989, it acquired the Thermos company manufacture's thermos bottles and outdoor products business of the Thermos Corporation from Household International. Thermos was the leading manufacturer of thermos bottles, a product that Nippon Sanso did not handle, but due to its slumping results, Nippon Sanso withdrew from production in the United States in 2001. In 1996, it recorded a loss from the liquidation of affiliates of 7.4 billion yen.[41]

- Ishihara Sangyo

In 1990, it acquired from major Swedish medical and pesticide manufacturer Fermenter, the US pesticide subsidiary SDS Enterprise. It changed its name to ISK Biosciences, and it acquired R&D and sales bases in the United States, but it sold SDS to Zeneca of the United Kingdom in 1997.

- Fujifilm

In 1996, it made UK printing equipment joint venture Crossfield into a wholly owned subsidiary, following the withdrawal of its US joint venture partner DuPont. Subsequently, after suspending the production of scanners, it sold the company to Crossfield's employees through an MBO.

Medical and Pharmaceutical

- Yamanouchi Pharmaceutical

In 1989, it acquired the US nutritional foods company Shaklee Corporation as a white knight through a tender offer. It attempted to diversify from pharmaceuticals, but in advance of the merger with Fujisawa Pharmaceutical in 2004, it sold Shaklee to the US private equity firm, Ripplewood. In 2001, it recorded a loss on the valuation of shares of 30.1 billion yen.[42]

- Shionogi & Co., Ltd.

In 1992, it acquired the hard gelatin pharmaceutical capsule business of Eli Lilly of the United States. Although it advanced overseas business expansion and diversification, it sold the business to Carlyle Group, a private equity firm, in 2005, in order to concentrate on its medical pharmaceuticals business.

- Chugai Pharmaceutical

In 1989, it acquired the US bio-diagnostics venture company Gen Probe through a tender offer and advanced into the diagnostics drugs business. In advance of joining the pharmaceutical Roche Group of Switzerland and due to the possibility of infringing antitrust laws in the United States, in 2002, it divested Gen Probe, selling the business through an allotment of shares without contribution to Chugai Pharmaceutical's shareholders.

- Fujisawa Pharmaceutical

In 1989, it acquired the US generic pharmaceuticals manufacturer Lyphomed, for which it had previously acquired a 30% stake. It intended to use Lyphomed as Fujisawa USA, its US sales bases, but it discovered that Lyphomed had incorrectly applied for a license for generics and in conjunction with this application, its products were recalled, and its results deteriorated. In 1998, it liquidated the business and withdrew from the US generics business. It recorded a loss on the liquidation of the subsidiary of 75 billion yen.[43]

Retail

- Seibu Saison

In 1988, it acquired InterContinental Hotels' chain of luxury hotels from the UK Grand Metropolitan. It sold it to Path Corporation of the United Kingdom in 1998 in order to repay its debts arising from the group companies' worsening financial conditions after the collapse of the bubble economy.

- Kyotaru

In 1990, it acquired the US restaurant chain RAI and Paragon Steakhouse. It embarked on a restaurant business in the United States, including through the additional acquisition of Mexican restaurants, but it declared bankruptcy in 1997 and filed for the application of the Corporate Rehabilitation Law.

- JUSCO

In 1988, it acquired Talbots, a chain of luxury women's apparel specialty stores in the United States. In 2006, through Talbots, it additionally acquired J. Jill, a US women's apparel chain, but its results did not improve and in 2010, it sold Talbots to a US investment fund. In 2009, it recorded an impairment loss of 55.5 billion yen.[44]

- Renown

In 1990, it acquired the UK luxury men's apparel company Aquascutum as a white knight through a tender offer. After the acquisition, it attempted to rebuild the company, including through 15 billion yen in additional investment, but it continued to record losses, and in 2009, it sold the business to the Broadwick Group of the United Kingdom. In the same year, it recorded a loss on the valuation of shares of 5.8 billion yen.[45]

- Sogo

In 1989, it acquired Paragon, a large-scale shopping center in Singapore. However, as its borrowing increased alongside its active development of stores domestically and overseas, it sold it to Singapore Press in 1996 with the objective of recovering funds. In 2000, it filed for the application of the Civil Rehabilitation Law and went bankrupt.

Steel

- Kawasaki Steel Corporation

In 1991, it acquired LNP Engineering, which possessed resin compound production bases in the United States and the Netherlands, from the UK chemicals manufacturer ICI. LNP was to be the pillar of its diversification from the steel business, but in advance of its management integration with NKK and following a review of its business portfolio, it sold LNP to General Electric of the United States in 2001.

- NKK

In 1990, it made steel manufacturer National Steel a subsidiary following the withdrawal of its joint venture partner NII of the United States. In 2002, National Steel filed for reorganization proceedings based on the United States Federal bankruptcy laws. NKK subsequently sold National Steel to US Steel, and in 2002, it recorded an extraordinary loss of 26 billion yen.[46]

- Kyoei Steel

In 1992, it acquired the electric furnace manufacturer Florida Steel from FLS Holdings of the United States. It changed the name to Ameristeel and aimed to rebuild its rebar steel bars and groove-type steel businesses, but it sold Ameristeel to the Brazilian electric furnace manufacturer Gerdau in 1999 in order to improve its financial condition following the deterioration of its domestic results.

Machinery

- Komatsu

In 1999, it acquired the silicon business of Union Carbide of the United States. After the acquisition, it focused on polycrystalline silicon as an advanced silicon material, but due to its slumping results, in 2005, it sold the business to Norwegian solar cell manufacturer REC. It recorded losses on the impairment of equipment of 13 billion yen in 2001 and 15.6 billion yen in 2002.[47]

- NSK

In 1990, it acquired United Precision Industries (UPI), a major UK bearings manufacturer. It acquired UK production bases in advance of the market integration in Europe, but its profits deteriorated due to the strengthening of the British pound, and in 2003, it liquidated the majority of UPI's businesses. In the same year, it recorded business structure-related costs alongside the liquidation.[48]

- JUKI

In 1988, it acquired Union Special Corporation, a major US knitwear sewing machine company, as a white knight. It attempted to rationalize Union Special and strengthen its development department, but the results were poor, and in 2005, it withdrew from the sewing machines business in the United States.

Glass

- Nippon Electric Glass

In 1993, it made the US CRT glass joint venture OI NEG into a wholly owned subsidiary following the withdrawal of joint venture partner

Owens. Due to the rapid decline in demand for CRT TVs following the expansion of the flat-screen TV market, in 2004, it withdrew from production in the United States, recording an extraordinary loss of 40 billion yen in the same year.[49]

- Asahi Glass

In 1999, it acquired the CRT glass manufacturer Hankuk Electric Glass from the South Korean Daewoo Group. However, due to the dramatic decline in demand following the expansion of the flat-screen TV market, in 2010, it terminated Hankuk Electric Glass and completely withdrew from the CRT glass business. That same year, it recorded an extraordinary loss of 9.5 billion yen.[50]

Nonferrous Metals

- Ryobi

In 1988, it acquired the motor products (household power tools) division of Singer of the United States. In addition to business use, it attempted to expand its power tools business in the United States, but its profitability deteriorated due to the slumping results of Sears, on which it relied for sales. In order to concentrate on its die-caster business, in 2000, it sold the acquisition to Techtronic Industries of Hong Kong. It recorded an allowance for subsidiary-adjusted losses of 14 billion yen.[51]

- Furukawa Electric

In 1990, it acquired Yates Industries, a major manufacturer of electrolytic copper foil, from Square D of the United States. Furukawa had entered the copper foil business in 1970 with a joint venture with Yates Industries. From the acquisition, it acquired bases in the United States, the United Kingdom, and Luxembourg, but it sold Yates in 1997 due to its poor results.

Transportation Equipment

- Mitsubishi Motors Corporation

In 2001, it made Dutch auto manufacturer NedCar into a wholly owned subsidiary following the withdrawal of its joint venture partner Volvo. After the acquisition, it planned joint operations with Daimler Chrysler, with which it had a capital partnership, but this goal was not realized, and its slumping results continued. Mitsubishi Motors withdrew from European production in 2012, recording an extraordinary loss of 25.1 billion yen in the same year.[52]

Construction

- Aoki Construction

In 1987, it acquired Westin Hotels, a chain of luxury hotels in 11 countries, from UAL of the United States. Its aim was to diversify from the construction business, but results deteriorated for its main business of construction, and it sold Westin to Starwood of the United States in 1995 to repay its debts.

Paper

- Daishowa Paper Manufacturing

In 1988, it acquired the North American business of Reed International, a major UK paper manufacturer. It managed the newspaper-use paper mills in Canada and the sales bases in North America and Europe as Daishowa Forest Products, but sold Daishowa to the ENRON Group of the United States in 2001 in order to concentrate management resources on its domestic operations.

Communications

- SoftBank

In 1995, it acquired the Interop exhibition business of Ziff-Davis of the United States. In the same year, it additionally acquired the exhibition business of the Interface Group, which operated the COMDEX computers trade fair. However, after it reviewed its policy of diversification and in 1988, it integrated with Ziff-Davis and then sold it through a public offering.

In 1995, it acquired the computer-related publishing company Ziff-Davis Publishing, which published PC Magazine and other publications, from the US investment company Forstmann Little.

However, again, it reviewed its policy of diversification, and in 2000, it sold Ziff-Davis Publishing to the US investment company Willis Stein & Partners.

In 1996, it acquired Kingston, a PC memory capacity and memory board manufacturer. However, following its decision to concentrate on its internet business, it sold Kingston back to the founder in 1999 and recorded a loss on the sale of 72.5 billion yen.[53]

Transportation

- Footwork

In 1991, it acquired the German transportation company Harry Hamaha. Due to the failure of its investments for diversification, including into overseas hotels and a jewelry business, in 2001, Footwork filed for the application of the Civil Rehabilitation Law and went bankrupt.

Food

- Suntory

In 1985, it acquired Kentwood Spring Water, a US natural water home delivery company. It acquired two other such companies in the United States but subsequently withdrew from the natural water business in the country.

Notes

1. Nihon Keizai Shimbun, November 27, 1990.
2. Nikkei Business, April 28, 2009 edition.
3. Nihon Keizai Shimbun, November 28, 1990.
4. Matsushita Electric Industrial annual securities report.
5. Nihon Keizai Shimbun, May 14, 1989.
6. Nikkei Sangyo Shimbun, February 4, 1989.
7. Nikkei Sangyo Shimbun, April 6, 2004.
8. Yamanouchi Pharmaceuticals press release, April 2, 2004.
9. Yamanouchi Pharmaceuticals annual securities report, March 2001.
10. Mitsubishi Motors Corporation Factbook, 2000.
11. Mitsubishi Motors Corporation press release, April 2, 2001.
12. Nihon Keizai Shimbun, February 7, 2012.
13. Mitsubishi Motors Corporation press release, December 17, 2012.
14. Nihon Keizai Shimbun, June 26, 1990.
15. Nihon Keizai Shimbun, May 14, 1990.
16. Nihon Keizai Shimbun, May 14, 1990.

17. Nihon Keizai Shimbun, April 26, 1990.
18. Nihon Keizai Shimbun, July 2, 1991.
19. AEON Group History.
20. Nihon Keizai Shimbun, October 2, 1990.
21. AEON press release, November 25, 2008.
22. Nihon Keizai Shimbun, June 10, 2009.
23. AEON press release, December 9, 2009.
24. Nihon Keizai Shimbun, August 27, 1987.
25. Nihon Keizai Shimbun, May 9, 1988.
26. Nikkei Sangyo Shimbun, December 21, 1987.
27. Dainippon Ink and Chemicals press release, September 12, 2005.
28. Dainippon Ink and Chemicals fiscal 2005 interim financial results briefing materials.
29. Nikkei Sangyo Shimbun, November 2, 1999.
30. Asahi Glass news release, June 17, 1999.
31. Asahi Glass news release, November 4, 2010.
32. Asahi Glass news release, December 24, 2010.
33. Nihon Keizai Shimbun, June 5, 1996.
34. Mitsubishi Electric annual securities report, March 1999.
35. NEC annual securities report, March 1999.
36. Fujitsu press release, April 22, 2004.
37. Matsushita Kotobuki Electronics Industries annual securities report, March 1999.
38. Nihon Keizai Shimbun, July 2, 1998.
39. Mitsubishi Corporation annual securities report, March 200l.
40. DIC fiscal year 2005 interim financial results briefing materials.
41. Nippon Sanso annual securities report, March 1997.
42. Yamanouchi Pharmaceuticals annual securities report, March 2001.
43. Astellas (formerly Fujisawa Pharmaceuticals) press release, March 30, 1998.
44. AEON annual securities report, February 2009.
45. Renown press release, April 8, 2009.
46. NKK press release, March 6, 2002.
47. Komatsu news releases, October 2, 2001, and March 1, 2002.
48. NSK annual securities report, March 2003.
49. Nippon Electric Glass press release, August 4, 2004.
50. Asahi Glass press release, December 24, 2010.
51. Ryobi annual securities report, March 2000.
52. Mitsubishi Motors Corporation press release, July 11, 2012.
53. SoftBank press release, July 15, 1999.

CHAPTER 5

The Nature of Failure: Why Do Companies Fail in Overseas Acquisitions?

5.1 What Separates Successes from Failures in Overseas M&A?

Up until the previous chapter, we considered the traps that lay in wait amid the benefits of overseas acquisitions and traced the consequences of failure. When we look at the comments made by Japanese acquiring companies at the time of the bubble economy, we find that they said they were aiming to expand the business overseas and to generate synergy by taking advantage of yen appreciation; we see that the ideas of managers today have hardly changed. Thus, there would seem to be lessons we should learn from the consequences of these past acquisitions in order to improve the current situation in which there are much more failures than successes.

While on one hand, there have been deals that have helped the acquiring company to achieve record profits at the fast pace of at least once in two years, on the other hand, there have been deals in which the company incurred a major loss and ended up selling or withdrawing from the acquired business. Thus, as we can see that the consequences after the acquisition diverge greatly, we ask, "What factors affect the success or failure of these acquisitions?" At the time they are conducted, the media and market label the company's acquisition "as an aggressive measure to launch itself onto the global market." However, after an acquisition fails and the company has to record an impairment loss and withdraw from the business, many voices criticize the acquiring company, saying that it "paid

S. Matsumoto, *Japanese Outbound Acquisitions*,
https://doi.org/10.1007/978-981-13-1364-6_5

too much," and that it failed because "its management after the acquisition was poor" or "its strategy was wrong." As there have been too many failures, there are also those that simply conclude that "Japanese companies are not good at overseas acquisitions." Yet, often, acquisitions that go well are attributed to factors like company-specific management approaches. Until now, the nature of the success or failure of outbound acquisitions has not been fully investigated.

In this chapter, we will examine in detail the cases determined to be either successes or failures in Chap. 3 and attempt to verify the factors that clearly separate the consequences (success and failure) of overseas acquisitions. The examination process is shown in Fig. 5.1. I set examination conditions that are considered to affect the success or failure of an acquisition (refer to Table 5.1) and investigated their correspondence with a total of 60 cases of successes and failures. With the results of statistical tests, I analyzed the relationships between the examination conditions and the successes and failures. Based on the results of this analysis, we will describe the nature of failure.

Setting the examination conditions is an important process in order to discover the nature of failure. Therefore, I would like to explain the reasons why I set these examination conditions and provide some context for them.

For those readers who are more interested in the results rather than in the grounds for setting the examination conditions and the process of the correspondence investigation, I recommend that you continue on to the end of the next section, "The Nature of Failure in Outbound Acquisition."

In addition, for those readers who are interested in the details of the investigation, I would like to refer you to my research thesis, "A long-term evaluation of company acquisitions – Case study research of cross-border acquisitions by Japanese companies" (in Japanese).

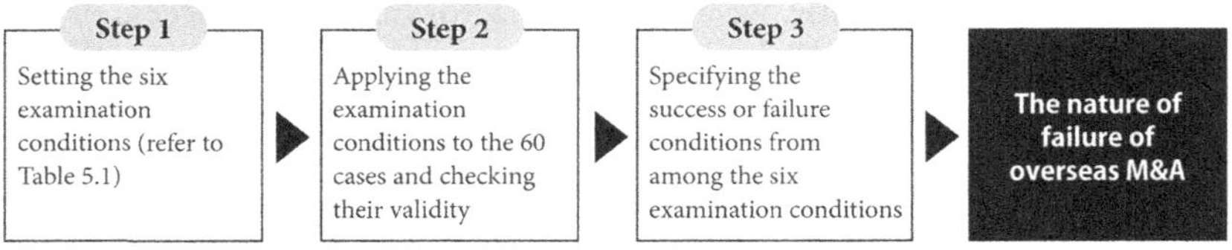

Fig. 5.1 The examination process in this chapter

Table 5.1 Step 1: Setting the six examination conditions

Target selection at the time of the acquisition	*Management after the acquisition*
1. Acquisition of related business for horizontal or vertical integration	4. Long-term commitment by top management, that is, the president at the time of the acquisition manages for at least 10 years after the acquisition
2. Acquisition with advantage of scale (at least double the sales or production capacity)	5. Additional acquisition in the targeted business area or region
3. Acquisition to rescue (white night) or buyout joint venture shares	6. Maintenance of the acquired business as a separate entity

Step ① Setting the Examination Conditions

When investigating what affects the success or failure of an M&A, the more comprehensive the conditions that are applied to the investigation, the better. Therefore, with reference to the hypotheses and the strategic theories within M&A research up to the present time, and also with reference to acquisition case studies, I set six conditions that corresponded to the actual conditions for overseas acquisitions by Japanese companies. I have divided them into the conditions for target selection at the time of the acquisition and for management after the acquisition, and I will explain the reasons for these divisions.

The Target Selection at the Time of the Acquisition

In M&A research prior to this point, elements, such as the method of acquisition, degree of hostility, debt ratio, and relatedness of the business, that may affect the success or failure of an M&A have each been investigated.

However, in the case of an overseas acquisition by a Japanese company, there are restrictions on acquisitions using a company's own shares, so rather than utilizing this method, Japanese companies use cash for their acquisitions. Moreover, the majority of the cases are friendly acquisitions. Therefore, as the acquisition method or the degree of hostility is not considered to have an effect on the success or failure of an overseas acquisition by Japanese companies, I did not consider these factors in the examination conditions.

① Acquisition of a related business for horizontal or vertical integration

However, the relatedness of the businesses of the acquiring and acquired companies has been investigated in many studies, and it is possible that this factor does affect the success or failure of acquisitions by Japanese companies. For example, Singh and Montgomery (1987) investigated the effects of acquisitions by listed companies in the United States and found that acquisitions in which the businesses were related produced a positive impact on share price. Moreover, Porter (1987, 3) discovered that among acquisitions by major US companies with the objective of diversification, more than half of the acquisitions were subsequently sold and therefore concluded that acquisitions not related to the existing business are not likely be successful.

To determine the relatedness of the businesses, prior research in the United States mainly used the Standard Industrial Classification (SIC) code, but it is not easy to objectively determine business relatedness and diversification. Therefore, in order to clearly determine the correspondence with this factor, I set as a condition the acquisition's horizontal or vertical integration with the existing business area and examined whether the relatedness of the businesses affected the success or failure of Japanese companies' acquisitions.

② Acquisition with advantage of scale (at least double the sales or production capacity)

This factor has hardly been investigated in research up until now, but it is worth noting that there are examples of an acquisition ending in failure when the acquired company was the same scale or even larger than the acquiring company. The leading examples of such failures in the United States are Daimler's acquisition of Chrysler in 1988 and AOL's acquisition of Time Warner in 2000. Similarly, the results of Pilkington of the United Kingdom, which was acquired by the smaller Nippon Sheet Glass in 2006, continued to struggle after the acquisition. These cases suggest it is not easy to get management on track in an acquisition in which the acquired company is the same scale or larger than the acquiring company. Therefore, we will consider if the acquiring company's larger size relative to the target company at the time of the acquisition affects its success or failure. Specifically, I added to the condition the presence of an advantage of scale for the acquiring company (at least double the sales or production capacity of the targeted company or business).

③ Acquisition to make a joint venture into a subsidiary following the withdrawal of the joint venture partner or to rescue the target company from a hostile takeover

In research on the United States, Bradley, Desai, and Kim (1988) reported on cases in which a rescue by a so-called white knight (in the form of a friendly acquisition) in a competitive or hostile bidding environment resulted in considerable damage to shareholder value. In the case of Japanese companies, there are many examples of acquisitions in response to a request to be rescued by a target company that was facing a hostile takeover in which the acquiring company had a minority stake. There are also many instances of a joint venture being made into a subsidiary following the withdrawal of the joint venture partner. When the target company is in trouble and wants to be rescued, or when the joint venture partner has severed its ties with the business, the rescue and business continuity tend to be given priority. Therefore, in order to investigate what effects the situation at the target company has on the success or failure of the acquisition, I set as a condition acquisition to make a joint venture into a subsidiary or to rescue a company in which it previously invested.

The Post-acquisition Management

What is important after an acquisition is generating sustainable profits by integrating the target company. Research up to the present time has focused on short-term share price performance, so there have been few attempts to investigate management after an acquisition. Therefore, here, rather than considering the integration process directly after an acquisition, we will consider the long-term effects of the management after the acquisition on success or failure.

④ Long-term commitment by top management (the president at the time of the acquisition manages for at least 10 years after the acquisition)

As the management after the acquisition needs to build an operational mechanism to achieve sustainable profit growth by generating synergy, I wanted to extract a corresponding condition from the theories and hypotheses in the field of strategy. For example, within the research on profit growth over the long term, Mishina (2004) focused on the presidents of highly profitable Japanese companies who served continuously in that position for over 15 years and pointed out that it was impossible to separate this necessity from strategy and operations. In order for strategy to take root in operations, it is absolutely essential that managers participate at work sites and that mistakes be corrected from an overall viewpoint. At the same time, it is necessary to have a process of correcting the strategy itself in response to partial problems occurring at work sites, and Mishina argued that a period of at least 10 years is required in order to excel in this process.

It would seem that long-term and consistent management is essential for an acquisition, which is the measure of embodying a strategy. Therefore, here, I set as a condition for investigation continuous management over the long term, that is, the president at the time of the acquisition manages for at least 10 years.

⑤Additional acquisition in related business or region

We have frequently seen examples of an acquiring company conducting additional acquisitions in order to fortify the target company's functions and customer base. IBM, which repeatedly conducted acquisitions of more than 100 software businesses in a 10-year period from the start of the 2000s, has been reborn as a company focused on providing business solutions to their clients and has improved profitability. As acquisitions can be a corporate activity in which companies advance the consolidation of their industry (Haspeslagh and Jemison 1991), a strategy of conducting roll-up acquisitions can also be a consistent behavior. Therefore, I investigated the relationship between success or failure and additional acquisition, that is, whether the company has been conducting additional acquisitions in the targeted business area.

⑥Maintenance of the acquired business as a separate corporate entity

The importance of integration with the target company in the management after an acquisition has frequently been noted. For integration after the acquisition, Haspeslagh and Jemison (1991) showed that a "coexistence" approach can be a middle way between the target company's "absorption" and "autonomy." The coexistence method involves strengthening the acquiring company's controlling stakes by initially maintaining the target company's management and then promoting codependence between the two companies through initiatives by the target company's management, thereby increasing the responsibilities allocated to the target company's management.

NIDEC Corporation President Shigenobu Nagamori, who is known for aggressively conducting acquisitions, explained what he considered to be important for overseas acquisitions.

> We look at the managers. As the personnel system and corporate culture are different, fundamentally it is unreasonable to expect Japanese can manage the acquired company. The key is whether or not there are people in the target company to whom the management can be entrusted. Even when indicating the major policies, we take a step back with the feeling of being the owner shareholder and entrust the management to them. While synergy effects and access to technologies are also important, they come next in the order of priorities.[1]

Therefore, here, I set as a condition keeping the acquired company or business as a separate entity after the acquisition, in order for the acquiring company to utilize the management resources it has acquired. I then investigated its effect on success or failure.

Step ② Validity Check: Verification Using the 51 Failures and 9 Successes

I verified the correspondence of the six conditions set in Step ① with each of the 60 successes and failures, based on publicly available information sources such as annual securities reports and company press releases. The results of this verification are summarized in Figs. 5.2 and 5.3. Below, I explain the correspondence and implication for each of the conditions (refer to Material 1 and Material 2 at the end of this chapter). The results support three of our hypothesis (see Table 5.2).

The Target Selection at the Time of the Acquisition

Condition 1: Acquisition of related business for horizontal or vertical integration

Within the 51 failure cases, there were 33 in the acquiring company's own business area. The remaining 18 cases were acquisitions outside of its existing business area, including acquisitions for the sake of diversification.

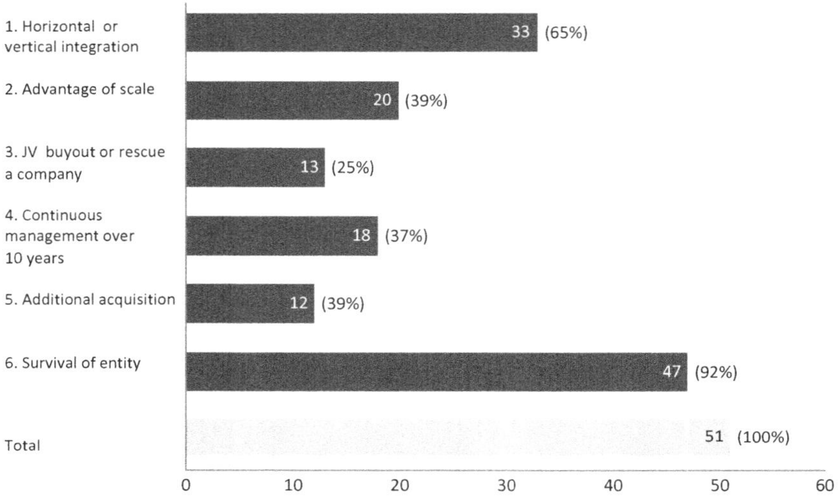

Fig. 5.2 Correspondence with the failure cases

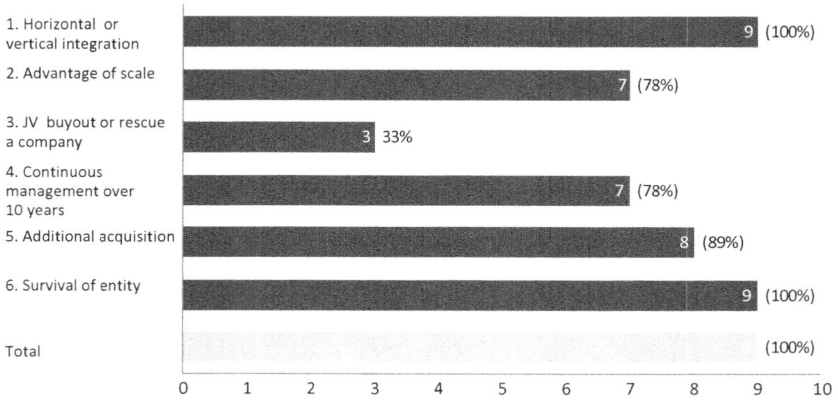

Fig. 5.3 Correspondence with the successful cases

Conversely, all nine of the success cases were acquisitions in the acquiring company's own business area. As more than 60% of the failures were acquisitions in the acquiring company's own business area, it would seem that simply being very knowledgeable about the target business is no guar-

Table 5.2 Corporate behaviors that affect success or failure (results of the statistical tests of correspondence with success or failure case studies)

Selection at the time of the acquisition	*Management at the time of the acquisition*
☐ Horizontal integration or vertical integration in the acquiring company's own business area	✓ Continuous management over the long term (the president at the time of the acquisition manages for at least after the acquisition)
✓ An advantage of scale (at least double the sales or production capacity of the targeted business)	✓ Additional acquisition in the targeted business area or region
☐ Acquisition to make a joint venture into a subsidiary or to rescue a company in which it previously invested	☐ Survival of the acquired business as a corporate entity

antee of success. In addition, in the statistical test, no significant relationship was observed between success or failure and whether or not the acquisition was in a related field.

For your reference, among all 116 acquisitions, 24 were outside of the acquiring company's own business area. Among these, there were no successes and 18 were determined to be failures. It has also been frequently reported in prior research that in many cases, acquisitions to diversify into a non-related field end in failure (Barney 2003).

Condition 2: Acquisition with advantage of scale (at least double the sales or production capacity)

Among the 51 failure cases, an advantage of scale (at least double the sales or production capacity of the targeted business) was present in only 20 cases. In other words, an advantage of scale was not present in more than 60% of the failures, while it was present in seven of the nine successes. In the statistical test, a significant relationship was observed between an advantage of scale and success or failure (refer to Material 3 at the end of the chapter).

For example, the acquisitions in the United States of Singer's household power tools business by Ryobi and the Thermos Corporation by Nippon Sanso are M&As within the existing industry. These were also acquisitions of brands that are highly recognized in the US market, yet they each ended in failure. In both these cases, the target company's sales exceeded those of the acquiring company at the time of the acquisition.

Conversely, even in the successes, those without an advantage of scale had to work hard to achieve their success. In the acquisition of Southland (7-Eleven Inc.) of the United States by Seven & i, after the acquisition it had to spend a long time restructuring 7-Eleven by investing additional capital in the United States. In Terumo's acquisition of the artificial heart-lung equipment business of 3M of the United States, it utilized various techniques after the acquisition, including transferring its own development and production departments to the target company in the United States. These examples show that the management after the acquisition will not be easy if the advantage of scale is not present at the time of the acquisition.

Condition 3: Acquisition to make a joint venture into a subsidiary following the withdrawal of the joint venture partner or to rescue the target company from a hostile takeover

Within the 51 cases of failure, 13 were following the withdrawal of a joint venture partner or to rescue a company it previously invested in from a hostile takeover, and so, they constituted only a small percentage of the total cases.

Among the nine successes, three were acquisitions to make a joint venture into a subsidiary or to rescue it. In the statistical test, no significant relationship was observed between success or failure and acquisitions to turn a joint venture into a subsidiary or to rescue the target company.

For your reference, out of all 116 acquisitions, 11 were to make an overseas joint venture into a subsidiary. Among these 11, the only success was Sumitomo Electric Industries' acquisition to make its UK wire harness joint venture into a subsidiary. There were seven failures, including Mitsubishi Motor's acquisition of NedCar of the Netherlands and NKK's acquisition of the US-based National Steel. When an overseas joint venture was made into an overseas subsidiary, there are many cases in which the partner to the joint venture did not see a future for the local business, and also of the results deteriorating after the acquisition.

The failures also stand out in the cases of a rescue of a company in which the acquiring company previously invested. These cases include instances when the acquired company was in the same business area and when the advantage of scale was present, such as the acquisition of Packard Bell by NEC and of Amdahl by Fujitsu. Thus, it can be said that caution is required for an overseas acquisition that is conducted for the convenience of the other party, whether to end a joint venture or to rescue the target company.

Management After the Acquisition

Condition 4: Long-term commitment by top management (the president at the time of the acquisition manages for at least 10 years after the acquisition)

In more than 60% of the failure cases, the president at the time of the acquisition had left the position less than 10 years from the time of the acquisition. Only 15 presidents remained in their positions for at least 10 years after the acquisition. Conversely, in seven of the nine successes, the president at the time of the acquisition continued to manage over a period of at least 10 years from the acquisition. In addition, in the results of the statistical test, a significant relationship was observed between success or failure and whether the president at the time of the acquisition remained in the position for at least 10 years.

For your reference, in the failure case studies, I compared the length of time the president at the time of the acquisition remained in the position to the length of time the business was owned until the sale or withdrawal, and found that in only 14 out of the 51 cases was the length of office of the president longer than the period that the business was owned. In 70% of the failures, the sale or withdrawal occurred after the manager who decided on the acquisition had left the position. This fact suggests that management tends to avoid reconsidering its ownership of the acquired business during the period in which the president at the time of the acquisition remains in office (refer to Material 4 at the end of the chapter).

Condition 5: Additional acquisition in the targeted business area or region

Among the 51 failure cases, only 12 conducted an additional acquisition.

Some companies were forced to change their strategy after the acquisition or carry out restructuring due to the deterioration of the target company's results, and consequently, did not conduct an additional acquisition. Conversely, among the nine successes, eight conducted horizontal or vertical integration through an additional acquisition. In the statistical test, a significant relationship was observed between success or failure and an additional acquisition. It would seem that together with the condition of continuous management, the consistency of a strategy over the long term affects whether the acquisition will be a success or failure.

Condition 6: Maintenance of the acquired business as a separate corporate entity

In 47 of the 51 failures and in all 9 of the successes, the target company survived as a corporate entity after the acquisition. Based on this finding, it was not possible to verify if this factor was related to success or failure. It is considered that the survival as a corporate entity is mainly derived from the lack of experience in overseas management in Japanese companies or integration into the group after the acquisition.

Lack of scale advantage	*Lack of continuous long-term management*	*No additional acquisition*
31/51 (all the failures)	32/51 (all the failures)	39/51 (all the failures)

Step ③ Specifying the Conditions that Affect Success or Failure

From the results of the investigation into the correspondence of the six conditions, a relationship was observed between success or failure and the presence of an advantage of scale at the time of the acquisition (at least double the sales or production capacity), continuous management over the long term (the president at the time of the acquisition manages for at least 10 years from the acquisition), and an additional acquisition in the targeted business area.

Conversely, no relationship was observed between success or failure and an acquisition within the company's existing field, an acquisition to make a joint venture into a subsidiary or to rescue the target company, or maintenance as a corporate entity.

5.2 The Nature of Failure in Outbound Acquisitions

We will next try to address the nature of failure based on our qualitative analysis about traps that lay in wait within the benefits, such as synergy effects and "buying time," and also from the quantitative analysis of the results on corporate behaviors that affect the success or failure of an outbound acquisition.

The Tunnel of Pitfalls

When Japanese companies consider acquisition opportunity overseas, they are extremely cautious and assiduously carry out due diligence before the acquisition. In addition, in many cases, they discuss and share their plans for business development with local management at the target company in advance. If the acquisition is in their own business area, to a certain extent they should be able to understand the target company's actual abilities. As the business culture and environment of the overseas target will be different, the acquiring company can also prepare itself to accept these differences.

However, from immediately after the acquisition, comments such as the following can often be heard: "We are not able to achieve planned revenue next year," "It is going to take more time than we thought to sell our own products through the acquired company's local distribution network," "The level of product development and quality control are very low," "As soon as we became a shareholder, labor disputes started to frequently occur," "Foreign capital has been placed at a disadvantage due to a change in policy by the local government," and also, "The local management does not listen to what we have to say," and ultimately, "The local managers are resigning one after another." When the situation becomes like this, the acquiring company may have little choice but to sigh disappointedly and start to think, "This acquisition seems to be a failure."

① shows a success pattern, in which the acquiring company escapes from the shallow pitfalls and maintains a consistent strategy after the acquisition. In fact, it corresponds to all the cases that were determined to be successes.

② pertains to cases of failure even when the pitfalls in the tunnel were shallow. It has two patterns. The first pattern involves failures resulting from a change of strategy. From the results of the verification in the previous section, we saw that in 32 of the 51 failure cases, the president at the time of the acquisition had left the position before 10 years had passed from the time of the acquisition. Further, in 39 failure cases, no additional acquisitions were made after the current acquisition and no consistent strategy could be seen.

The second pattern is when the acquiring company is ultimately unable to escape from the pitfalls and the business subsequently stalls. This pattern corresponds to the case of Asahi Glass, which acquired a South Korean manufacturer that was smaller in scale and acquired the leading share of the CRT glass global market, but which was subsequently forced to withdraw from this business due to the rapid growth in popularity of LCD TVs. It is a pitfall of market share.

③ are cases of failure in which the acquiring company brings into its group a business that is larger than itself, and as a result, it ends up falling into a deep pitfall in the tunnel that it is unable to overcome. In Dainippon Ink and Chemicals' acquisition of Reichhold, the scales of their resin businesses were antagonistic. Therefore, it entrusted management after the acquisition to the local management team and did not waiver from this strategy, even conducting additional acquisitions proposed by Reichhold. However, the synergy with its Japanese business was not generated and Reichhold's results did not improve. Dainippon Ink and Chemicals finally sold it 18 years after the acquisition, recording a loss in excess of 50 billion yen. This is a pitfall of cross-border synergy.

④ are cases in which the acquiring company does not have an advantage of scale and the pitfalls are deep, but while struggling, it keeps its strategy consistent and escapes from the deep pitfalls. However, this is limited to cases that achieved the considerable feat of restructuring the acquired business, like Bridgestone's rebuilding of Firestone.

The results of the categorization into patterns ② to ④ for each of the deals that failed owing to the five pitfalls, as described in Chap. 2, and that resulted in a sale or withdrawal, as described in Chap. 3, are shown in Table 5.3.

Perhaps readers with experience in overseas acquisition may have had these same thoughts on one or two occasions.

However, it is not unusual for problems to accumulate on a seemingly daily basis within local operations after an acquisition, which is far from achieving synergy. To say this in another way, to a greater or lesser extent, all acquiring companies must pass through the "tunnel of pitfalls." This tunnel refers to the number of years following the acquisition that the acquiring company suffers owing to the gap between its understanding before the acquisition and the actual situation after the acquisition. During this period, the acquiring company can't avoid these pitfalls but must struggle to correct this gap.

In fact, there are few cases in which there is no gap between the reality and the acquiring company's understanding before the acquisition.

Table 5.3 The tunnel of pitfalls: categorization of the failed cases

② **Had advantage of scale but failed**	
Failed because company changed strategy	
Mitsubishi Motors' acquisition of NedCar	Changed strategy due to the dissolution of the alliance with Daimler
Failed because company could not overcome pitfalls	
Renown's acquisition of Aquascutum	"Buying time" pitfall (could not make up for delay in overseas expansion)
NKK's acquisition of National Steel	Synergies pitfall (no synergy effects by assisting technological support)
Asahi Glass' acquisition of Hankuk Electric Glass	Market share pitfall (even though had leading market share, the market disappeared)
③ **No advantage of scale; failures from falling into a deep pitfall**	
Failed because company changed strategy	
Matsushita Electric Industrial's acquisition of MCA	Replaced president three years after the acquisition. Returned to prioritizing consumer electronics
Failed company could not overcome from deep pitfalls	
Yamanouchi Pharmaceutical's acquisition of Shaklee	Synergies pitfall (no synergies with pharmaceuticals business)
JUSCO's acquisition of Talbots	Acquisition-by-management team pitfall (loss increased due to additional acquisitions)
Dainippon Ink and Chemicals' acquisition of Reichhold	Synergies pitfall (no progress made in cooperation with domestic business)
[a]Nippon Sheet Glass' acquisition of Pilkington	Market share pitfall (suffered more from recession in Europe)
[a]Furukawa Electric's acquisition of a fiber-optic cable business	Market share pitfall (sales declined severely upon the collapse of the IT bubble)
④ **No advantage of scale; fell in to a pitfall, but was able to rebuild the target company**	
Did not change strategy over the long term and escaped from the pitfalls	
[a]Bridgestone's acquisition of Firestone	Pitfalls in "buying time," capturing market share, acquiring a management team, and generating synergy effects Get out from pitfalls through a drastic restructuring

[a]Indicates that the company still owns the acquired company

Further, cases where a company can generate synergy straight away are rare. Therefore, entering this "tunnel of pitfalls" is not in itself an essential cause of failure.

The essential causes of a failure are present only after the acquiring company has entered into the tunnel. One cause is that even though the acquiring company steps on the accelerator, it cannot escape from the various traps that lay in wait in this tunnel, while another is that after escaping from the pitfalls, the acquiring company itself changes course, causing the business to stall.

I would like to specifically explain this situation from the three conditions verified in the previous section, namely an advantage of scale, long-term management, and additional acquisitions.

First, the advantage of scale condition expresses the depth of the pitfalls in the tunnel after the acquisition. If the acquiring company is larger in scale than the target company at the time of the acquisition, then the pitfalls will be shallow and easy to escape. However, if the scales are antagonistic and the target company is larger than the acquiring company, then the pitfalls will be deep and hard to overcome. For example, when the scales are antagonistic, after the acquisition, the acquiring company inevitably ends up having to rely on the target company's management team, because it would be difficult for it to manage an overseas company that is larger than itself. However, when the management is left up to local managers, there is the deep pitfall in which local managers may resign as results start to deteriorate. Moreover, if a recession occurs after acquiring a large-scale business and occupying greater global market share, the acquiring company will not be able to adjust production and carry out restructuring with the same flexibility as it could when it was a standalone. Thus, it will fall into a deep pitfall, be buffeted by bigger waves, and suffer a loss many times greater than it would have when it was independent.

In such a situation, no matter how hard the acquiring company tries to keep the acquired company over the long term, it will not be able to escape from the pitfalls. Ultimately, it will end up selling or withdrawing from the target business.

Next are cases in which, even if the acquiring company escapes from the "tunnel of pitfalls," it ends up failing because it did not conduct good, long-term management, possibly due to the resignation or removal of the acquiring company's president, or it changed its strategy for the target business or for the region in which it is located. When the acquired business is no longer a priority as a result of a management change, the acquiring company tends to become passive about additional acquisitions and capital investment. It may then deviate from its track to profit growth. Acquisitions may end in failure when the strategies at the time of the acquisition and that after the acquisition lack consistency.

Please look at Fig. 5.4, "The tunnel of pitfalls." ① and ② are cases where the acquiring company is larger in scale at the time of the acquisition, while ③ and ④ are cases where the acquiring company does not have this advantage of scale at the time of the acquisition. If the acquiring company

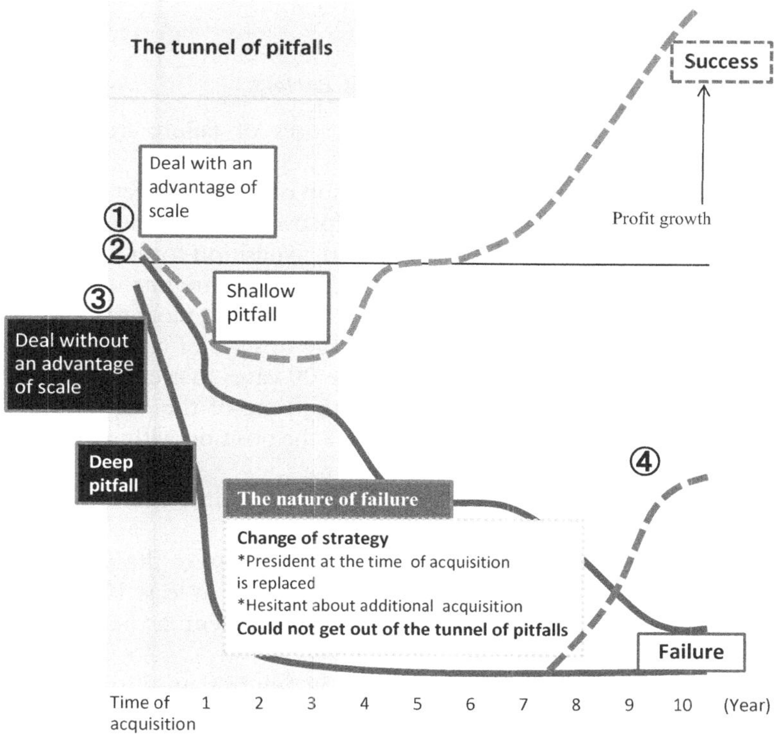

Fig. 5.4 The tunnel of pitfalls (1. Here, the five pitfalls within the benefits introduced in Chap. 2, namely "buying time," obtaining global market share, generating synergy effects, acquiring local, competent managers and engineers, and utilizing the strong yen. 2. ① and ② are deals with an advantage of scale at the time of the acquisition. ③ and ④ are deals without an advantage of scale at the time of the acquisition)

has the advantage of scale, the pitfalls in the tunnel are shallow, but if it does not have this advantage, they are deep. However, in both cases, the pitfalls in the tunnel are unavoidable.

Thus, the essential causes of a failure are to be found after entering into the "tunnel of pitfalls." When the acquiring company replaces its top management so that it lacks consistency of strategy, it is unable to overcome the pitfalls it encounters, resulting in failure. Moreover, when the existing business of the acquiring company is smaller in scale than the target at the time of the acquisition, the pitfalls in the tunnel become deeper and more difficult to get escape.

Combination of Factors

I would like to explain the essential causes of failure from another viewpoint.

Independent factors, such as the selection of a good target company at the time of the acquisition, or ownership over the long term after the acquisition, cannot by themselves guide an acquisition to success.

When we look at the details of all the cases of failure introduced in the previous section, we see that 47 out of the 51 cases, or more than 90%, did not satisfy either the condition of advantage of scale or continuous management over the long term. In 13 of the 20 cases that ended in failure, despite having an advantage of scale at the time of the acquisition, the president at the time of the acquisition left the position within 10 years of the acquisition.

Had advantage of scale, but management was in place for less than 10 years.

Conversely, in 14 of the 18 cases that failed despite the fact that the president at the time of the acquisition managed for at least 10 years from the acquisition, the advantage of scale was not present at the time of the acquisition (Fig. 5.5).

Further, there are no cases that ended in failure that satisfied all three conditions: advantage of scale, continuous management over the long term (10 years), and additional acquisition. In other words, all of the failure cases did not satisfy at least one of these three conditions. What this result shows is that the acquisition ends in failure when the acquiring company is unable to demonstrate its ability to combine these three factors over the long term.

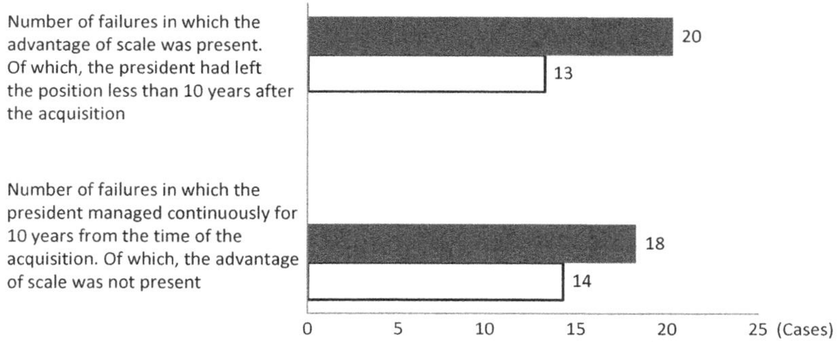

Fig. 5.5 Analysis of the advantage of scale at the time of the acquisition and the long-term management after the acquisition. (Prepared by the author from the companies' press releases and annual securities reports)

Lack of either scale advantage of long-term management	*Lack of long-term management despite having scale advantage*	*Lack of scale advantage despite long-term management in place*
47/51 (all the failures)	13/20 (had scale advantage)	14/18 (had long-term management)

For the acquiring company, an overseas M&A is a measure used to redefine its own business domains. This task entails vertical integration to expand the business in the upstream and downstream, or developing its business horizontally overseas, while a sale or withdrawal is itself also a redefinition. The definition of the business area is the foundation of a corporate strategy and the basis on which a company builds its profit growth over the long term. An overseas acquisition is the embodiment of strategy, and its success or failure will answer the question of whether or not the company was able to get management on track in its newly defined business domains. If the management team is not strongly aware of this when they consider acquisitions, it will be unable to combine these success factors.

In fact, the acquired business will not go well if even one of these factors is missing. In AEON's acquisition of Talbots of the United States, it conducted long-term management after the acquisition and made additional acquisitions locally (J. Jill of the United States), but these efforts only served to deepen the wounds it suffered. Ultimately, it ended up selling the business. It did not have an advantage of scale at the time of the acquisition in the area of luxury women's apparel specialty stores, so it did not have the combination of factors to prevent Talbots' resulting slump. Although Mitsubishi Motors had an advantage of scale in its acquisition of NedCar, it also failed, as it replaced its top management after the acquisition due to its capital alliance with Daimler and its later dissolution, and it did not define a strategy.

When the acquiring company brings into its group an overseas business of a larger scale than itself, the redefined business domain becomes more difficult. Thus, even though it has taken the trouble to newly define its business domain through the overseas acquisition, when it changes managers during the process, the position of the target company becomes somewhat indeterminate. Despite the fact it should correct and adjust the target company's business in response to local conditions, such as through additional acquisitions, the head office leaves its criteria for the business unchanged and it loses its competitiveness locally.

If just one of the three conditions outlined in the previous section, namely an advantage of scale at the time of acquisition; continuous, long-term management; and additional acquisitions, is not met, then the business will face difficulties after the acquisition, or in other words, after the business domain has been redefined. We believe that this is the essential cause of failure in overseas acquisition.

Ultimately, the management capability to lead overseas acquisitions to success involves rebounding from the temporary contraction after the acquisition, seizing the initiative in management and correcting operations, and adapting to the local environment to expand the target company's business domain. If the acquiring company has cash, completing the acquisition itself will not be that difficult. If it seems that, gradually, the deal negotiations are proceeding smoothly, this may be simply because the other party, the seller, is prepared to compromise as it understands the problems that will be faced after the acquisition. What is most important is not the valuation but confidence that the acquiring company can manage the target company after the acquisition.

"Can you demonstrate the ability to secure and combine those factors over the long term after the acquisition?" Based on the consequences of overseas M&A up to the present time, this would seem to be the essential question to ask management when it is considering an acquisition.

Material 1 The cases of success with the corresponding conditions

Acquiring company	*Targeted business*	*At the time of acquisition*			*After the acquisition*		
		Condition 1	*Condition 2*	*Condition 3*	*Condition 4*	*Condition 5*	*Condition 6*
		Related business	*Scale advantage (at least double sales or production capacity)*	*Joint venture into a subsidiary or to rescue the target company*	*Continuous management by the president at the time of the acquisition for at least 10 years*	*Additional acquisition in the target business area or region*	*Survival as a corporate entity*
Shin-Etsu Chemical	Vinyl chloride resin	Yes	Yes	No	Yes	Yes	Yes
Kuraray	Poval resin	Yes	Yes	No	Yes	Yes	Yes
Seven & i	Convenience store chain (Hawaii 7-Eleven)	Yes	Yes	Yes	Yes	Yes	Yes
	Convenience store chain (Southland main company)	Yes	No	Yes	Yes	Yes	Yes
Japan Tobacco	Tobacco	Yes	Yes	No	No	Yes	Yes
Terumo	Artificial heart-lung business	Yes	No	No	Yes	Yes	Yes

(*continued*)

Material 1 (continued)

Acquiring company	*Targeted business*	*At the time of acquisition*			*After the acquisition*		
		Condition 1	*Condition 2*	*Condition 3*	*Condition 4*	*Condition 5*	*Condition 6*
		Related business	*Scale advantage (at least double sales or production capacity)*	*Joint venture into a subsidiary or to rescue the target company*	*Continuous management by the president at the time of the acquisition for at least 10 years*	*Additional acquisition in the target business area or region*	*Survival as a corporate entity*
Sumitomo Electric Industries	Wire harness business	Yes	Yes	Yes	Yes	Yes	Yes
Ricoh	Office equipment sales	Yes	Yes	No	Yes	Yes	Yes
TORAY	Polyester film	Yes	Yes	No	No	No	Yes

Source: Prepared by the author based on the annual securities reports, company press releases, Thomson Reuters data, and newspaper articles

Material 2 The failure cases' correspondence with the conditions

Acquiring company	*Targeted business*	*At the time of acquisition*			*After the acquisition*		
		Condition 1	*Condition 2*	*Condition 3*	*Condition 4*	*Condition 5*	*Condition 6*
		Related business	*Scale advantage (at least double sales or production capacity)*	*Joint venture into a subsidiary or to rescue the target company*	*Continuous management by the president at the time of the acquisition for at least 10 years*	*Additional acquisition in the target business area or region*	*Survival as a corporate entity*
Matsushita Electric Industrial	Entertainment	No	No	No	No	No	Yes
TDK	Semiconductors	No	No	No	Yes	No	Yes
Mitsubishi Electric	Computers	Yes	Yes	No	No	No	Yes
NEC	Computers	Yes	Yes	Yes	No	Yes	Yes
	Computers	Yes	Yes	Yes	No	No	Yes
Fujitsu	Computers	Yes	Yes	Yes	No	No	Yes
Hitachi Koki	Printers	No	Yes	Yes	Yes	No	Yes
Toshiba	Semiconductor memory	Yes	Yes	Yes	No	No	Yes
Matsushita Kotobuki Electronics Industries	Magnetic heads	Yes	No	No	No	No	Yes

(continued)

Material 2 (continued)

Acquiring company	*Targeted business*	*At the time of acquisition*			*After the acquisition*		
		Condition 1	*Condition 2*	*Condition 3*	*Condition 4*	*Condition 5*	*Condition 6*
		Related business	*Scale advantage (at least double sales or production capacity)*	*Joint venture into a subsidiary or to rescue the target company*	*Continuous management by the president at the time of the acquisition for at least 10 years*	*Additional acquisition in the target business area or region*	*Survival as a corporate entity*
Akai Denki	AV	Yes	No	No	No	No	Yes
Yuasa Battery	Industrial batteries	Yes	Yes	No	No	No	Yes
NISSEI Electric	Capacitors	Yes	No	No	N/A	No	Yes
Mitsubishi Kasei	Floppy disks	No	No	Yes	Yes	No	Yes
Mitsubishi Corp.	Resins	No	No	No	No	No	Yes
Settsu	Printing	No	No	Yes	Yes	No	Yes
Dainippon Ink and Chemicals	Synthetic resins	Yes	No	No	No	Yes	Yes
	Polyester	Yes	Yes	No	No	Yes	No
	Coating resin	Yes	Yes	No	No	Yes	No
	Polyester	Yes	Yes	No	No	No	No
Nippon Sanso	Thermos bottles	Yes	No	No	No	No	Yes
Ishihara Sangyo	Pesticides	Yes	No	No	Yes	No	Yes
Fuji film	Printing	Yes	Yes	Yes	Yes	No	Yes
Yamanouchi Pharma	Health foods	No	No	Yes	Yes	No	Yes
Shionogi	Capsules	No	No	No	No	No	Yes

(*continued*)

Material 2 (continued)

Acquiring company	*Targeted business*	*At the time of acquisition*			*After the acquisition*		
		Condition 1	*Condition 2*	*Condition 3*	*Condition 4*	*Condition 5*	*Condition 6*
		Related business	*Scale advantage (at least double sales or production capacity)*	*Joint venture into a subsidiary or to rescue the target company*	*Continuous management by the president at the time of the acquisition for at least 10 years*	*Additional acquisition in the.target business area or region*	*Survival as a corporate entity*
Chugai Pharmaceutical	Diagnostic drugs	No	No	No	No	No	Yes
Fujisawa Pharmaceutical	Generic drugs	Yes	Yes	No	Yes	No	Yes
Seibu Saison	Hotels	No	No	No	No	No	Yes
Kyotaru	Restaurant chain	No	No	No	No	Yes	Yes
	Restaurant chain	No	No	No	No	Yes	Yes
JUSCO	Luxury women's apparel specialty stores	No	No	No	N	Yes	Yes
Renown	Apparel	No	No	Yes	No	No	Yes
Sogo	Commercial facilities	Yes	Yes	No	No	No	Yes
Kawasaki Steel Corporation	Resin compounds	No	No	No	No	Yes	Yes
NKK	Steel	Yes	Yes	Yes	No	No	Yes
Kyoei Steel	Electric furnaces	Yes	No	No	No	No	Yes

(continued)

Material 2 (continued)

Acquiring company	*Targeted business*	*At the time of acquisition*			*After the acquisition*		
		Condition 1	*Condition 2*	*Condition 3*	*Condition 4*	*Condition 5*	*Condition 6*
		Related business	*Scale advantage (at least double sales or production capacity)*	*Joint venture into a subsidiary or to rescue the target company*	*Continuous management by the president at the time of the acquisition for at least 10 years*	*Additional acquisition in the target business area or region*	*Survival as a corporate entity*
Komatsu	Polycrystalline silicon	Yes	No	No	No	No	Yes
NSK	Bearings	Yes	Yes	No	No	Yes	Yes
JUKI	Knitwear sewing machines	Yes	Yes	Yes	Yes	No	Yes
Nippon Electric Glass	CRT glass	Yes	Yes	Yes	No	Yes	Yes
Asahi Glass	CRT glass	Yes	Yes	No	Yes	No	Yes
Ryobi	Electric tools	Yes	No	No	Yes	No	Yes
Furukawa Electric	Electrolytic copper foil	Yes	No	No	Yes	No	Yes
Mitsubishi Motors	Automotive	Yes	No	No	No	No	Yes
Aoki Construction	Hotels	No	No	No	Yes	No	Yes
Daishowa Paper	Paper manufacturing	Yes	Yes	No	No	No	Yes

(continued)

Material 2 (continued)

Acquiring company	*Targeted business*	*At the time of acquisition*			*After the acquisition*		
		Condition 1	*Condition 2*	*Condition 3*	*Condition 4*	*Condition 5*	*Condition 6*
		Related business	*Scale advantage (at least double sales or production capacity)*	*Joint venture into a subsidiary or to rescue the target company*	*Continuous management by the president at the time of the acquisition for at least 10 years*	*Additional acquisition in the target business area or region*	*Survival as a corporate entity*
SoftBank	Exhibition business	No	No	No	Yes	Yes	Yes
	Exhibition business	Yes	No	No	Yes	No	No
	Publishing	No	No	No	Yes	No	Yes
	Memory boards	No	No	No	Yes	No	Yes
Footwork	Transportation	Yes	No	No	Yes	No	Yes
Suntory	Natural water home delivery	No	No	No	Yes	Yes	Yes

Source: Prepared by the author based on annual securities reports, company press releases, Thomson Reuters data, and newspaper articles

Material 3 Analysis of the advantage of scale

Acquiring company	*Targeted business*	*Target company*	*Sales or production capacity of the target business in the acquiring company at the time of the acquisition*	*Sales or production capacity of the target company at the time of the acquisition*	*Advantage of scale*
Matsushita Electric Industrial	Entertainment	MCA	No corresponding business	626.3 billion yen	No
TDK	Semiconductors	Silicon Systems	No corresponding business	130 million dollars	No
Hitachi Koki	Printers	Dataproducts	39.1 billion yen	350 million dollars	No
Matsushita Kotobuki Electronics Industries	Magnetic heads	Quantum's magnetic head business	No corresponding business	2 factories in the United States, 1 factory in Indonesia	No
Akai Denki	AV	Konwa	58.9 billion yen	39.6 billion yen	No
NISSEI Electric	Capacitors	Arcotronics	15 billion yen	17 billion yen	No
Mitsubishi Kasei	Floppy disks	Verbatim	50% joint venture in Japan, Kasei Verbatim	45 billion yen (factories in 11 countries)	No
Mitsubishi Corporation	Resins	Aristech Chemicals	No corresponding business	1.065 billion dollars	No
Settsu	Printing	Uarco	62.7 billion yen	524 million dollars	No
Nippon Sanso	Thermos bottles, outdoor ware	Thermos Corporation	5.9 billion yen	194.4 million dollars	No
Ishihara Sangyo	Pesticides	SDS Enterprise	15.9 billion yen	26 billion yen	No
Yamanouchi Pharmaceutical	Health foods	Shaklee	No corresponding business	627 million dollars	No
Shionogi	Capsules	Capsule business of Eli Lilly	Joint venture with Eli Lilly	15 billion yen, factories in Europe and North America	No

(*continued*)

Material 3 (continued)

Acquiring company	*Targeted business*	*Target company*	*Sales or production capacity of the target business in the acquiring company at the time of the acquisition*	*Sales or production capacity of the target company at the time of the acquisition*	*Advantage of scale*
Chugai Pharmaceutical	Diagnostic drugs	Gen Probe	No corresponding business	5.8 million dollars	No
Seibu Saison	Hotels	Intercontinental Hotels	16 hotels	110 hotels around the world	No
Kyotaru	Restaurant chain	RAI	No corresponding business	32 billion yen	No
	Restaurant chain	Paragon Steakhouse	No corresponding business	15.5 billion yen	No
JUSCO	Luxury women's apparel specialty stores	Talbots	No corresponding business	48 billion yen	No
Kawasaki Steel Corporation	Resin compounds	LNP Engineering	No corresponding business	100 million dollars	No
Kyoei Steel	Electric furnaces	Florida Steel	95.7 billion yen	63 billion yen	No
Komatsu	Polycrystalline silicon	Union Carbide's polycrystalline silicon business	No corresponding business	Annual production capacity of 11.8 million tons	No
Ryobi	Electric tools	Singer's household electric tools business	17.6 billion yen	300 million dollars	No
Furukawa Electric	Electrolytic copper foil	Yates	Joint venture with Yates in Japan	50% market share in Europe, 25% in the United States	No
Aoki Construction	Hotels	Western Hotels	No corresponding business	40.9 billion yen	No
SoftBank	Exhibition business	Interop	No corresponding business	10 billion yen	No
	Exhibition business	Interface	10 billion yen	15 billion yen	No
	Publishing	Ziff-Davis Publishing	No corresponding business	70 billion yen	No
	Memory boards	Kingston	No corresponding business	1.3 billion dollars	No

(*continued*)

Material 3 (continued)

Acquiring company	*Targeted business*	*Target company*	*Sales or production capacity of the target business in the acquiring company at the time of the acquisition*	*Sales or production capacity of the target company at the time of the acquisition*	*Advantage of scale*
Footwork	Transportation	Harry Hamaha	20.7 billion yen	60 billion yen	No
Suntory	Natural water home delivery	Kentwood Spring water	No corresponding business	3rd in the US market	No
Mitsubishi Electric	Computers	Apricot Computers' PC business	812.4 billion yen	17.5 billion yen	Yes
NEC	Computers	Packard Bell	3.7429 trillion yen	3.9 billion dollars	Yes
	Computers	Packard Bell's European business	3.7219 trillion yen	Additional acquisition	Yes
Fujitsu	Computers	Amdahl	4.5034 trillion yen	1.5 billion dollars	Yes
Toshiba	Electronic devices/ semiconductor memory	Dominion Semiconductors	1.2508 trillion yen	US joint venture with IBM	Yes
Yuasa Battery	Industrial batteries	Exide's industrial battery division	59.7 billion yen	23 billion yen	Yes
Dainippon Ink and Chemicals	Synthetic resins	Reichhold	89.3 billion yen	823 million dollars	No
	Coating resins	Spencer Kellogg	Reichhold additional acquisition	100 million dollars	Yes
	Polyester	Koppers' unsaturated polyester business	Reichhold additional acquisition		Yes
	Polyester	Jotun Polymer	Reichhold additional acquisition		Yes
Fujifilm	Printing	Crossfield	110 billion yen	Joint venture with DuPont	Yes
Fujisawa Pharmaceutical	Generic drugs	Lyphomed	183.4 billion yen	127.89 million dollars	Yes

(*continued*)

Material 3 (continued)

Acquiring company	*Targeted business*	*Target company*	*Sales or production capacity of the target business in the acquiring company at the time of the acquisition*	*Sales or production capacity of the target company at the time of the acquisition*	*Advantage of scale*
Renown	Apparel	Aquascutum	49.1 billion yen	14 billion yen	Yes
Sogo	Commercial facilities	Paragon SC	262 billion yen	1 site in Singapore	Yes
NKK	Bearings	National Steel	1.38 trillion yen	2.5 billion dollars	Yes
NSK	Bearings	UPI	205.7 billion yen	30 billion yen	Yes
JUKI	Knitwear sewing machines	Union Special	55.6 billion yen	18 billion yen	Yes
Nippon Electric Glass	CRT glass	OI NEG	117.5 billion yen	Joint venture with Owens of the United States	Yes
Asahi Glass	CRT glass	Hankuk Electric Glass	108.5 billion yen	45 billion yen	Yes
Mitsubishi Motors	Automotive	NedCar	Production performance: 1,298,664 units	200,000 units	Yes
Daishowa Paper Manufacturing	Paper manufacturing	Reed International's North American paper business	Annual production: 2,216,475 tons	Annual production: 435,000 tons	Yes
Shin-Etsu Chemical	Vinyl chloride resin	Robin	2.15 million tons	400,000 tons	Yes
Kuraray	Poval resin	Clariant's Poval resin business	80 billion yen, 144,000 tons	18 billion yen, 50,000 tons	Yes
Seven & i	Convenience stores	Southland Hawaii (Hawaii 7-Eleven)	3954 stores, 780.3 billion yen	58 stores, 69 million dollars	Yes

(*continued*)

Material 3 (continued)

Acquiring company	*Targeted business*	*Target company*	*Sales or production capacity of the target business in the acquiring company at the time of the acquisition*	*Sales or production capacity of the target company at the time of the acquisition*	*Advantage of scale*
Japan Tobacco	Tobacco	RJ Reynolds International	2.6216 trillion yen, 272.5 billion cigarettes	298.4 billion yen, 186.7 billion cigarettes	Yes
Sumitomo Electric Industries	Automobile wire harness business	Lucas SEI Wiring System	29 factories, 550.2 billion yen	5 factories	Yes
Ricoh	Office equipment sales	Gestetner	941.8 billion yen	180.8 billion yen	Yes
TORAY	Polyester film	Rhône-Poulenc's polyester film business	281.9 billion yen	17 billion yen	Yes
Seven & i	Convenience stores	Southland	4629 stores 1.818 trillion yen	7500 stores 8.6 billion yen	No
Terumo	Artificial heart-lung business	3M's artificial heart-lung business	7.2 billion yen	12 billion yen	No

Note: Sources of the sales and production capacities are listed at the end of the book

Material 4 The length of time until the president at the time of the acquisition left the position and the number of years of ownership until the sale or withdrawal

Acquiring company	*President*	*Number of years until leaving position*[a]	*Number of years until sale/withdrawal*[b]
Matsushita Electric Industries	Akio Tanii	4	6
TDK	Hiroshi Sato	10	8
Mitsubishi Electric	Moriya Shiki	5	10
NEC	Hisashi Kaneko	2	3
	Hisashi Kaneko	1	8
Fujitsu	Tadashi Sekizawa	7	7
Hitachi Koki	Hiroshi Kenmori	10	13
Toshiba	Taizo Nishimuro	5	4
Matsushita Kotobuki Electronics Industries	Takashi Honjo	2	3
Akai Denki	James Ting	6	6
Yuasa Battery	Teruhisa Yuasa	9	10
NISSEI Electric[c]	Tamiji Imai	N/A	11
Mitsubishi Kasei	Masahiko Furukawa	10	9
Mitsubishi Corporation	Shinroku Morohashi	7	11
Settsu	Yoshihisa Masuda	6	11
Dainippon Ink and Chemicals	Shigekuni Kawamura	7	19
	Shigekuni Kawamura	5	17
	Shigekuni Kawamura	5	17
	Takemitsu Takahashi	4	9
Nippon Sanso	Hideo Kurobuchi	8	13
Ishihara Sangyo	Takashi Akisawa	14	9
Fujifilm	Minoru Ohnishi	19	11

(*continued*)

Material 4 (continued)

Acquiring company	*President*	*Number of years until leaving position*[a]	*Number of years until sale/withdrawal*[b]
Yamanouchi Pharmaceutical	Shigeo Morioka	11	16
Shionogi & Co., Ltd.	Yoshihiko Shiono	8	8
Chugai Pharmaceutical	Hajime Sano	4	14
Fujisawa Pharmaceutical	Tomokichiro Fujisawa	10	11
Seibu Saison	Seiji Tsutsumi	4	11
Kyotaru	Hiroshi Tanaka	3	8
	Hiroshi Tanaka	3	8
JUSCO	Hidenori Futagi	9	22
Renown	Yasuo Kaneda	8	20
Sogo	Hiroo Mizushima	8	8
Kawasaki Steel Corporation	Shinobu Kiyosaki	6	11
NKK	Yoshinari Yamashiro	7	13
Kyoei Steel	Koichi Takashima	9	8
Komatsu	Akira Anzai	5	7
NSK	Toshio Arata	9	14
JUKI	Takeo Yamaoka	23	18
Nippon Electric Glass	Seisaku Kishida	8	12
Asahi Glass	Shinya Ishizu	10	12
Ryobi	Hiroshi Urakami	25	13
Furukawa Electric	Shingo Tomomatsu	12	8
Mitsubishi Motors	Takashi Sonobe	4	13
Aoki Construction	Hiroyoshi Aoki	13	9
Daishowa Paper Manufacturing	Takashi Saito	7	14
SoftBank	Masayoshi Son	20[d]	7
	Masayoshi Son	20	7
	Masayoshi Son	20	6
	Masayoshi Son	19	5

(*continued*)

Material 4 (continued)

Acquiring company	*President*	*Number of years until leaving position*[a]	*Number of years until sale/withdrawal*[b]
Footwork	Wataru Ohashi	11	11
Suntory	Keizo Saji	15	N/A

[a] Counted as the number of years as the chairman of the board of directors. Includes the year of acquisition and the year the person left the position

[b] Number of years includes the year it was acquired and sold

[c] It is not known when NISSEI Electric President Tamiji Imai left his position

[d] As of 2014, Masayoshi Son was still president of SoftBank

Each company's annual securities report and press releases

Note

1. Nihon Keizai Shimbun, August 10, 2012.

References

Barney. J. B (2003) *Corporate strategy theory* (Volumes 1, 2, & 3) (Masahiro Okada, trans.) Diamond, Inc.

Bradley. M, A. Desai, and E. Han Kim (1988) "Synergistic gains from corporate acquisitions and their division between the stockholders of target and acquiring firms." *Journal of Financial Economics* (21) 1: 3–40.

Haspeslagh. P, and D. Jemison (1991) *Managing acquisitions: Creating value through corporate renewal.* Free Press.

Mishina. K (2004) *The logic of strategy failure.* Toyo: Keizai, Inc. (in Japanese).

Porter. M (1987) "From competitive advantage to competitive strategy." *Harvard Business Review* (May–June): 43–59.

Singh. H, and C. Montgomery (1987) "Corporate acquisition strategies and economic performance." *Strategic Management Journal* 8 (4), https://doi.org/10.1002/smj.4250080407.

PART II

Ways of Fighting for Success

CHAPTER 6

Case Studies of Eight Successful Deals that Realized Sustainable Profit Growth After Acquisitions

In Part 1, we considered the essential factors behind failed overseas acquisitions. Of course, it is important to analyze and learn from failures, but a question that company managers also want an answer to when considering an acquisition is, "How do we succeed in an overseas acquisition?" In Part 2, we will identify the post-acquisition strategies for outbound acquisitions common to all deals that have successfully achieved profit growth.

In this chapter, I will introduce the eight case studies listed on the next page. These eight cases were determined to be successes in Chap. 3, as they realized accelerated profit growth after the acquisition. These successful companies, such as Kuraray and Terumo, have become global leaders in their respective fields through the use of outbound acquisitions.

In the following case studies, we will, again, consider these successes from four angles: the idea at the time of the acquisition, the managers, the management and challenges after the acquisition, and the consequences. We will search for and identify the points in common among all these successful companies.

6.1 The Idea at the Time of the Acquisition

What are the objectives when conducting a large-scale acquisition overseas? The investment of considerable management resources in order to acquire an overseas company represents a company's strategy. In this section, I summarize the goals and thought processes behind these acquisitions,

S. Matsumoto, *Japanese Outbound Acquisitions*,
https://doi.org/10.1007/978-981-13-1364-6_6

extrapolated from the management issues at the time of the acquisition, the management environment of the targeted business, and the strategic direction of the deal.

1. Acquisition of Clariant AG's POVAL resin business by Kuraray
2. Acquisition of Lucas SEI Wiring Systems by Sumitomo Electric Industries (SEI)
3. Acquisition of Gestetner by Ricoh
4. Acquisition of Southland (7-Eleven) by the Ito-Yokado Group
5. Acquisition of 3M's Cardiovascular Division by Terumo
6. Acquisition of RJ Reynolds International (RJRI) by Japan Tobacco (JT)
7. Acquisition of Rovin NV by Shin-Etsu Chemical
8. Acquisition of Rhône-Poulenc's (RPF) polyester film business by Toray Industries

The Managers

What kinds of managers have guided the deals to success? A manager's true colors will appear most vividly when acquiring an overseas company, and his or her subsequent responsibilities will also be heavy. In Japanese companies, as well as in Western companies, we have frequently seen cases of managers being forced to resign in order to take responsibility for the fact that, despite investing enormous sums of money, the results of an acquisition were poor, even to the point where the acquiring company's business deteriorated. In this section, I summarize the thought process of managers in acquisitions that have realized profit growth and their relationships with the targeted business, including from media interviews conducted at that time.

The Management and Challenges After the Acquisition

What kind of management did the successful companies conduct after the acquisition? Also, what challenges did they face and overcome during this period? Even in cases where the management was placed under a spotlight at the time of the acquisition, the management after the acquisition may not be that well known.

In this section, I summarize the management conducted after acquisitions that realized accelerated growth in profits through strategies such as incorporating the target company into the group and supplementing its functions with additional acquisitions.

The Consequences

What were the final outcomes of these acquisitions? In this section, we will finally look at the consequences of the deals, and we will consider the role played by the acquisitions within the acquiring companies' corporate strategies.

6.2 Case Study 1: Kuraray

Case 1 Acquiring company: Kuraray
Target company: Clariant AG's poval resin business (Germany)
Shareholders: Clariant (Switzerland)
Target business: Poval (polyvinyl alcohol, PVA) resin
Acquisition year: 2001

The Idea at the Time of the Acquisition

At the time of the acquisition, Kuraray was faced with two management issues: restructuring its rayon business, which had been its mainstay business up to that time and developing its vinyl acetate-related business to become an earnings pillar. The acquisition of Clariant AG's poval resin business was a large-scale investment that was to be the touchstone in Kuraray's conversion from a textile business to a chemicals business.

The targeted business, poval resin, is the raw material for the synthetic vinyl fiber that Kuraray commercialized in 1950. It was the first fiber to be produced domestically in Japan, and by 1958, it had pioneered the industrialization of functional resins. It was initially used as packaging for shirts, but currently, it is one of the main materials in the polarizing plates used for liquid crystal displays (LCDs) on TVs and smartphones.

At the time of the acquisition, Kuraray had a total poval resin production capacity of 144,000 tons, comprised of 124,000 tons at its Okayama and Niigata Nakajo factories, and 20,000 tons in Singapore (half of a total production of 40,000 tons equally owned in a joint venture with the Nippon Synthetic Chemical Industry (Nippon Gohsei)[1]), but it had no production bases in Europe. Through this acquisition, it would acquire in Europe not only the production capacity for 50,000 tons of PVA (polyvinyl alcohol), but also for 16,000 tons of PVB (polyvinyl butyral) resin, which is the film material used for the interlayer in construction-use glass and vehicle windshields. As Kuraray did not have a PVB resin business, the acquisition would also enhance its product lineup.

The president at the time of the acquisition was Mr. Yasuaki Wakui, who said, "If we do not go ahead with this acquisition, it is likely that one of our competitors will. We are concerned that they will overtake us in terms of market share and we will lose our price supremacy."[2] From this comment, it would seem that he was strongly aware of the competition in the global poval resin market. The acquisition took place prior to the explosive expansion in demand for optical poval film for LCD TVs, but Kuraray ranked first in global market share for poval resins, followed by Celanese of Germany and Nippon Gohsei, which was affiliated with Mitsubishi Chemical. Through this acquisition, Kuraray increased its global market share from 23% to 31%.

The Managers

Mr. Wakui was promoted to president in 2000, from his former position of managing director for public relations, and the acquisition was conducted in the following year. At the same time, the company withdrew from the rayon business, its original business, and greatly reduced the scale of its polyester business. The fact that President Wakui quickly conducted an acquisition and withdrawal after his appointment makes clear his strategy of transferring Kuraray's core business to chemical manufacturing.

Since the 1970s, Kuraray had attempted to diversify into other fields of business, such as real estate and beverages, owing to the recession in the textile market. However, practically all of these attempts at diversification ended in failure, and it had been unable to develop a new earnings pillar. President Wakui, when he was a member of the planning department, had also been responsible for reconstructing those diversified businesses after slumping results. There had also been a period in which he was busy closing businesses, such as in 1979, when he was involved in the business reorganization and sale of the soft drink manufacturer Kuraray Kyoei. In this way, his experience taught him how diversification conducted without full consideration could result in a major loss. Thus, in the background to the concentration of management resources in poval resin, which was a niche market with little competition, was the fact that Kuraray's fibers business had become embroiled in price competition and the painful experiences of the failures of its previous attempts at diversification into businesses in which it was not independently competitive.

As an example of the superiority of Kuraray's technologies, in 2006, the price of liquid crystal panels fell by 16% in one year, and the prices of polarizing plates and filters also fell by 20%, yet in contrast, Kuraray raised the price of poval film by 15%, as it was a critical material.[3]

Subsequently, President Wakui consistently focused on the chemicals business, and in 2007, Kuraray's sector code on the Tokyo Stock Exchange was changed from "textile" to "chemicals."[4] In 2008, he was appointed chairman of the board of directors and served in that position until 2013. In sum, he developed the poval business globally by his long-term commitment as a top management.

The Management and Challenges After the Acquisition

Kuraray launched its poval resin business by transferring the acquired business into Kuraray Specialties Europe (KSE), which was established specifically for this expansion. After the acquisition, it strengthened the production capacity of its poval resin factories. Furthermore, it pursued forward-vertical integration through the additional acquisition of a film business.

In 2004, Kuraray acquired the PVB film business of HT Troplast of Germany. As PVB film is strong against impact, it is used for vehicle windshields and construction purposes. Kuraray explained the objectives for this additional acquisition as follows:

> In line with this strategy, at the end of 2001, Kuraray acquired the PVA and PVB businesses of Clariant AG, Germany. Those businesses are now operated by Kuraray Specialties Europe GmbH ("KSE"), which was founded for the succession of those businesses. In August 2003, KSE started the expansion of its PVA plant in order to meet the growing market demand and developed applications in Europe.
>
> There is a fifty-year commercial relationship between HT Company's PVA film business and KSE's PVB resin business. This transaction is deemed as a business development towards the downstream of the "vinyl acetate chemical chains business," which will enable Kuraray to establish a consistent production flow from PVA resin to PVB resin and PVB film. Furthermore, through integrated operation of research and development activities and realization of synergy effects brought by this transaction, Kuraray will take proper actions to respond to the diversified needs in the growing architectural and automotive safety laminated glass industries in Europe, United States and Asia, with a purpose to achieve middle and long-term business expansion.[5]

This explanation suggests a strategy in which Kuraray had started to shift its focus from poval resin to downstream parts. At the ceremony for the acquisition in front of the employees of HT Troplast, President Wakui said, "We have not carried out restructuring and reduced employee numbers by even a single person at Clariant, which we previously acquired, and have instead increased its facilities. We want to develop this business together with you as colleagues."[6]

Kuraray subsequently strengthened its poval business through additional acquisitions overseas. In Europe, in 2008, it acquired the German PVB company Wacker Polymer Systems GmbH & Co., and in Asia, in 2008, it made into a wholly owned subsidiary a Singapore poval resin joint venture it had established with Nippon Gohsei. In the United States, in 2012, it acquired MonoSol, a manufacturer of poval film for individual packaging, such as for detergents, pesticides, and dyes, as well as industrial uses. Then in 2014, it acquired a vinyl acetate business from DuPont, which was primarily a poval resin and film business.

Kuraray is strong in the optical field, such as for polarization film for LCDs. In a situation that involves the growth of the smartphone market on the one hand and a slump in the LCD TV market on the other, it has also expanded its business into the downstream of industrial film. Another feature of its management after the acquisition is that it segregated production, with the production of optical film for LCD polarizing plates taking place in Japan and the production of film for construction and vehicle windshields in Europe.

It was the restructuring of its fibers business, which had a long history that made possible this series of investments of management resources in the poval business. It positioned synthetic fiber as one chemical item, and it drastically cut its unprofitable business. At the start of the 1990s, the fibers business provided the majority of Kuraray's total sales, but by 2005, its share of total sales had fallen to around 33% and by 2012, to as low as 17%. It would be unable to invest management resources into the chemical business while continuing to maintain the low-profitability fibers business. Thus, restructuring was essential in order to make the poval business a success, and Kuraray took on and succeeded with this challenge.

The Consequences

In the acquired business, Dr. Matthias Gutweiler is president of Kuraray Europe GmbH (KEG), which currently functions as the supervisory company for Kuraray in Europe, and he also serves as a senior executive officer

Fig. 6.1 Breakdown of operating profit and operating profit margin in Kuraray's business segments (fiscal year ended March 2016). (Kuraray's annual securities report 2017)

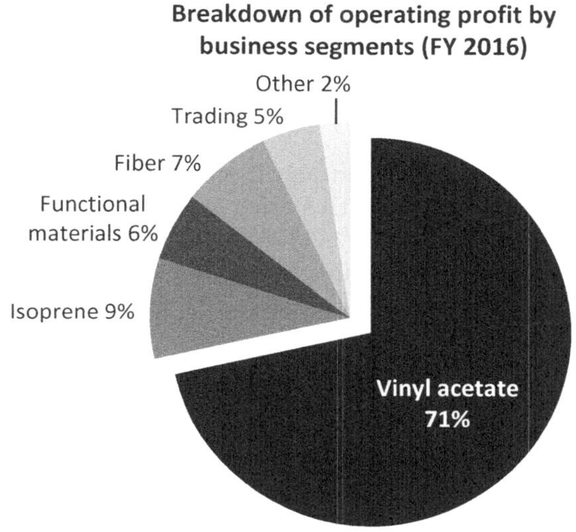

Operating profit margin(%) of business segment FY 2016

Vinyl acetate	**23.1**
Isoprene	13.6
Functional materials	8.9
Fiber	12.3
Trading	3.2
Other (outside the segment)	3.2

at the Kuraray parent company. This acquisition was a horizontal integration for the poval resin business, but subsequently, Kuraray combined it with forward-vertical integration following the acquisition of a film business. It built a unified structure of the poval resin and film businesses through vertical integration, which resulted in accelerating profit growth.

In fiscal year 2016, the operating profit of the vinyl acetate business segment, which is primarily poval resin and film products, was 58.5 billion yen, constituting 71% of Kuraray's total operating profit. The vinyl acetate business's operating profit margin was 23.1%, which greatly exceeds all other Kuraray business segment (refer to Fig. 6.1). Thus, Kuraray used an acquisition and developed its poval business so that it became a foundation for earnings, just as intended.

6.3 Case Study 2: Sumitomo Electric Industries

Acquiring company: Sumitomo Electric Industries (SEI)
Target company: Lucas SEI Wiring Systems (United Kingdom)
Shareholders: Lucas Parity/TRW (United Kingdom/United States)
Target business: Automotive wiring harnesses
Acquisition year: 1999

The Idea at the Time of the Acquisition

Sumitomo Electric Industries' (SEI) automotive wiring harness business has a long history, and its current subsidiary, Sumitomo Wiring Systems, started production of wiring harnesses for four-wheeled vehicles in 1961 in Japan. Wiring harnesses are an aggregation of parts, such as electric cables and connectors, and are an electric wiring system connecting vehicle information and energy. Electric cables were SEI's original business, from which it expanded to various other areas, one being the wiring harness business.

SEI was quick to develop overseas, having established a wiring harness manufacturing and sales base in the US state of Kentucky in 1986. Then in 1990, it established Lucas SEI as an automotive wiring harness joint venture with Lucas Industries, a leading UK automotive parts manufacturer, thereby also advancing into Europe. SEI's initial stake in the joint venture was 30%, and production was launched by transferring the production of Lucas Industries' factory in Wales to the joint venture. The joint venture mainly supplied wiring harnesses to the UK factories of Rover, Ford, Honda, and Nissan.

The background to SEI's making this joint venture with Lucas Industries into a wholly owned subsidiary involves the two management issues it faced with European business. The first issue was it had been unable to expand its customer base to Europe's leading auto manufacturers. This was because it had been shackled by the limitations placed on direct transactions with non-Japanese auto manufacturers during the period of the joint venture arrangement.

The second European management issue was the sharp appreciation of the British pound against the euro, which meant its production was losing price competitiveness. A trend could also be seen among its auto manufacturer customers of reducing production in or withdrawing from the United Kingdom, so developing production bases in Eastern Europe had become an urgent task. Thus, the time had arrived when SEI needed to go beyond its UK joint venture framework to develop its wiring harness business in Europe.

In 1996, its joint venture partner, Lucas Industries merged, with the US automotive parts manufacturer Parity, and in 1999, it was acquired by the US major parts supplier TRW Automotive. Consequently, TRW became its new joint venture partner, but TRW was not looking to focus on wiring harnesses, so SEI turned the joint venture into a wholly owned subsidiary through an acquisition.

At the time of the acquisition, sales from SEI's automotive business, which was mainly wiring harnesses, were 550.2 billion yen[7] and production was carried out by its 29 factories[8] around the world. Lucas SEI had three factories in the United Kingdom and two factories in Eastern Europe, and its sales were on the scale of 20 billion yen.[9] By making the joint venture into a wholly owned subsidiary, SEI acquired the opportunity to flexibly rebuild its European business.

The Managers

SEI's president at the time of the acquisition was Mr. Norio Okayama, who was appointed president in 1999, and then served as chairman from 2004 to 2008. Serving under President Okayama was Mr. Masayoshi Matsumoto, who was in charge of the automotive wiring harness business as managing director and then became senior president. Mr. Matsumoto was continually involved in the wiring harness business from his appointment as the head of the automotive planning division in 1992 up to his appointment as president in 2004.

During the 1990s, SEI was in the spotlight for its information communications businesses, such as fiber optics. In contrast, however, within the company, its wiring harness business had become a candidate for restructuring[10] because it was labor intensive and had a less than 10% share of the global market.

However, in 1995, Mr. Matsumoto overcame strong opposition within the company and established the Harness Technologies Development Research Facility within Sumitomo Wiring Systems, with the objective of enhancing its technological development capabilities.[11] Together with the acceleration of the overseas advances of Japan's auto manufacturers, it developed production bases in North America, Asia, and Europe.

Reflecting on that time, Mr. Matsumoto said, "The question was how to rebuild and expand the wiring harness business. I thought it essential that we enhance our technological development capabilities and expand our market share through M&A."[12]

After his appointment as president, Mr. Matsumoto said, "I considered to exit our businesses in which we were not in the top three for global market share," and he reviewed SEI's business portfolio. In its automotive business, SEI made Sumitomo Wiring Systems, which up to that time had been responsible for wiring harness products development, into a wholly owned subsidiary, and it established a unified system, from development through to production. However, in contrast, in 2007, it sold its automotive brake systems business, which was profitable and recording sales close to 60 billion yen, to Aisin Seiki because its share of the global market was low.

The Management and Challenges After the Acquisition

SEI moved quickly after it went from a joint venture into a wholly owned subsidiary. After the acquisition, it changed its name to Sumitomo Electronics Wiring Systems Europe (SEWSE) and started restructuring the production bases. At that time, SEWSE had three factories in the United Kingdom and a factory in both Poland and Slovakia. However, after the acquisition, it ended operations of its UK Sunderland factory. It also ended a joint venture agreement with a state-owned company in Hungary and brought the joint venture under the umbrella of SEWSE. Additionally, in conjunction with the increase in production in Eastern Europe by Toyota Motor Corporation, it redeployed and increased production capacity at its production bases in Europe, including by building a second factory in Poland.

It also solidified its local customer base through additional acquisitions. In 2001, it acquired the Italian automaker Fiat's wiring harness parts business, thereby launching a full-fledged business in Italy.[13] In 2006, it acquired the wiring harness parts business of the German Volkswagen Group,[14] changed its name to Sumitomo Electric Bordnetze GmbH, and established its wiring harness products development base in Europe. In this way, SEI succeeded in expanding its customer base locally by acquiring the in-house wiring harness businesses of European auto manufacturers. In 2002, it acquired the Japanese wiring harness business of Calsonic Kansei Corporation,[15] a major supplier of Nissan, and, in 2007, it became a wholly owned subsidiary through an exchange of shares in Sumitomo Wiring Systems, which is responsible for wiring harness product development.[16]

While the management of the wiring harness business proceeded smoothly, immediately after the acquisition, SEI faced a major test of its management. Its information communications business, which was centered on fiber optics, and up to that time had been one of its mainstay businesses, fell significantly following the collapse of the so-called IT bubble. As a result, in the fiscal year that ended March 2003, SEI recorded a loss for the first time in its history.

Normally, during times of emergency, regardless of the industry, the tendency is to maintain or reduce business scale, such as through freezing capital investment. However, even in this difficult situation, SEI continued to invest in its wiring harness business and focused on expanding its customer base through acquisitions.

SEI's decision to take a long-term viewpoint and continue to invest in its wiring harness business, despite the temporary changes to its management environment, subsequently resulted in sustainable profit growth.

The Consequences

SEI combined horizontal and vertical integration in Europe and Japan to not only expand its customer base locally, but also to build an integrated structure for wiring harnesses, from development through to sales. Currently, sales in its automotive business exceed one trillion yen and constitute the majority of its total sales. Although the recovery of earnings from its information communications business, which was formerly its "star" business, has not proceeded as expected, the automotive business presently represents more than 60% of its total operating profit (refer to Fig. 6.2).[17]

SEI is currently operating its wiring harness business in more than 30 countries, and it is one of the world's "Big Three" wiring harness suppliers, alongside Yazaki Corporation of Japan and Delphi Corporation of the United States. Currently, SEWSE in the United Kingdom continues to function as the supervisory base for its wiring harness business in Europe.

6.4 Case Study 3: Ricoh

Acquiring company: Ricoh
Target company: Gestetner (United Kingdom)
Shareholders: Tender offer (United Kingdom)
Targeted business: Office equipment sales
Acquisition year: 1995

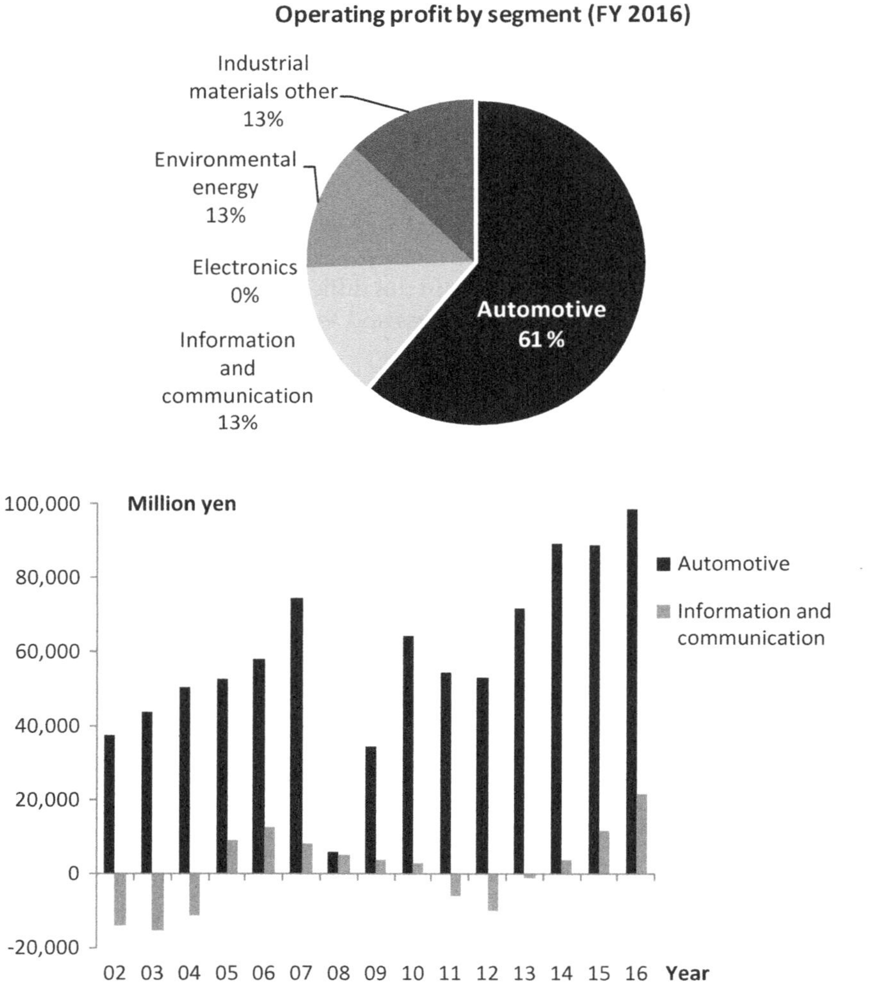

Fig. 6.2 Breakdown of operating profit by business segment FY 2016 and Trends of operating profit in SEI's business segments (FY 2002 to FY 2016). (SEI's annual securities reports)

The Idea at the Time of the Acquisition

At the time of the acquisition, Ricoh was facing two management challenges: increasing awareness of its own brand, RICOH, overseas and building its overseas sales and services network.

In the second half of the 1980s, Japanese copier manufacturers, including Ricoh, were actively exporting their products, and Japanese-made copiers had a more than 80% share of the European market. Owing to the development of trade friction with the European Community (EC), Japanese manufacturers embarked on local production in Europe. Ricoh also began production in the United Kingdom and France, but sales of Ricoh brand products did not grow as expected. At that time, the two pillars of Ricoh's business were sales of copiers and fax machines under the Ricoh brand and under the brands of local office equipment distribution companies. Therefore, there was little incentive for local distributors to actively sell Ricoh brand products. This situation was in stark contrast to that of Canon, whose export ratio at that time exceeded 80%. Canon succeeded in growing its own brand awareness overseas.

Further, Ricoh had been relying on a leading, local office equipment distribution company that sold Ricoh's products under its local brand name. In fact, the local brand was more recognized than Ricoh at that time. Therefore, it had been unable to build its own direct sales and services network. The profit margin from the sales of office equipment itself is low, so its entry into more profitable businesses such as maintenance services and sales of consumables, including toner and paper, was necessary. However, Ricoh had not made progress in increasing awareness of its own brands or in fully developing its direct sales network overseas.

In order to overcome these management issues, in 1991, Ricoh carried out equity participation to acquire a 28.81%[18] stake in the major UK office equipment distribution company Gestetner, which, in 1995, Ricoh made into a wholly owned subsidiary through a tender offer. Ricoh had been a copier and fax machine supplier to Gestetner since 1968, with its products being sold locally under the Gestetner brand. At the time of the acquisition in Europe, the awareness of the Gestetner brand was higher than that of the Ricoh brand.

Gestetner was an office equipment distributor with a long history, having been founded in 1881. It had a sales network in 40 countries and sales of 180.8 billion yen,[19] making it the world's leading independent distributor of office equipment.

Through the acquisition, the number of Ricoh's overseas sales subsidiaries increased from 17 to 80. The president of Ricoh at the time of the acquisition of Gestetner was Mr. Hiroshi Hamada, who said,

> Gestetner's sales network in 40 countries was attractive, but the biggest reason we made it a subsidiary was that it was necessary to respond to the digitization of office equipment and drastically change our strategy. We could not compete with our competitors solely through sales of equipment such as copiers that are used on a standalone basis. But it was essential that we expand sales by promoting the entire system, including multifunctional devices, printers, and fax machines, that emphasize compliance with computer networks.[20]

Ricoh, through a forward-vertical integration from the acquisition of a leading distribution company, obtained the opportunity to increase awareness of its own brand and to build its own sales and service networks in Europe.

The Managers

President Hamada, who conducted the acquisition, had experience mainly in the area of sales, having built a nationwide office equipment sales and maintenance services network in Japan. He was one of the key creators of Ricoh's competitive sales force. He was appointed president in 1983 at the relatively young age of 49.

Ricoh's business environment was not easy at the time he was appointed president. Ricoh was trying to catch up to Canon and Sharp with its core product, the plain paper copier (PPC), but it also had to bail out Ricoh Watches, which had incurred excessive debts. In addition, it was undertaking a heavy financial burden with its investment in the semiconductor business, which Ricoh had entered to diversify its business portfolio. Moreover, during that period, while it had built a strong sales network in Japan, Ricoh still relied on original equipment manufacturer (OEM) sales through local distributor' brand names and had only just started to export its self-branded products. At the time he was appointed, President Hamada said,

> The 4000 series PPC that we launched in the middle of last year has become a product revived from near death. We also started exports from this year, but a situation in which we are receiving hardly any orders is continuing. In the last two to three years, we were forced to go on the defensive against the attacks of other companies, but from now onwards, we will start our full-scale counter attack.[21]

Thus, he started as president by stating his intention to turn the situation around.

While Ricoh's exports to Europe increased rapidly, and it had begun local production, it was not progressing as expected with the building of a direct sales network for its products under its own brand. Then, in 1991, it conducted equity participation to obtain its largest OEM customer, Gestetner, and built closer relationships with it as a shareholder. Four years later, Gestetner's share price fell dramatically following a slump in the business of its Canadian subsidiary, and it was brought into the Ricoh Group through a friendly acquisition. Discussing the objective of the acquisition, Mr. Hamada said, "We are a company with an immature direct sales network in Europe, so the sales network of Gestetner has always been attractive to us."[22] In the year after the acquisition when he was appointed Chairman of the board, he commented on his fondness for Gestetner, saying, "In terms of our overseas business offensive through the acquisition of Gestetner, I am ready to be in charge of the president's tasks as the CEO."[23] As a result of focusing on the sales of its own brand, by 2003, when Mr. Hamada left the position of CEO, Ricoh's overseas sales exceeded its domestic sales, and it occupied a 30% share of the European market.[24]

At that time, many Japanese companies had attempted local production in Europe but had been unable to increase profits because they relied on local companies for sales. Mr. Hamada, from his sales experience in Japan, prioritized building Ricoh's own local sales network, which was achieved with this acquisition and led to the development of its overseas business.

The Management and Challenges After the Acquisition

After the acquisition of Gestetner, Ricoh made series of acquisitions to enhance its sales networks in Europe and the United States (Table 6.1). It acquired Danka Business Systems, which was strong in corporate sales and had sales and maintenance business operations in 12 European countries; IKON Office Solutions, a major US company in the sales of information devices; and a large-scale printing business from Hitachi.

It brought into the Ricoh Group the digital printer equipment business of IBM, aiming to complete both its sales network and product lineup. The Gestetner acquisition became the foundation for Ricoh's subsequent

Table 6.1 Ricoh acquisitions in Europe and the United States

1995	Acquired UK office equipment distribution company Gestetner through a tender offer
	Acquired US office equipment distribution company Savin Corporation
2001	Acquired US office equipment distribution company Lanier Worldwide through a tender offer
2004	Acquired Hitachi Printing Solutions, from Hitachi
2006	Acquired the European office equipment sales and maintenance business from Danka Business Systems
2007	Acquired the digital printer office equipment business from IBM
2008	Acquired major US information devices distribution company, IKON Office Solutions through a tender offer
2009	Acquired Swedish IT services and office equipment distribution company Carl Lamm
2011	Acquired Australian office equipment IT services company Print Solutions
	Acquired Indian IT services company Momentum Infocare
2012	Acquired German IT services company Das SystemHaus GmbH

active overseas development, and at the same time, helped it to seize the initiative in terms of the movement or trend of office equipment manufacturers vertically integrating by acquiring distribution companies.

Ricoh president Mr. Shiro Kondo praised the activities of local management, saying,

> Thanks to the hard work of managers in the acquired U.K. company (Gestetner), in Europe, we have created a gap of 10% between us and the company with the second largest share. The local managers are from the U.K. company, and in the same way, going forward, we want to utilize those human resources on a global scale, such as transferring European managers to the United States.[25]

After the acquisition of Gestetner, one of the challenges Ricoh faced was how to increase the awareness and sales of its own Ricoh brand. In the initial period after the acquisition, awareness of the Gestetner brand was already widespread across the market, so it was difficult to give priority to the Ricoh brand as a so-called manufacturer-affiliated distribution company. However, it continuously launched Ricoh brand copiers and fax machines with new features and superior quality, and it spent time on brand-awareness measures, thereby successfully increasing awareness of its own brand in Europe.

The Consequences

Building a direct sales and services network through the acquisition of Gestetner enabled Ricoh to achieve accelerating profit growth in Europe. It can be said to have used this acquisition to build a blueprint for Ricoh's Japanese success model in Europe. In both the successes and failures, we have seen many examples of horizontal integration through overseas acquisitions by Japanese companies, but this case study is an example of forward-vertical integration functioning effectively to solidify a local sales network.

Ricoh's sales figures show that the European segment contributes 20% of total sales (fiscal year ending March 2012). In that year, Ricoh recorded an operating loss for its entire business due to the impact of the strong yen and other factors, but the European segment still recorded an operating profit of 17.7 billion yen. These results were achieved despite the economic recession in Europe due to the European financial crisis triggered by the non-performing debt problem in some southern European countries as well as a strong yen and weak euro, which once again indicate the strength of Ricoh's European business.

Also, compared to the Americas segment, the European segment has achieved stable profit growth (refer to Fig. 6.3).

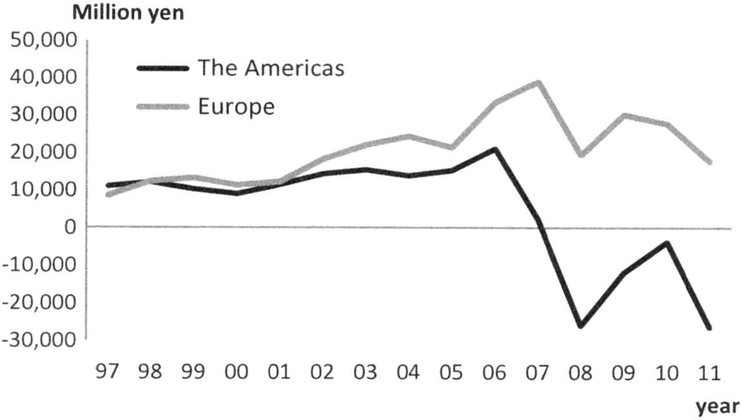

Fig. 6.3 Trends in operating profit for Ricoh's regional segments (the Americas and Europe: fiscal year 1997 to fiscal year 2011). (Ricoh's annual securities report)

6.5 Case Study 4: Ito-Yokado Group

Acquiring company: Ito-Yokado Group (currently, Seven & i)
Target company: Southland (7-Eleven in the United States)
Shareholders: Southland founder (United States)
Targeted business: Chain of convenience stores
Acquisition year: 1991

The Idea at the Time of the Acquisition

In 1973, Ito-Yokado concluded an area licensing agreement for Japan with Southland of the United States, which operated the nationwide chain of 7-Eleven stores. After the licensing agreement, its business in Japan expanded. At the time it acquired Southland in 1991, its scale had grown to the extent that 7-Eleven Japan had a network of 4629 stores[26] that were generating sales of 162.8 billion yen[27] (sales from all its chain stores nationwide were 1.82 trillion yen[28]).

The negotiations for this acquisition started with Southland, which, after its business in the United States had become deadlocked, requested rescue from its license partner Ito-Yokado and 7-Eleven Japan. To help us better understand the motivation for the acquisition, I will briefly describe the history of Southland and its situation up to that time. Southland, which initially conducted retail sales of ice, launched its convenience store business in response to customer demand in the 1930s, when refrigerators were still not widely owned in homes, for sales of food items like bread and milk. The stores were open from seven in the morning until 11 at night, which is where it got its name 7-Eleven, and it began to develop a nationwide chain. The founders of Southland, the Thompson family, became famous in Texas, its state of origin, as a family that built its wealth from something other than oil and natural gas.[29]However, dark clouds began to gather over Southland when it stumbled in its attempts to diversify its business. It tried its hand at various other businesses, including real estate, an automotive parts retail chain, and the oil and gas refinery business, but its results deteriorated when the price of land in Texas slumped due to factors such as the freeze on space development projects following the Challenger space shuttle disaster in 1986.

An investment fund had proposed an acquisition by tender offer to the Thompson family, and it responded by conducting a buyback of its own shares through a leveraged buyout (LBO) in order to defend its control of the company.

It issued corporate bonds in order to repay this large debt, but it could not find buyers for them following the Black Monday stock market crash in 1987; these corporate bonds became junk bonds with a yield of 16%, and its business became deadlocked. In 1991, it filed for the application of the Federal Bankruptcy Act and requested rescue from Ito-Yokado.

Ito-Yokado agreed to the rescue on the condition that the owners of the junk bonds respond to its request to exchange their bonds with newly issued low-yield corporate bonds and shares. Southland at the time of the acquisition was be described as "the main family being saved by a relative." Ito-Yokado did not want a situation in which the lights were turned-off at 7-Eleven, which had become a familiar presence to it for over 17 years. Mr. Toshifumi Suzuki, who at that time was vice president of Ito-Yokado and president of 7-Eleven Japan, commented as follows: "We understood that if we did not assist Southland, its interest payment would further increase and ultimately, it would end up selling its trademark rights to an as yet unknown party. It would not be an ideal situation for the trademark rights to be owned by the corporate bond holders either."[30]

At the time of the acquisition in 1991, it was unlikely that Ito-Yokado had the ambition to develop its convenience store business globally. Rather, the major reason for conducting the acquisition was to protect its convenience store business in Japan, which had become its major source of earnings within the group. If the 7-Eleven trademark rights were transferred to another company, reviewing the licensing conditions for its Japanese business, which was its greatest success, would become inevitable, and depending on the circumstances, even the ongoing survival of this business might be placed in jeopardy. From this sense of crisis, Ito-Yokado chose to step up and turnaround 7-Eleven in the United States.

The Managers

The president of 7-Eleven Japan at the time of the acquisition was Toshifumi Suzuki. Mr. Suzuki served as president and CEO of 7-Eleven Japan from 1978 until recently, as president of Ito-Yokado from 1992, and as CEO of Seven & i Holdings from its establishment in 2005.

Mr. Suzuki, who had previously visited the United States for Ito-Yokado employee training, found 7-Eleven in the United States and subsequently concluded the licensing agreement with Southland. Southland's initial proposal was for a joint venture, and the opening of 7-Eleven stores would be limited to eastern Japan, with Japan divided into two areas. However, in the negotiations, Ito-Yokado was finally able to reach an agreement for all of Japan, with the stores to be operated by its independent subsidiary.

The subsequent powerful advance of 7-Eleven stores through techniques unique to Japan, such as management of products that sold well through a point-of-sale (POS) information management system, joint delivery with manufacturers, and joint product development, is well known today. Five years following the opening of the first store in 1974, 7-Eleven Japan was listed on the Tokyo Stock Exchange, and by the time it acquired Southland in 1991, it had grown to become the second-ranked company in the retail sector in Japan in terms of ordinary profit.

However, the convenience store business was not always smooth sailing in the beginning. At the time of the negotiations with Southland to bring 7-Eleven stores to Japan, it is said that most of the management within Ito-Yokado were opposed to this convenience store business and did not think it would be a success. Although this opposition was overcome, and the licensing agreement was concluded, the 7-Eleven management manual it had received from Southland was not something Ito-Yokado could use unchanged for managing stores in Japan. There were few employees within the company who wanted to be transferred to the convenience store business, which had initially been opposed, so it essentially had to start from scratch, including gathering mid-career hires with no retail experience. Mr. Suzuki described in his own book how from this situation, they used various creative techniques to independently grow the 7-Eleven business and to establish the first convenience store business in Japan.

Even while serving as the president of Ito-Yokado and the CEO of Seven & i, Mr. Suzuki continued to serve as both the president and chairman of 7-Eleven Japan for more than 35 years.

The Management and Challenges After the Acquisition

The turnaround of 7-Eleven in the United States after the acquisition was not easy. Directly after the acquisition, Mr. Suzuki explained that they could not be optimistic about the turnaround, saying, "Looking at the actual situation from the position of a close relative, the management conditions are worse than we anticipated. Items are sold cheaply equivalent to at a discount, and unashamedly on the shelves of the stores are frozen fast foods that they themselves would not want to eat."[31]

Directly after the acquisition in 1992, the restructuring proved costly and the business recorded a deficit of 130 million dollars. In 1993, Ito-Yokado refurbished 1500 7-Eleven stores, or one quarter of the total of 6300 stores, in the United States, and closed 360 unprofitable stores. It would need another three years before 7-Eleven in the United States returned to profitability.

The cash flow situation at 7-Eleven in the United States was severe due to the closure of unprofitable stores and the refurbishment of some stores, and in 1998, it issued 12.5 billion yen of collateralized securities, with the royalties received from 7-Eleven Japan serving as collateral, in order to invest in the opening of new stores and other aspects of the company. Further, in 2000, the Ito-Yokado Group provided an additional investment of 540 million dollars.

7-Eleven Japan supported product development and the upgrading of store management in the United States, and rather than focusing on directly managed stores, it focused its attention in increasing the number of franchise stores. As a result of developing local community-centered franchise stores in the United States, the ratio of these stores to directly managed stores reversed, and in 2012, franchises accounted for 70% of all stores.[32] This outcome improved the profit structure of 7-Eleven in the United States.

In addition to stabilizing management at 7-Eleven, Ito-Yokado continued to make acquisitions in the United States, and in 2006, it acquired White Hen Pantry (WHP), which operated 200 White Hen convenience stores in Chicago, and then in 2010 and 2011, it acquired from Exxon Mobil 183 convenience stores in Florida and 51 stores in Texas, respectively. In 2017, it also announced to purchase 1110 stores from Sunoco in the United States.

The Consequences

Ito-Yokado protected the 7-Eleven trademark through the acquisition, and, for more than 20 years, its convenience store business in Japan maintained a high level of profits and achieved profit growth. The acquisition also enabled it to retain the royalties that it paid to Southland prior to the acquisition. Further, by acquiring the 7-Eleven trademark, it was able to embark on the global development of its convenience store business.

Seven & i maintained 7-Eleven as a corporate entity after the acquisition as 7-Eleven, Inc., and even today in the United States, 7-Eleven, Inc. owns the trademark rights to and is the licensor of 7-Eleven. While the turnaround after the acquisition was not easy, in the fiscal year that ended

Table 6.2 Seven & i Holdings operating profit by company (fiscal year ending February 2017)

	Billion yen
7-Eleven Japan	243.4
7-Eleven Inc.	76.6
Ito Yokado	0
York Benimaru	18.7
Sogo and Seibu	4.3

Seven & i Holdings' financial results briefing materials

February 2017, 7-Eleven, Inc. recorded an operating profit of 76.6 billion yen and its contribution to the total profit of the Seven & i Group was second only to 7-Eleven Japan among the various group companies. Its operating profit was greater than the group's department store and supermarkets business (refer to Table 6.2). Currently, it operates the 7-Eleven business in 17 countries and regions, and its store numbers have grown to 63,000, including 8670 stores in North America and 20,033 stores in Japan.

6.6 Case Study 5: Terumo

Acquiring company: Terumo
Target company: The Cardiovascular Division of 3M (United States)
Shareholders: 3M (United States)
Targeted business: Artificial heart-lung systems
Acquisition year: 1999

The Idea at the Time of the Acquisition

At the time of the acquisition in the second half of the 1990s, Terumo was standing at a crossroads in terms of its overseas business development. It had entered into the United States in 1971, but its business of locally produced glass and plastic blood-collection tubes was overwhelmingly weaker than those of US companies such as Johnson & Johnson, and it ended production in 1996 following losses. As it had been unable to increase profits in its commodity products business, Terumo decided to shift its focus to high-end products for their overseas business and chose the artificial lung business in the United States,[33] and in 1997, it transferred its production base for artificial lungs from its Ashitaka factory in Japan to the United States. However, sales in the United States did not pick up even after the production base transfer. The sales of its artificial lung business before the acquisition were 7.2 billion yen, which meant it ranked a lowly fifth place in the global market.

The targeted business, artificial lungs, refers to medical devices that, during heart surgery, derive blood from outside of the body and play the role of lungs to replace oxygen and carbon dioxide in the bloodstream. The artificial heart-lung system is the collective name for a combination of devices, including a tube called a cannula that removes blood from the veins, a tube blood circuit that connects the artificial lung to the body, sensors to monitor oxygen saturation and blood gas partial pressure, a reservoir to collect the blood that is temporarily taken out of the body, and a roller pump that plays the role of the heart outside of the body.

In 1982, Terumo was the first company in the world to develop and sell a hollow fiber artificial lung. This device used a hollow fiber membrane and had a large number of micropores, and, through the blood flowing inside and gas outside the hollow fibers, oxygen and carbon dioxide were transported via the membrane, which enabled stable gas exchange. Up to that time, artificial lungs had involved a gas exchange through oxygen bubbles flowing in the bloodstream and direct contact between the oxygen and carbon dioxide, but this process frequently caused damage to the bloodstream, so postoperative complications were common.

While Terumo possessed product development capabilities, it had been slow to build a sales network for the local hospitals in the United States that used artificial lungs. Also, its own product lineup was not able to meet the needs of doctors who expected the delivery not just of artificial lungs as a single device, but also the individual components of artificial lung systems such as cannulas, tubes, and sensors. Further, a consolidation of artificial lung suppliers was underway, including the acquisition in 1998 of Avecor by Medtronic of the United States, and of COBE of the United States by Sorin of Italy. Therefore, an urgent task for Terumo was achieving a full lineup of the products that comprised the artificial lung system, including products from other companies, and thereby supporting sales in the largest market for medical equipment, the United States.

For Terumo, the acquisition of US-based 3M's artificial heart-lung systems business (the Cardiovascular Division) was appealing for the following three reasons. First, the revenue of 3M's artificial heart-lung systems business was 12 billion yen sales and the division ranked fourth in global market share, but with this acquisition, Terumo would become the third ranked company. Owing to the industry consolidation, it would be difficult for companies ranked fifth and below to survive. The second reason was that in addition to artificial lungs, the product lineup in 3M's artificial heart-lung systems business included all types of devices used for extracorporeal circulation, including blood gas monitors, roller pumps, and cannulas. Thus, the acquisition would complete Terumo's product family and enable it to provide a full lineup of products to hospitals. The third reason is that it would acquire a sales network and customer base in the United States, the home of the cardiovascular field.[34]

The president at that time, Mr. Takashi Wachi, explained the acquisition as follows:

> Survival in international competition is not guaranteed for companies outside of the top three for global market share. (The Cardiovascular Division's) businesses have high market share, including the catheter system guide wire business and the blood bag filter business. We utilize acquisitions when we would not be able to enter into the top three by our own efforts. This idea formed the basis for our acquisition of 3M's artificial heart-lung systems business.[35]

The Managers

The president at the time of the acquisition, Mr. Wachi, was requested by Terumo to join the company in 1989, when he was a director of the Fuji Bank; he joined Terumo as managing director.

At that time, Terumo had invested excessively in overseas production facilities and had recorded a net loss for three consecutive years, despite being at the peak of the bubble economy in Japan. Upon joining the company, Mr. Wachi first reviewed Terumo's overseas businesses, which resulted in its dissolution of its Australian subsidiary, withdrawal from most of its European business, and a discontinuation of the local production of blood-collection tubes in the United States, which was having profitability problems.

Mr. Wachi become known for turning around Terumo based on "management with a respect for people," as he did not simply use methods like reducing personnel and rationalization. At the time he was appointed president, he visited all the bases in Japan and overseas and explained his philosophy of "management focused on employees" directly to the all of the group's 5500 employees. He called employees "associates" and gave each of them autonomy, requiring that they demonstrate both their individuality and ability to work in a team.

From 1995, when he was appointed president, to 2005, Terumo's revenues doubled, its recurring profit tripled, and its market capitalization increased fivefold. Revenues increased for 14 consecutive fiscal years from 1997, while profits increased for eight consecutive fiscal years from 2001. What supported this profit growth was a business founded on the twin axes of the general-purpose products businesses, such as syringes, and the cutting-edge devices businesses, including the artificial heart-lung systems. The overseas business also contributed to this expansion, through acquisitions in the United States and Europe as well as local production in Asia.

Reflecting on previous efforts to advance overseas, Mr. Wachi cited the following reasons for their failure. "Due to the excessive rush to establish the business, the focus was placed on production capacity and as a result, quality could not keep up and funds were wasted on producing a large number of defective products." He also said, "Japan-initiated management ideas can be harmful, as in the long run, they may delay localization, the transfer of technologies and skills, and the entire business."

Also, he stated that even when Terumo conducts an acquisition,

> We do not acquire companies with poor results and try to improve them, as one of our cardinal rules for M&A is to acquire companies at a level where we can keep its managers and employees. Since an 'occupying force' does not work well after an acquisition, we only dispatch one or two managers from Terumo and entrust management to local employees.[36]

Terumo aimed to systemize its businesses by acquiring leading Western companies in the medical equipment sector that possessed superior technologies and products. Under the guidance of Mr. Wachi, Terumo conducted more than 10 overseas acquisitions, mainly of cutting-edge Western medical equipment suppliers, with the acquisition of 3M's artificial heart-lung systems business being the forerunner.

The Management and Challenges After the Acquisition

After it acquired 3M's artificial heart-lung systems business, Terumo established the Terumo Cardiovascular Systems (TCVS) Corporation in US.

In the year after the acquisition, it brought under the umbrella of TCVS the Terumo's own factory producing the artificial lungs in the US state of Maryland and integrated it. In addition to establishing a full lineup of products for the artificial heart-lung system, it built an integrated structure for their development, production, and sales in the United States. Terumo did not absorb the acquired 3M business into its own US base; instead, it did the reverse, incorporating its own development division and production bases so they were under the control of the acquired business. This business required that certain management techniques be utilized, as the scale of 3M's artificial heart-lung systems business was bigger than its own business, but in 2001, the Americas regional segment was able to achieve profitability in a single fiscal year.

Terumo conducted additional acquisitions overseas with the objective of completing its product lineup for its cardiovascular business including artificial lung systems (refer to Table 6.3). It has acquired a complete lineup of products that are indispensable when selling artificial heart-lung systems to its customers, hospitals, including blood circuit tubes, roller pumps, gas monitors, cannulas, hemoconcentrators, and artificial blood vessels. Even prior to this acquisition, it had acquired Olsen Medical of the United States, a manufacturer of blood circuits (tubes) that constitute one part of the artificial heart-lung system.

Table 6.3 Terumo's acquisitions of overseas companies in the cardiovascular field

Year	*Country*	*Target company*	*Targeted business*
1997	United States	Olsen Medical	Blood circuit tubes
1999	United States	3 M Cardiovascular Division	Artificial heart-lung devices, roller pumps, and blood gas monitors
2002	United States	Lifestream	Cannulas and hemoconcentrators
	United Kingdom	Vascutek	Artificial blood vessels
2005	Japan	Edwards Lifesciences	Distributor of the artificial heart-lung business in Japan
	United States	Mission Medical	Blood product preparation devices
2006	United States	MicroVention	Endovascular coils for cerebral aneurysms
2011	United States	Harvest Technologies	Blood and bone marrow centrifuges used for organ surgery

Terumo press releases

Mr. Wachi, the president at that time, said, "I want us to gradually learn the lessons from M&A in the United States. In terms of technologies, generating synergy effects is a condition for M&A."[37] From this comment, it would seem he was taking a long-term viewpoint for acquisitions.

Terumo utilized the lessons learned from its past failures in its overseas business for both the acquisitions and the management after the acquisition. The basic policy it had formulated at that time is described in the company's history.

> We aim to conduct the world's optimal production, sales, and research and development. We produce high-quality products wherever their production takes place.
>
> It is not efficient to move in the direction of spreading widely but too thinly over the world. We keep in mind discerning Terumo's power, utilizing its strength, and identifying the characteristics of and different conditions in each respective country, and we aim for prioritized and efficient business deployment.
>
> We shall deploy our businesses while conducting selection and concentration in each area and business field. We shall incrementally shift the production of technologically matured products to Asia. For our businesses, we shall focus on the catheter and cardiovascular fields, blood-related businesses, and the artificial heart-lung systems business. We shall also keep watch for partnerships and M&A as the methods to achieve this.
>
> We shall integrate our bases in Japan and overseas, and coordinate to advance a global strategy.[38]

The Consequences

The company Terumo's acquired was entrusted with a supervisory function in its artificial heart-lung systems business, and subsequently, its business in the cardiovascular field grew significantly (refer to Fig. 6.4). Currently, Terumo's shares of the artificial lung markets are 50% of the domestic market and 30% of the global market.

The operating profit margin in Terumo's cardiovascular field segment, which includes the artificial heart-lung systems business, is consistently higher than its total operating profit margin. Further, its acquisitions in the United States have subsequently contributed greatly to its overseas business, reflected by the fact that TCVS Corporation CEO Mark Sutter has also been appointed an executive officer at the Terumo parent company.[39]

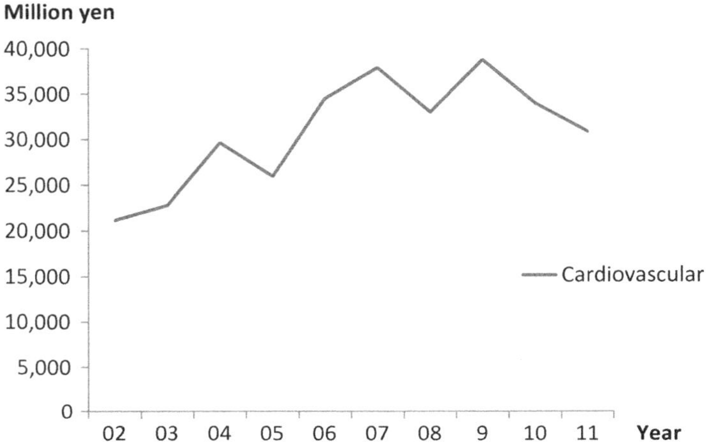

Fig. 6.4 Trends in Terumo's operating profit for the Cardiovascular business segment (2002–2011). (Terumo's annual securities reports)

6.7 Case Study 6: Japan Tobacco

Acquiring company: Japan Tobacco (JT)
Target company: RJ Reynolds International (RJRI, Switzerland)
Shareholders: RJR Nabisco (United States)
Targeted business: Tobacco
Acquisition year: 1999

The Idea at the Time of the Acquisition

The management issue facing JT, which was listed on the Tokyo Stock Exchange at the same time the Japanese government sold some of its shares in JT, was the decline in domestic demand for tobacco. Through rationalizing its domestic production structure, in the 10 years from its launch in 1985, it had closed 11 manufacturing plants in Japan. However, it had not been able to find an earnings pillar to replace its domestic tobacco business.

Mr. Masaru Mizuno, who was appointed president in 1994, said,

> While tobacco sales are stable, we must develop new businesses to be sources of earnings. In order to develop diversification businesses, we have in sight acquisitions of related companies in fields such as foods, restaurants, and

> pharmaceuticals, and also large-scale collaborations. The leading tobacco companies overseas operate in non-tobacco fields such as foods, which provide around half of their sales, and we are aiming to catch up through diversification.[40]

In this way, JT actively worked to diversify its businesses.

In 1993, JT entered the switching power supply business. It acquired Unimat's soft drinks business and Torii Pharmaceutical in 1998 and then the foods business of Asahi Kasei in 1999. However, the cumulative loss of its power supply business had reached 7 billion yen, and it sold the business, while its pharmaceutical business at the time was also recording a loss in excess of 5 billion yen per year. In this situation, it was unable to get its diversification strategy on track. Also, while it had begun exports of its Mild Seven brand to China and South Korea, the profitability of its export business was low because of its obligation to purchase the entire volume of domestically produced tobacco. Despite having ample cash from the revenue of its domestic tobacco business, JT could not see prospects for its diversification and export businesses.

Therefore, JT decided on a course of acquiring(RJR), a tobacco company outside of the United States, in order to obtain leading overseas brands and make its overseas tobacco business a pillar of earnings in the future.

The acquisition amount was the most that a Japanese company had ever paid for an overseas acquisition, and JT used its own cash to cover this amount without incurring any debt. In fact, after the acquisition of Rothmans of the United Kingdom, which ranked fifth for market share, by British America Tobacco (BAT), which ranked second for market share at the start of 1999, a two-company oligopoly situation had developed in the global tobacco industry, in which Philip Morris ranked first and BAT ranked second.

President Mizuno described the objective of the acquisition as follows:

> The five major global brands are Mild Seven, Marlboro, L&M, Winston, and Camel, but this acquisition will secure us three out of these five brands. We have only developed our business for the overseas market in East Asia, mainly countries such as South Korea and Taiwan, while RJ Reynolds has developed its business widely in 70 countries, including in Europe, Africa, and the Middle East. While mutually completing each other's overseas divisions, the acquisition will make it possible for us to reduce costs through rationalization.[41]

The Managers

Mr. Mizuno, who was president at the time of the acquisition of RJRI, worked as the head of the Budget Bureau of the Ministry of Finance and the Director General of the National Tax Administration Agency before being appointed president of JT in 1994. During his term as president, he mainly focused on domestic acquisitions toward the goal diversification. He left the position of president in 2000, the year after the acquisition of RJRI. Under the leadership of Mr. Mizuno, Vice President Katsuhiko Honda took control of the RJRI acquisition, and in 2000, became the first JT career employee to be appointed president. Mr. Honda joined the company in 1965 from the former Japan Tobacco & Salt Public Corporation, and after leading the team responsible for privatization in 1985, when JT was launched, he became executive director of personnel and labor relations. In preparation for the lifting of the ban on importing tobacco, he was responsible for streamlining employee numbers from 32,000 to 25,000, and he was said to be "the vanguard of establishing a de-bureaucratized structure."[42] In 2001, Mr. Honda attended the Financial System Council Tobacco Industry Subcommittee of the Ministry of Finance, where he argued that "It is preferable that the government release all of its shares in JT and completely privatize it," and said that the acquisition of RJRI was "from a feeling of wanting to break the sense of stagnation within the company"[43]; his desire for the privatization to be a success seemed unusually strong, even to the people involved.

Mr. Honda changed the name of the acquired company RJRI to JT International BV (JTI), while maintaining its location it in Switzerland, and used it as the supervisory company for JT's overseas business. Based on the differences at that time between his own company's bureaucratic constitution and RJRI's corporate culture, he deliberately did not integrate it with the parent company in Japan and entrusted a large part of the overseas business to its local management. On the occasion of the negotiations between Mr. Honda and Nabisco, he sent then company director Mr. Hiroshi Kimura to serve as the vice president of JTI and implemented cost reductions and a restructuring of production bases.

In 2006, Mr. Kimura succeeded Mr. Honda as president. Mr. Kimura, the second president who started his career at JT, conducted the acquisition of the major UK tobacco company Gallaher Group plc. at a cost of over 2 trillion yen in 2007, shortly after he was appointed president. During the time he was vice president of JTI, Mr. Kimura had initiated the outsourcing of production and sales in Poland and the United Kingdom to Gallaher Group, so he was familiar with conditions in Europe.[44]

Reflecting on the overseas tobacco business, Mr. Kimura said,

> Through the two large-scale M&A in the past, we have acquired a full-fledged business platform and brand portfolio overseas, which are contributing greatly to growth. In an era in which we cannot implement a tobacco advertising strategy globally, inherently, the best method has been to acquire companies and the brands of those companies, which in addition to obtaining human resources with expertise and intelligence, also enables us to obtain a share of attractive markets.

He also explained JT's approach to acquisitions, stating,

> What we focus on for an acquisition is obtaining 100% of the shares. Also, we do our best to conduct extremely friendly acquisitions so that all employees work their hardest from the day after the contract for the acquisition is signed. In an M&A, the integration after the acquisition is important, so at an early stage, we formulated integration plans for the deployment of specific personnel and bases.[45]

Over the course of 10 years, Mr. Honda and Mr. Kimura, who were the first and second JT career men, respectively, to become its president, took charge of the large-scale acquisitions of overseas companies and developed JT's overseas tobacco business into a source of earnings exceeding those of its domestic tobacco business.

The Management and Challenges After the Acquisition

However, management of RJRI got off to a rough start immediately after the acquisition. At the time of the acquisition, the forecast for RJRI's financial results was a profit of 25.8 billion yen, but it actually recorded a net loss of 5.1 billion yen, and in the fiscal year that ended March 2000, JT, Inc.'s consolidated net profit was down 36%.

Speaking at a press conference at that time, President Mizuno was forced to admit that they had been too optimistic about the outlook, saying, "There is not a word I can say about the fact that we did not foresee the global economic situation,"[46] and the press ridiculed the acquisition as "an acquisition by the former state owned enterprise."

JT quickly embarked on major restructuring. In 1992, the year after the acquisition, it decided to close the tobacco factory it had acquired in the United Kingdom (formerly Manchester Tobacco), and at the same time, resolved to reduce by 20% its 12,000 overseas employees. It then continued RJRI in the form of JTI; integrated JT International, which was the overseas division of the Japan Tobacco parent company located in Tokyo up to that time, with JTI; and unified the organization by making it the supervisory company for its overseas tobacco business.

Moreover, it closed or upgraded the facilities at the aging tobacco factories of the former RJRI, and introduced high-speed tobacco rolling equipment for low-tar, low-nicotine cigarettes in order to comply with regulations in Europe. In such ways, it actively invested in improving production efficiency, and its overseas tobacco business achieved profitability in fiscal year 2000, one year ahead of its target.

Borrowing the expertise of the local management team, it positioned Mild Seven, Camel, Winston, and Salem as the global flagship brands (GFBS) and established a structure focused on sales and marketing.

In 2007, as an additional acquisition, it once again broke the record for the highest amount paid by a Japanese company for an acquisition, bringing the major UK tobacco company Gallaher into the group for a total of 2.25 trillion yen. The president at that time, Mr. Kimura, explained the objectives of the acquisition of Gallaher as "an important step in order to become the globally leading tobacco company. Currently, we are the second or first in market share in three countries and regions, but with this acquisition, this will increase to 10 markets."[47] Immediately after the acquisition, it integrated the functions of JTI in Switzerland and the Gallaher head office and conducted restructuring and rationalizing of the manufacturing bases and sales organization, and by 2010, it had realized cost reductions of 300 million dollars compared to 2006. JT drew out synergy effects by using horizontal integration from the rationalization following the RJRI acquisition and utilizing the marketing expertise it acquired through the Gallaher acquisition (refer to Fig. 6.5).

The Consequences

In terms of JT's current tobacco sales by number of cigarettes, it ranks third globally, following Philip Morris of the United States and BAT of the United Kingdom. In 2017, sales in JT's overseas tobacco business were 1.2 trillion yen, almost twice as much as its domestic tobacco sales of

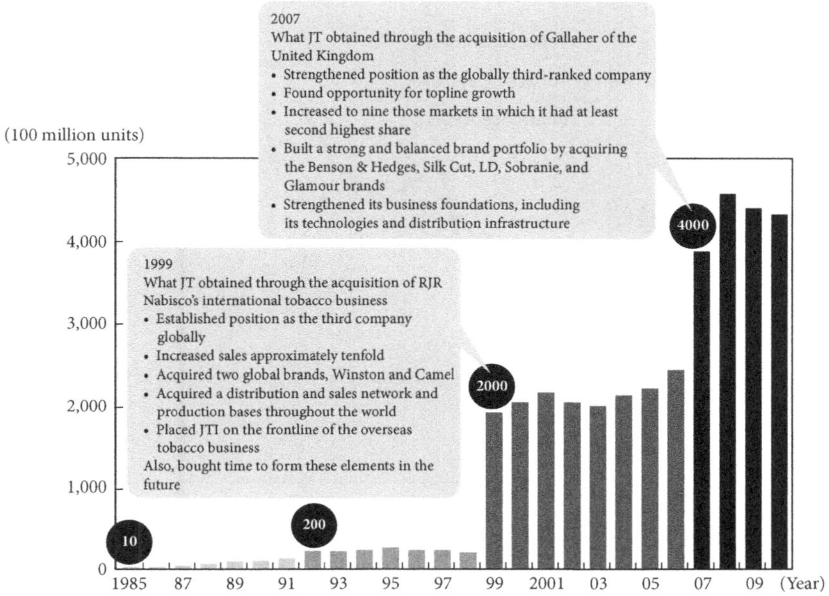

Fig. 6.5 Trends in the sales volumes of JT's overseas tobacco business (1985–2010). (Materials on the website of Japan Tobacco, Inc.)

635.3 billion yen. The overseas tobacco business' operating profit of 351.3 billion yen also exceeded that of the domestic tobacco business of 232.2 billion yen. In contrast, its other businesses, such as pharmaceuticals, which was supposed to be the centerpiece of its diversification strategy, were not currently contributing to earnings (refer to Fig. 6.6).

Through the acquisition, JT built its overseas tobacco business to be a pillar of earnings. However, the trajectory it followed to reach this point involved walking the path of privatization by leveraging its overseas business, to which the bureaucratic constitution of the former state-owned company would not apply.

6.8 Case Study 7: Shin-Etsu Chemical

Acquiring company: Shin-Etsu Chemical
Target company: Rovin NV (the Netherlands)

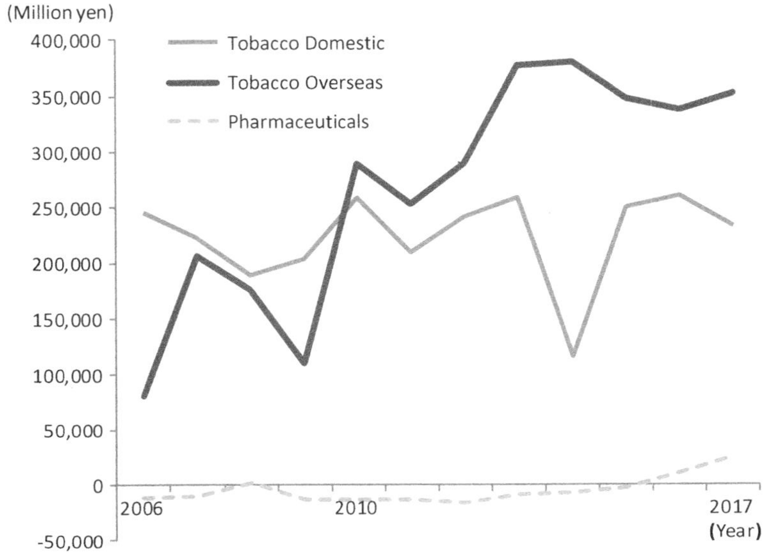

Fig. 6.6 Trends in Japan Tobacco's (JT) operating profit by segment (2006–2017). (JT's annual securities reports)

Shareholders: Shell Chemicals (United Kingdom) and Akzo Nobel (the Netherlands)
Targeted business: Polyvinyl chloride (PVC)
Acquisition year: 1999

The Idea at the Time of the Acquisition

At the time of the acquisition, Shin-Etsu Chemical was competing with Occidental Chemical of the United States, which was the leader in terms of global production of PVC with 2.2 million tons. It had repeatedly increased production at Shintech, its US subsidiary, which was producing 1.45 million tons annually, while its Kashima factory in Japan was producing 550,000 tons and its joint venture in Portugal 150,000 tons, for a total production capacity of 2.15 million tons.

Shin-Etsu Chemical entered into the PVC business in 1957, the last company to do so in Japan. Many of Japan's PVC manufacturers are derivative companies that, as subsidiaries, undertake the downstream functions of their parent companies' original businesses, such as chlorine and petrochemicals, like Tosoh. In contrast, Shin-Etsu Chemical's core business was PVC itself. Also, its competitors' material production bases are in Japan, so they have mainly produced PVC domestically, but since the 1970s, Shin-Etsu Chemical had repeatedly increased the production capacity of its base in the United States.

Due to the introduction of the euro as a single currency in Europe, the number of Japanese companies entering into Europe increased during the 1990s; it became necessary to form a three-region structure of Japan, the United States, and Europe for global supply, and in 1999, Shin-Etsu Chemical acquired Rovin of the Netherlands. Rovin was a joint venture between Shell Chemical of the United Kingdom and Akzo Nobel of the Netherlands, and it was a business derived from the upstream industry of petrochemicals, which are the raw materials used in the production of PVC. Rovin, which was located in the suburbs of Rotterdam, had an annual production capacity of 400,000 tons. Thus, after the acquisition, Shin-Etsu Chemical's production capacity increased to 2.55 million tons, making it the world's largest producer of PVC.

In addition to its factory for PVC, Rovin had a vinyl chloride monomer (VCM) factory with an annual production on the scale of 500,000 tons, which Shin-Etsu Chemical inherited together with 170 employees. Before the acquisition, Rovin had recorded a loss for three consecutive fiscal periods, which was why its parent companies Shell Chemical and Akzo Nobel decided to sell it. As these parent companies supplied Rovin with raw materials, Shin-Etsu Chemical, in anticipation of the management after the acquisition, negotiated with these parent companies to set a condition for the supply of raw materials over a period of a year and a half from the time of entering into the basic agreement.

The Managers

Shin-Etsu Chemical's president at the time of its acquisition of Rovin in 1999 was Mr. Chihiro Kanagawa. Mr. Kanagawa had worked in Shin-Etsu Chemical's overseas sales division and had primarily been involved in PVC plant exports. He was appointed president in 1990 and has served as the chairman since 2010. During the time that Mr. Kanagawa was president, from 1996 until 2008, Shin-Etsu Chemical achieved record profits for 13 consecutive fiscal years, growing its businesses to acquire globally leading shares in the PVC and semiconductor silicon markets.

In his biography, Mr. Kanagawa conveyed that his management of the US PVC subsidiary became the origin of his subsequent rational management, writing that "The foundation of my management method was established through managing Shintech"[48] (Kanagawa 2011, 163–164). So, what sort of management did he conduct in the US PVC business?

In 1973, Mr. Kanagawa negotiated with the world's largest PVC pipe company, Robintech, to establish Shintech as a joint venture. In 1976, Shin-Etsu Chemical began negotiations with Robintech to acquire its stake in this joint venture and make Shintech its subsidiary.

These negotiations were around the time of the oil shocks, and in 1978, Shin-Etsu Chemical reduced by 600 its 2800 employees in Japan. Also, the annual production of its North American PVC business was 100,000 tons, and it had no more than a 3% share of the US market and few prospects. Therefore, there were many members of Shin-Etsu Chemical's board of directors who were opposed to making it a subsidiary by acquisition. The funds required for the acquisition were 2.8 billion yen, and, considering that the net profit of Shin-Etsu Chemical at that time was 650 million yen, it is understandable that some within the company were opposed to the acquisition.

Mr. Kanagawa overcame the opposition within Shin-Etsu Chemical and made Shintech a subsidiary, and was appointed Shintech president in 1978, a position he held until recently, and he remains its chairman. The management of Shintech was based on the rational management of a small number of highly skilled workers, and while it has increased production capacity more than tenfold up to the present day, it still has a sales team of only six people. It implements extremely rational management; as of 2011, it had a production capacity of 2.6 million tons, a utilization rate of 100%, 460 sales employees, annual sales of 2 billion dollars, and a recurring profit of 200 million dollars. Mr. Kanagawa said, "In a business dealing with PVC, which is a general-purpose product, the only way to survive is to be competitive through cutting costs. By thoroughly implementing this approach, Shintech is virtually the only company in the global PVC industry that constantly achieves profitability."

Mr. Kanagawa also said, "We cannot achieve profits unless we secure raw materials,"[49] and Shintech's business expanded based on an agreement with Dow Chemical for the long-term supply of VCMs. The United States has an abundance of the basic raw materials: natural gas and industrial salt, which is why Shin-Etsu Chemical has increased production capacity of PVC in the United States. Subsequently, it expanded in-house production of the intermediate materials VCMs and caustic soda, and consolidated its production facilities, thereby reducing its reliance on Dow Chemical.

Mr. Kanagawa would subsequently apply the management methods he used in Shintech to the management of the PVC business. Shin-Etsu Chemical's domestic PVC business had suffered in the recession in the industry as a whole, and for two years, in 1981 and 1982, it had recorded losses of 4 billion yen. However, it was able to return to profitability, including through reviewing its methods of transporting products and its raw materials suppliers, and by increasing sales of exports. After the acquisition, the Shintech management methods were also incorporated into the management of Rovin, which was recording a loss, and the company became profitable. Reflecting on the negotiations with Rovin's parent companies Shell and Akzo, Mr. Kanagawa said, "We started the negotiations for an agreement on the supply of raw materials and labor, while keeping in mind incorporating the management methods of Shintech," also pointing out that "As long as we did not make a mistake in the method of proceeding, we would be able to buy time through the acquisitions."

The Management and Challenges After the Acquisition

After the acquisition, Shin-Etsu Chemical changed the name of Rovin to Shin-Etsu PVC and conducted a thorough rationalization of the company, from raw materials purchase through to the personnel, and it achieved profitability in the first year after the acquisition.

As it continued to operate at full capacity for three years after the acquisition, in 2003, it raised its production capacity of VCMs, from 500,000 tons to 620,000 tons. After that, based on the increase in the demand for PVC in Europe, including for pipes for water supply and sewage systems, automotive parts, and insulating window frames for energy-saving measures, in 2006, it invested 7 billion yen to increase the production capacity of its PVC factory by 20% to 540,000 tons.[50] Further, in 2011, with the aim of strengthening its production and sales in southern Europe, it acquired CIRES of Portugal, which had an annual production capacity of 200,000 tons,[51] making it into a wholly owned subsidiary.

The success of Rovin after the acquisition was because Shin-Etsu Chemical utilized its experience managing Shintech in the United States. As there is practically no differentiation for PVC, because it is a general-purpose product, cost competitiveness is the most important factor.

Shin-Etsu Chemical thoroughly practices rational management, producing its products in close proximity to consumers and suppliers and keeping the number of personnel to the absolute minimum.

In contrast to Shin-Etsu Chemical's increase in production facilities and acquisitions in the United States and Europe, restructuring has been repeatedly carried out in the PVC industry in Japan since the second half of the 1990s owing to reasons such as the slump in public works projects. In 1995, three companies, namely Sumitomo Chemical, Nippon Zeon, and Tokuyama, integrated their PVC businesses and established Shin Dai-Ichi Vinyl Corporation, while in 1996, Mitsui Toatsu, Tosoh and Denki Kagaku Kogyo integrated their PVC businesses and established Taiyo Vinyl. In 1999, Taiyo Vinyl eradicated its cumulative loss through a reduced capital increase, and Tosoh acquired it and initiated its turnaround. At the same time, Shin Dai-Ichi Vinyl was also being restructured under the leadership of Tokuyama, including the disposal of excess facilities.

In 2000, Mitsubishi Chemical and Toagosei, which ranked fifth and sixth respectively, for domestic production capacity, integrated their PVC businesses and established Vtec. Then in 2004, Mitsubishi Chemical raised its stake in Vtec to 85%. In 2002, Kureha Chemical Industry transferred the trade rights to its PVC business to Taiyo Vinyl and withdrew from the PVC business, while Chisso also withdrew by selling its PVC business to Kaneka Corporation. This restructuring has continued in the context of the decline in demand in Japan, such as by companies reducing and disposing of production facilities through consolidation.

In 1995, there were 13 companies in the PVC industry in Japan, but by 2004, those had been consolidated into five companies: Taiyo Vinyl, belonging to the largest domestic company Tosoh; Kaneka; Vtec, belonging to Mitsubishi Chemical; Shin Dai-Ichi Vinyl, belonging to Tokuyama; and Shin-Etsu Chemical. However, subsequently, other than Shin-Etsu Chemical, these companies have repeatedly reduced their domestic production capacity. Shin-Etsu Chemical has not participated in the consolidation of the domestic PVC industry and has instead taken its own path. The objective of the consolidation was eliminating excess facilities to maintain price, and each company has aimed to rationalize its operations, for example, through integrating their businesses and disposing of facilities. However, Shin-Etsu Chemical has maintained the production capacity of its Kashima factory at 550,000 tons.

Also, companies such as Tosoh have attempted to increase their cost competitiveness and capture the rising demand from emerging countries through local production in Southeast Asia and China. However, Shin-Etsu Chemical has not entered into Asia in search of cheap labor and industrial parks, and instead, after the acquisition, all its increases in production facilities have taken place in the United States and Europe. A condition of its production locations is the ability to procure the raw materials, natural gas and industrial salt, and also the intermediate material VCM through long-term supply agreements, which it has with Dow Chemical in the United States and Shell in Europe. Shin-Etsu Chemical has demonstrated insight into where the source of cost competitiveness can be found. Also, in contrast to Mitsubishi Chemicals' advance into the downstream area of PVC processing, Shin-Etsu Chemical notably has continued to invest in upstream businesses, specifically in the production of raw materials like chlorine and ethylene and intermediate materials such as VCMs.

The PVC businesses of its domestic competitors exist as the sales destinations for their own raw materials and intermediate materials businesses, but in contrast, Shin-Etsu Chemical's core business is PVC, and its profitability has always been important. This is the reason for the important positioning of the PVC business within Shin-Etsu Chemical and why it has taken a different path from that of its competitors.

The Consequences

Since the 1990s, Shin-Etsu Chemical has built a global, three-region structure for production and sales of PVC, centered on Japan, the United States, and Europe. Through increasing production facilities in the United States and acquisitions in Europe, it has developed this business to rank first in the world for production capacity (refer to Table 6.4).

Table 6.4 The Shin-Etsu Chemical Group's PVC production capacity (as of 2013)

		(10,000 tons/year)
Japan	Kashima factory	55
United States	Shintech	263
Europe	Shin-Etsu PVC	45
	CIRES	20
Total		383

Shin-Etsu Chemical press release of June 19, 2013

According to its annual securities report, in the fiscal year that ended March 2017, Shin-Etsu Chemical recorded sales, an operating profit, and an operating profit margin of 1.346 trillion yen, 238.7 billion yen, and 17.7%, respectively.

The operating profit of the PVC business was 53.1 billion yen, which accounted for 22% of the total operating profit. This figure is in stark contrast to those of its domestic competitors, which were unable to maintain the profitability of their PVC businesses.

In the second half of the 1990s, Shin-Etsu Chemical probably looked at the PVC industry, particularly in Japan, and considered integrating its PVC businesses with those of other companies. However, based on its independent management policy, it instead has repeatedly increased production facilities and conducted acquisitions in the United States and Europe. In the context of the falling demand domestically, each of the other companies in Japan has spent a lot of time and effort on maintaining the profitability of their PVC businesses by disposing of excess facilities and restructuring their sales networks. However, despite these efforts, in the current severe conditions, the profitability of these businesses continues to be determined by the price of oil and domestic public works projects (refer to Fig. 6.7).

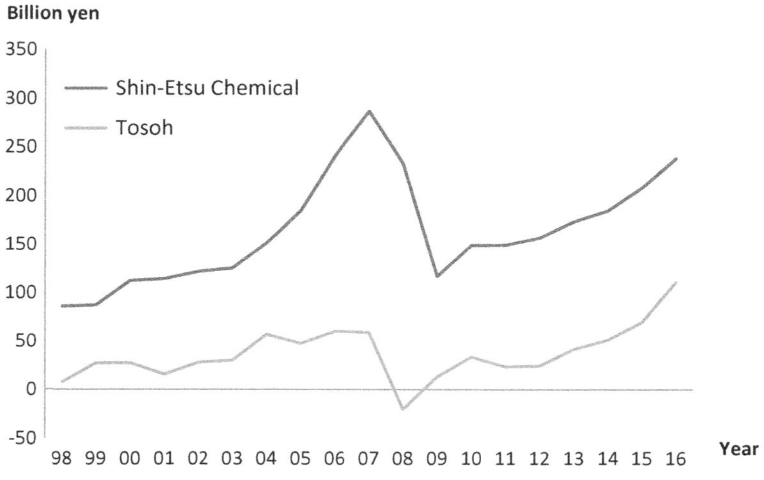

Fig. 6.7 Trends in the operating profits of Shin-Etsu Chemical and Tosoh (1998–2016). (Shin-Etsu Chemical's and Tosoh's annual securities reports)

6.9 Case Study 8: Toray Industries

Acquiring company: Toray Industries
Target business: Rhône-Poulenc's (RPF) polyester film business (France)
Shareholders: RPF (France)
Targeted business: Polyester film
Acquisition year: 1996

The Idea at the Time of the Acquisition

In the 1990s, earnings had fallen in Toray Industries' fibers business due to the yen appreciation, and in this context, it was focusing on its plastics business, which included polyester film, as a new pillar of earnings. In particular, in conjunction with the overseas advances of its main customers, electrical appliance manufacturers, a challenge it faced was to produce polyester film locally.

Toray Industries established its plastics business division in the second half of the 1950s, and in 1959, it opened the Mishima factory for the industrial production of its Lumirror polyester film.

The subsequent growth of Toray Industries' polyester film business coincided with the business development of Japan's electrical appliance manufacturers. In the second half of the 1970s, demand from Sony and other such companies increased for home video magnetic tape. After that, the applications for electronic parts and capacitors as well as industrial materials, like insulation, widened; meanwhile, Toray Industries' business also expanded to packaging for food and pharmaceuticals. Further, owing to the rapid increase in demand for optical polyester film from 2000 onwards for use with LCDs and flat panel displays (FPDs), it became Toray Industries' mainstay business.

Toray Industries began overseas production in the United States in 1991 with Lumirror, but it had no bases in Europe. Then, in 1996, it acquired the polyester film business of the French chemical manufacturer Rhône-Poulenc (RPF), thereby securing a system for local production in Europe. At that time, RPF ranked third in Europe with sales of 17 billion yen, and Toray Industries acquired its factory in the suburbs of Lyon, France, which had an annual production capacity of 30,000 tons of polyester film and 410 employees. Toray Industries' objective for the horizontal integration through this acquisition was "to advance its strong business independently, not as a joint venture,"[52] also stating that "Polyester film is a product in which Japan leads the world for quality. In conjunction with the entering into Europe of tape manufacturers such as Sony and TDK, it is vital that we begin local production as soon as possible." With this acquisition, Toray Industries established a three-region structure of Japan, the United States, and Europe.

Consolidation of chemical industry was progressing at that time. Hoechst and Monsanto sold their synthetic fiber businesses, RPF and SNIA Fibre integrated their nylon businesses, while ICI and DuPont exchanged their nylon and acrylic fibers businesses. In such ways, each company was actively working to concentrate on their specialty field.

Toray Industries' acquisition was also triggered by RPF's focus on its pharmaceuticals business. The restructuring at that time was mainly in the form of business swaps among Western chemical companies, but this acquisition was a deal in which a Japanese company became fully involved in the global restructuring, and for Toray Industries, "It was possible because it held the top share for products."[53]

At the time of the acquisition, each of the companies in the polyester film industry was actively working to develop its businesses globally. Mitsubishi Chemical (at that time, Mitsubishi Kasei) established Hoechst Diafoil GmbH (launched in 1992) with Hoechst of Germany as a Japan-US-Germany joint venture. It had a production capacity of 100,000 tons, while the major UK chemical company ICI also had a production capacity of 100,000 tons in Europe. DuPont of the United States and Teijin of Japan launched a magnetic tape film joint venture. Although Toray Industries increased its production capacity to 140,000 tons by adding the 30,000 tons from its acquisition of RPF, the production capacity of each company was still close.

In the background of Toray Industries' outbound acquisition was the consolidation of the chemical industry following the restructuring and swapping of businesses among Western companies to refine their business portfolios. In addition, the expansion of the production capacities of its competitors alongside the increase in the number of uses for polyester film motivated Toray to participate in global competition.

The Managers

The Toray Industries president at the time of the acquisition was Mr. Katsunosuke Maeda, who served as president from 1987 to 1997, and then served as chairman and CEO from 1997 to 2004. At the time of his appointment as president in 1987, Toray Industries was looking to reduce its reliance on its textile business and stabilize its management through "the expansion of the non-fibers businesses." While on the one hand it was reducing personnel in its textile business, on the other hand it had started to actively invest in its polyester film and resin businesses. During his period in office, Mr. Maeda consistently invested management resources in the development of the polyester film business, including the acquisition of RPF, and in its global development.

He served as president for more than 10 years until he was appointed chairman in 1997, and even after leaving his position as president, he returned to top management in 2002 as CEO following the deterioration of Toray Industries' results and took charge of its management reforms.

The Management and Challenges After the Acquisition

After the acquisition, Toray Industries changed the name of RPF to Toray Plastics Europe (TPE) and invested 13 billion yen in order to increase its annual production capacity from 30,000 tons to 40,000 tons. It suspended exports from Japan to Europe, introduced Toray Industries' latest technologies into TPE's industrial materials production facilities, such as for food packaging and electrical insulating materials, and established a new production line for magnetic tape.

In 1999, Toray Industries established a base within TPE's factory for polyester film vapor disposition, thereby establishing a unified system of production. In 2008, it decided to invest 60 million euro in TPE, to produce the "Toreyfan" functional film, and in 2010 it begun full operations.[54]

In addition to increasing production in Europe, Toray Industries needed to respond to the demand from Japan's electrical appliance manufacturers that had advanced into the Asian region, and in 1998, it spent 30 billion yen to establish a polyester film production base in Malaysia (annual production capacity of 24,000 tons) that specialized in industrial materials, including electrical insulation materials, thereby building a four-region structure of Japan, the United States, Europe, and Asia. Subsequently in 1999, it collaborated with Saehan of South Korea, a major materials manufacturer, and, in 2001, with Yihua Group Corporation in Jiangsu Province in China, to establish polyester film production factories. During this period, demand for polyester film had consistently increased alongside the expansion of its uses, from conventional uses like packaging and insulation, to uses in high-performance fields, such as optical film.

On the other hand, the industry's shift toward an oligopoly was advancing at the same time. In 1998, DuPont of the United States acquired the

UK polyester film business of ICI, and it integrated its polyester film business with that of Teijin, building a structure with a production capacity in excess of a total of 300,000 tons from bases in Japan, the United States, Indonesia, China, the United Kingdom, the Netherlands, and Luxembourg.

At that point, the DuPont-Teijin alliance came to have the world's leading production capacity, overtaking that of Toray Industries.

Furthermore, Hoechst of Germany withdrew from the polyester film business in order to concentrate on the pharmaceuticals business, and in 1998, it sold its stake in the Hoechst Diafoil joint venture to Mitsubishi Chemical. As an independent business, Mitsubishi Chemical had built an integrated production system, from raw materials through to final products. The polyester film industry advanced toward an oligopoly condition and competition that was based on increasing production between DuPont, which had integrated its business with Teijin, Toray Industries, which had acquired RPF, and Mitsubishi Chemical, which had turned its joint venture with Hoechst into a subsidiary.

The Consequences

Through its acquisition of RPF, Toray Industries was able to participate in the consolidation of chemical industry and the shift to the oligopoly condition that was taking place in the polyester film business at that time. The acquisition constituted one part of the important process for Toray Industries' building of a global polyester film production and sales system.

The demand for tape for home videos, which was the mainstream product at that time, shrank after the acquisition, and the price of general-purpose polyester film for packaging and industrial uses also fell. As a result, the profitability of the polyester film business deteriorated at the start of the 2000s.

However, in the field of optical polyester film for computers, and LCDs and FPDs for plasma TVs, Toray Industries dominated respective markets with its products, such as the Lumirror film for light-reflecting plates and Lumiclear high-performance, anti-reflection film, and so has been able to achieve profit growth. Currently, with its polyester film business, Toray Industries has a 20% share of the global market.[55]

With regard to operating profit by business segment for the fiscal year that ended March 2017, the textile was 66.3 billion yen, and plastics and chemicals together with information related devices, which includes the film business, was 64.2 billion yen; Toray Industries has positioned its plastics and chemicals segment as a key business. Thus, it has realized its plan for RPF at the time of the acquisition: making its non-textile business a pillar of earnings. Also, in its information devices and materials business, optical polyester film has grown to constitute nearly half of this segment's sales, and the film business accounts for a high percentage of Toray Industries' total profits.

In contrast, the chemical products business segment of Teijin, which integrated its polyester film business with DuPont, contributes only 8% to its total profits (refer to Fig. 6.8). Since the time of the acquisition in the second half of the 1990s, Toray Industries' operating profit has exceeded

Fig. 6.8 Breakdown of operating profit by business segment in Toray Industries and Teijin. (Toray Industries' and Teijin's annual securities reports)

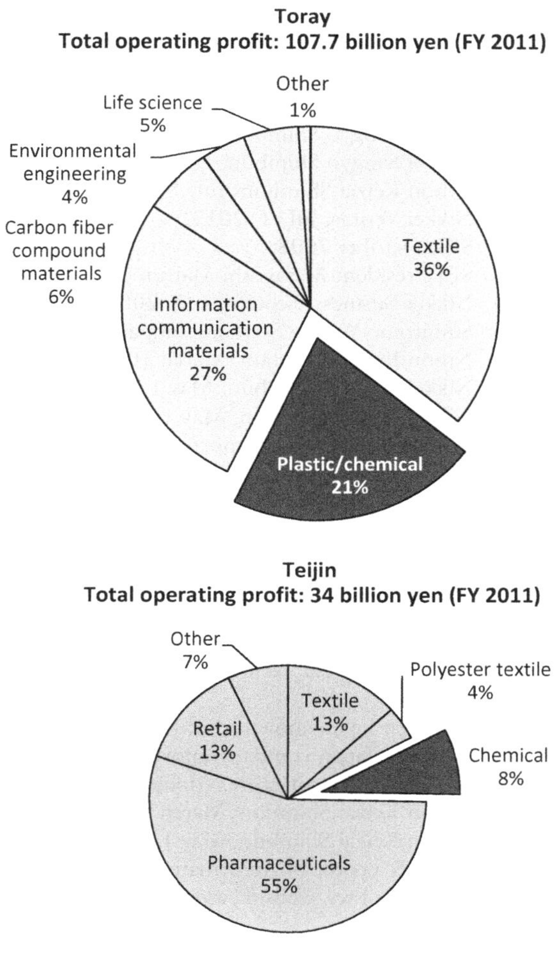

that of Teijin practically every year. Its approach of advancing a business in which it is strong independently rather than through a joint venture has proven successful.

Notes

1. Nihon Keizai Shimbun, July 10, 2001.
2. Nikkei Kinyu Shimbun, August 15, 2001.
3. Nikkei Sangyo Shimbun, January 12, 2007.
4. List of changes to industry categories on the Tokyo Stock Exchange, October l, 2007.
5. Kuraray press release, November 8, 2004.
6. Nikkei Sangyo Shimbun, February 17, 2006.
7. Kuraray company overview; list of officers, as of June 20, 2014.
8. Nikkei Sangyo Shimbun, April 24, 2000.
9. Nikkei Sangyo Shimbun, December 10, 1999.
10. Nihon Keizai Shimbun, July 8, 1999.
11. Nikkei Veritas, July 1, 2012.
12. SEI, October 2008.
13. SEI President Masayoshi Matsumoto's blog, October 12, 2007.
14. Nikkei Business, September 3, 2007 edition.
15. Sumitomo Wiring Systems company overview; history.
16. Nihon Keizai Shimbun, March 10, 2006.
17. Nikkei Sangyo Shimbun, May 13, 2002.
18. Nihon Keizai Shimbun, May 12, 2007.
19. SEI annual securities report, fiscal year 2012.
20. Nihon Keizai Shimbun, July 28, 1995.
21. Nihon Keizai Shimbun, July 14, 1995.
22. Nikkei Sangyo Shimbun, July 8, 1983.
23. Nikkei Sangyo Shimbun, November 8, 1995.
24. Nikkei Sangyo Shimbun, July 25, 1996.
25. Nikkei Kinyu Shimbun, February 6, 2003.
26. Nikkei Veritas, November 14, 2010 edition.
27. 7-Eleven Japan company information; trends in store numbers (domestic).
28. 7-Eleven Japan annual securities report, February 1992.
29. 7-Eleven Japan company information; trends in store information; trends in sales of all chain stores (domestic).
30. Nihon Keizai Shimbun, March 9, 1991.
31. Nihon Keizai Shimbun, May 12, 1991.
32. Seven & i company information; the Seven & i overseas strategy.
33. 7-Eleven, Inc., website, as of June 2014.

34. Terumo's company history.
35. Terumo's company history.
36. Nihon Keizai Shimbun, July 15, 1998.
37. Quarterly Journal of Public Policy & Management, Vol. 3, 2008.
38. Nihon Keizai Shimbun, July 28, 1998.
39. Terumo's company history.
40. Terumo company information; list of officers, as of June 28, 2012.
41. Nihon Keizai Shimbun, December 16, 1997.
42. Nihon Keizai Shimbun, March 10, 1999.
43. Nihon Keizai Shimbun, August 5, 2001.
44. Nihon Keizai Shimbun, August 20, 2001.
45. Nihon Keizai Shimbun, December 16, 2006.
46. Kinyu Facsimile Shimbun, March 5, 2012.
47. Nihon Keizai Shimbun, February 3, 2000.
48. Nihon Keizai Shimbun, December 16, 2006.
49. Nikkei Sangyo Shimbun, December 8, 2004.
50. Shin-Etsu Chemical press release, January 20, 2005.
51. Shin-Etsu Chemical press release, August 17, 2009.
52. Nihon Keizai Shimbun, January 24, 1996.
53. Nihon Keizai Shimbun, January 24, 1996.
54. Toray Films Europe's website.
55. Toray Industries' website.

Reference

Kanagawa, Chihiro. 2011. *Managers must fight precisely because there is a crisis!* Tokyo: Keizai, Inc. (in Japanese)

CHAPTER 7

A Model of M&A: Lessons from IBM's Acquisitions and Divestitures

7.1 Why Learn from IBM?

When considering overseas M&A, we should feel misgivings about referring to only a limited number of successful cases involving Japanese companies. We should also refer to successes involving local, leading companies on their home ground.

General Electric (GE), which has successfully conducted M&A in the United States, the home of M&A, is frequently cited as a model company. It has refined its business portfolio from its clear policy of only conducting a business in which it has the leading or second place share of the global market. It has incorporated into its group, through acquisitions, a wide range of businesses, from finance to medical equipment and broadcasting, thereby building a highly profitable conglomerate. GE's method of conducting M&A has also been introduced to Japan as the GE Way, together with its management training system and six sigma strategy.

Can GE's approach to M&A serve as a model for Japanese companies? In Japan, there are many diversified companies that have derived new business segments from their original businesses and technologies. However, there are few companies that have diversified through acquisitions like GE has done. Further, even in Japan's most diversified companies, in many cases, the head of each business division serves as a director, that is, as the "representative of its (the business division's) interests," and even if top management tries to boldly replace a business within its portfolio, it may not be able to do so owing to the opposition of the board of directors.

S. Matsumoto, *Japanese Outbound Acquisitions*,
https://doi.org/10.1007/978-981-13-1364-6_7

In fact, GE itself corrects its course on the path of diversification. It has even abandoned the businesses it acquired in Japan – an insurance business in 2006, a plastics business in 2007, and a consumer finance business in 2008. In 2009, it sold NBC Universal and withdrew from the media business. GE has rebuilt its own business portfolio over the last 10 years and has spoken of transforming itself from being an "industrial conglomerate" into "an infrastructure industry leader."[1] It would seem to have reached a turning point for its method of using M&A to boldly replace businesses in its portfolio and thereby realize a high profit margin as a whole, even if there are no synergy effects among its businesses. There are many things we can learn from GE's diversification management using M&A, but it is unrealistic to think that it can serve as a model for Japanese companies.

The companies that should serve as models are those that have points in common with Japanese companies and that have used M&A to overcome the same management challenges that currently face Japanese businesses. We will consider a model for Japanese companies based on the management issues that they must overcome and an approach to acquisitions.

The first, and even second, management issue facing Japanese companies is that their profit growth compares unfavorably to their rivals overseas. Even if sales are increasing, this does not lead to profits. It is not unusual even for leading companies to set an operating profit margin target for the first three years of their medium-term management plans at the low level of 3–5%. There are Japanese companies, like the TV business of a major electrical appliance manufacturer, that are concerned by the fact that their increasing sales never seem to translate into profits. In research comparing the profit margins of the leading companies in Japan and the United States, in the main 12 industry categories, it was reported that the operating profit margin of Japan's leading companies, after averaging over 20 years from 1985 to 2005, was 6.0%. In contrast, it was 9.1% for the leading US companies. There was only a single case in which the operating profit margin of a Japanese company, averaged over 20 years, exceeded that of the corresponding US company (Itami 2006, 18). Thus, a low profit margin is an issue that Japanese companies must overcome, and therefore, companies that have achieved high-profit growth through M&A should serve as a model for them.

Also, since the collapse of the bubble economy, Japanese companies have been cautious about leveraging, and quite a few of them conduct practically debt-free management. Even if their balance sheets are strong, they do not conduct investment that goes beyond their means owing to the trauma of being unable to repay their debts after the bubble collapsed. This management policy is unlikely to change in the near future.

Therefore, western companies that repeatedly conduct acquisitions using leverage as the method cannot serve as a model for Japanese companies. The only realistic model for them is companies that conduct acquisitions using their own financial resources.

In the case of Japanese companies, there are many examples of horizontal integration and vertical integration within their core business areas, and in the majority of cases, the acquired company or business is kept over the long term, regardless of its success or failure. There have been only a few cases where the objective was diversification or to enter into a new business. Therefore, overseas companies that have achieved long-term growth through repeatedly conducting acquisitions in their main business fields can also serve as models for Japanese companies.

To summarize, the model company for Japanese businesses is one "that achieved profit growth by conducting acquisitions utilizing its own core competence, while maintaining a strong balance sheet." Next, I would like to introduce IBM as such a model for M&A.

7.2 10 Years of IBM; 10 Years of Fujitsu (2002–2011)

IBM is a company that has used M&A to achieve incredible profit growth. In the 10 years from 2002 to 2011, its operating profit has more than tripled and its operating profit margin has grown from 8.4% to 19%. Its free cash flow has also increased from 6.17 billion dollars to 15.45 billion dollars, and its return on equity (ROE) from 15.4% to 73%. In the last 10 years, which has included the global financial crisis, IBM has achieved record profits nine times, achieving picture-perfect profit growth. Also, over these 10 years, IBM's sales have grown only 31% and its interest-bearing debt balance only 20%, so this case is not one in which it has relied on scale and leverage to realize profit growth[2] (refer to Fig. 7.1).

To demonstrate how IBM's growth stands out from that of its industry peers, we will compare it to that of Fujitsu over the 10-year period (refer to Fig. 7.2). Both companies had many points in common, such as having their home countries, namely the United States and Japan, respectively, as major markets, and up to the start of the 2000s, offering a

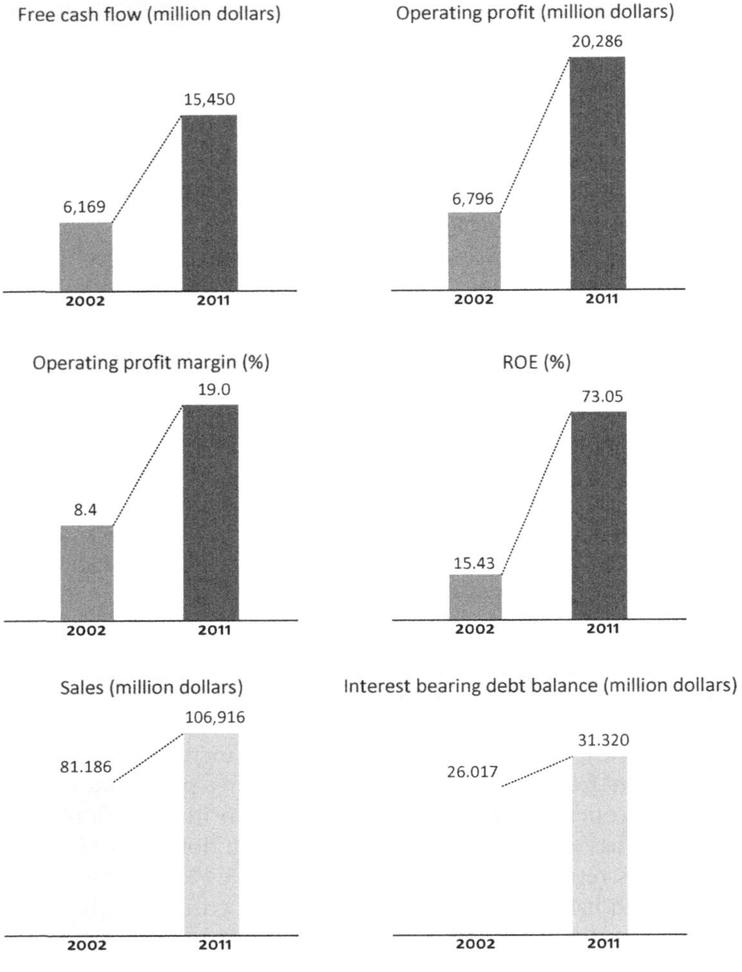

Fig. 7.1 IBM's main financial indicators in 2002 and 2011 (IBM realized profit growth without relying on sales scale or on leverage)

lineup of hardware products, from large-scale computers to PCs. However, the gap between the earnings of IBM and Fujitsu continuously widened during this 10-year period. While IBM's operating profit margin grew to reach close to 20%, during the same 10 years, Fujitsu's never reached 5%.

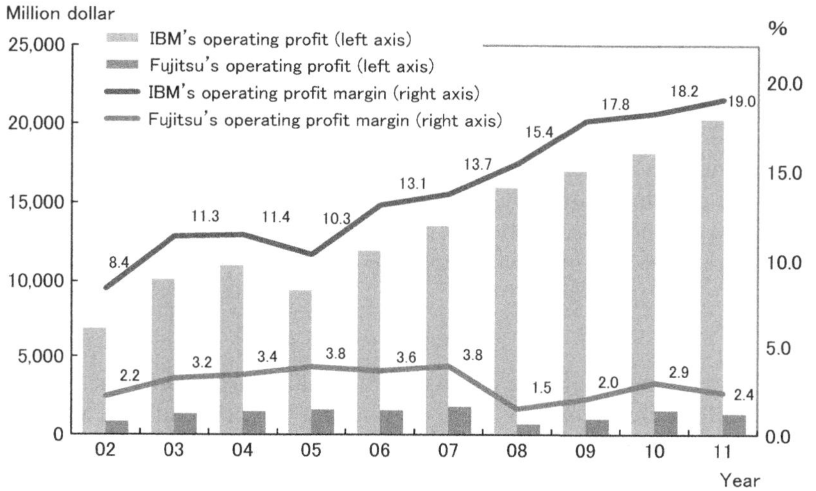

Fig. 7.2 Trends in operating profit and operating profit margin at IBM and Fujitsu over 10 years (2002–2011). (Prepared by the author from IBM's 10Ks and Fujitsu's annual securities reports)

In 2011, Fujitsu's operating profit was 105.3 billion yen, and IBM's was 20.3 billion dollars, roughly 20 times that of Fujitsu. In the 1980s, IBM had difficulty dealing with an IBM-compatible mainframe that was developed by Fujitsu and was involved in a long-term dispute with Fujitsu over a copyright infringement. There had been a period in which Fujitsu was a threat to IBM, but over these 10 years, IBM opened up a considerable lead over Fujitsu.

Its competitor in the United States, Hewlett Packard, also did not achieve an operating profit margin of 10% during these 10 years, and it recorded an operating loss in 2012. In comparing IBM's growth to that of Fujitsu and Hewlett Packard, we understand that its outstanding performance was not simply the result of fair winds blowing in its industry, but conversely, was achieved despite being buffeted by head winds.

7.3 Points in Common Between IBM's Management and that of Japanese Companies

There are experts in Japan who look at the success of Western companies and note that there are things that Japanese companies should learn from them. However, even if we have such a model on the table, as Western and

Japanese companies' management styles are different, such an approach would be unrealistic on many points. As previously explained, GE's style of conducting M&A would not be a suitable model for Japanese companies.

Conversely, there are many points in common between Japanese companies and IBM's management and M&A. Also, profit growth, in which IBM has excelled, is the biggest challenge facing Japanese companies. So next, I would first like to confirm that IBM is a realistic model by indicating its points in common with Japanese companies.

The Managers

IBM's M&A and profit growth were not realized by a superstar manager headhunted from outside of the company, but by CEO Samuel Palmisano, who worked at IBM continuously for 30 years. "Converting from a hardware to a software business and to a high value-added business" is not an approach exclusive to IBM; rather, over the last 20 years, it has been repeatedly advocated by Japan's leading electrical appliance manufacturers. Mr. Palmisano used the M&A method over 10 years to execute this approach, and similarly, the majority of managers in Japanese companies work continuously for 30 or 40 years in the same company, being promoted through the ranks from within.

A Strong Balance Sheet

Rather than using leveraging, IBM uses its operating cash flow as the source of funds for its acquisitions. Over the 10 years discussed, it spent 30 billion dollars on acquiring software businesses, but during this period, its interest-bearing debt balance rose by only 5.3 billion dollars. In fact, its balance sheet became stronger over these 10 years. As previously described, Japanese companies are cautious about increasing their borrowing from their experiences after the collapse of the bubble economy. Thus, another point in common between IBM and Japanese companies is that they conduct acquisitions while maintaining a stable balance sheet.

Monozukuri *(Manufacturing Excellence)*

IBM has a 100-year history. Its original business was manufacturing scales and time recorders, but later, from the 1960s, it grew significantly thanks to its computer mainframe business, and it has handled a range of products including PCs, semiconductors, HDDs, printers, and point-of-sale (POS) systems. Up to the present day, it remains a manufacturing giant. Upon entering the 2000s, based on its "e-business" and "Smarter Planet" vision, it shifted its center of gravity to the solutions business. The IBM way overlaps on many points with the management issues facing Japanese companies that focus on manufacturing.

Growth After Restructuring

It is not the case that IBM's profit growth proceeded in a straight line from its past success in its mainframes business. There was a period when IBM's results worsened significantly because its bureaucratic corporate culture, which had become widespread throughout its organization, caused it to become inflexible. Thus, it has not always been smooth sailing for IBM, and in 1992, it experienced the shock of recording a loss for the first time since its foundation. Feeling a sense of crisis, the board of directors at that time invited Louis V. Gerstner, Jr. from outside the company, who, despite not having a background in computers, succeeded in breaking IBM out of the deadlock it had found itself in. A current issue for Japanese companies, which can finally take a breath thanks to the quantitative easing by the Bank of Japan and the recovery of domestic economy, is what kind of growth strategy to envisage. This is the same issue IBM faced after its results recovered following its restructuring.

Acquisitions Around the Core Business

IBM has conducted more than 130 acquisitions, all of which have been in the field of software and services for corporate clients. It has achieved profit growth by honing its solutions business in the field of systems integration for corporate customers, which is its main business, and its method of diversifying is not simply collecting businesses with high profit margins. Japanese companies also advocate utilizing their own strengths to conduct overseas M&A (refer to Fig. 7.3).

In this way, there are many points in common between today's Japanese companies and IBM in terms of management environment and approach to M&A.

Acquisition by career manager

CEO Samuel Palmisano (2002 to 2011) worked at IBM for 38 years

Acquisitions using operating cash flows

IBM spent $30 billion on acquisitions over 10 years, but its free cash flows also increased by $9 billion

Acquisitions by *Monozukuri* (Manufacturing excellence) company

IBM is a manufacturing giant with 100 years of history

Acquisitions after restructuring

IBM successfully turned itself around in the 1990s to achieve profit growth

Acquisitions in the main business

IBM has enhanced its core system integration business instead of diversification

Fig. 7.3 Features that IBM has in common with Japanese companies

IBM's success is not due to it being "a special US company," and it would also seem its management could serve as a model for Japanese companies.

7.4 How Has IBM Realized Profit Growth?

How has IBM used M&A to realize profit growth? In this section, we will consider the answer to this question from three viewpoints: its roll-up acquisitions, its exit from the commodities business, and the long-term commitment of its top management.

Acquiring 130 Software Businesses for 30 Billion Dollars

During a 10-year period from 2002, IBM spent around 30 billion dollars to acquire more than 130 software and service businesses.

In 2000, IBM's software business segment contributed 27% of its total profit, but by 2011, this had increased to 44%,[3] which in monetary terms was around a fourfold increase. The profits obtained from long-term maintenance and services contracts also grew greatly, by around 2.5 times. This situation was in contrast to that of profits in the hardware business segment, which had hardly increased at all (refer to Fig. 7.4).

IBM's acquisitions in its software business can be traced back to 1995, when it acquired Lotus Development Corporation. This was around the time that IBM had started to become aware that software would be indispensable to its future development. Through this acquisition, it obtained Lotus 1.2.3, which is a spreadsheet software that at the time was greatly supported in the market, and also the groupware Lotus Notes. It is said that the IBM management team at the time did not fully understand Lotus, but what is extremely interesting is that this acquisition was conducted using a semi-hostile method, which can be considered to express the sense of crisis at IBM during that period.

Subsequently, when evaluating the acquisition of Lotus on a standalone basis, it is difficult to say whether it was a successful deal when compared to the relentless advance of Microsoft's Windows Office. In fact, a few months after the acquisition, the Lotus management team, including the CEO, left the company, while the person responsible for the development of Lotus Notes, its flagship product, also left two years later.

Given the corporate culture in Big Blue (a nickname for IBM), it is not difficult to imagine that it was not easy for it to integrate with an up-and-coming software company. While from the second half of the 1990s IBM conducted an "e-business" by incorporating e-commerce into its mainframes, transactions, and networks, it still considered software products to

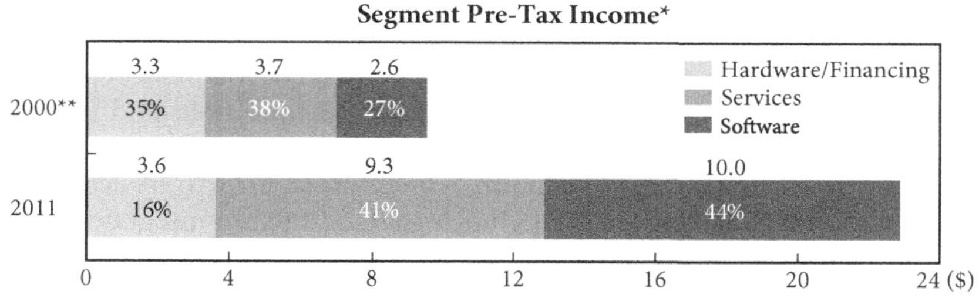

Fig. 7.4 IBM's segment pre-tax income (PTI) (billion dollars) from IBM's 2011 annual report (*Sum of external segment PTI not equal to IBM's PTI. **Excludes enterprise investments and not restated for stock-based compensation. 2000 Segment PTI is reclassified to conform to the 2011 presentation)

be merely "gimmicks" that were necessary for the sales of hardware, its main business.

However, this acquisition of Lotus served as the basis for IBM's acquisitions of many software businesses over the next 20 years. For the 10 years from 2002, IBM acquired software businesses at a pace of more than 10 per year. Moreover, these were not necessarily small acquisitions, and it announced billion-dollar deals on seven separate occasions.

During its repeated acquisitions of software businesses, IBM's approach to sales also changed greatly. Upon entering the second half of the 2000s, IBM's sales team would first propose to customers "a solution," then "a service," and finally, "a product." In 2008, it created its "Smarter Planet"[4] vision of using IT to solve the management issues facing companies, towns, and cities, and it developed throughout the world its sales approach of using "data analytics," "marketing," "the Cloud," and "next-generation commerce – Smarter Commerce," as the openings for sales.

By supplementing its software businesses through acquisitions, IBM became able to propose in-depth solutions to customers. In the data analytics field, it acquired the data analysis company Cognos for 5 billion dollars, the statistical analysis company SPSS for 1.2 billion dollars, and the data warehouse company Netezza for 1.7 billion dollars.

Also, in the marketing field, it brought into its group software businesses for Cloud-based retail analysis, digital marketing optimization, and website visitor behavior analysis. In the commerce field, it spent 1.4 billion dollars to acquire Sterling Commerce, a provider of software to integrate and to increase the sophistication of business-to-business transactions. In addition, in the security field, it acquired Internet Security Systems (ISS) for 1.3 billion dollars (Table 7.1).

Each of these fields is also becoming essential to corporate management in Japan. According to Road Map 2015, IBM's 2015 annual report, it planned to spend a further 20 billion dollars on acquisitions and to have the software business segment provide half of its total profits.

However, it is not an easy thing to achieve profit growth by acquiring companies at a pace of more than 10 per year and then to integrate them. At the time of the acquisition, at the very least, it would be necessary to investigate two or three times as many possible target than are actually acquired. The acquisitions would not be a success unless IBM had a concrete mindset, that is, clarifying what is to be targets (selection), understanding the value of the software business (valuation), and determining how it would use the business after the acquisition (integration). It is well

Table 7.1 IBM's software business acquisitions (2002–2011)

Release date	*Target company*	*Cost of acquisition*	*Target company business*
September 17, 2002	Holosofx, Inc.	Undisclosed	Business integration software
November 6, 2002	Tarian Software	Undisclosed	Electronic records management software
December 10, 2002	Rational Software	Approx. 2.1 billion dollars	Software development environment
May 15, 2003	Think Dynamics	Undisclosed	Software to automatically allocate computing resources
July 16, 2003	Aptrix	Undisclosed	Web contents management software
October 21, 2003	CrossAccess	Undisclosed	Information integration
December 19, 2003	Green Pasture Software	Undisclosed	Enterprise contents management
March 12, 2004	Trigo Technologies	Undisclosed	Product information management middleware
April 2, 2004	Candle	Undisclosed	Infrastructure management
July 22, 2004	Alphablox	Undisclosed	Analytical information such as purchasing and customer trends
August 30, 2004	Venetica	Undisclosed	Company content integration software
March 15, 2005	Ascential Software	Approx. 1.1 billion dollars	Data integration software
October 20, 2005	DataPower	Undisclosed	Improving security and processing speed of computer transactions
December 22, 2005	Bowstreet	Undisclosed	Integration of information on companies as a whole
December 27, 2005	Micromuse	Approx. 865 million dollars	Network management software
January 31, 2006	CIMS Lab	Undisclosed	Software to ascertain usage conditions of computing resources
May 23, 2006	Rembo Technology	Undisclosed	Software to automate installation of software onto thousands of PCs and servers
August 8, 2006	Webify Solutions	Undisclosed	Industry-specific software and services suitable to build SOA (service-oriented architecture)
August 8, 2006	MRO Software	Approx. 740 million dollars	Asset/service management software and consulting

(*continued*)

Table 7.1 (continued)

Release date	*Target company*	*Cost of acquisition*	*Target company business*
August 15, 2006	FileNet	Approx. 1.6 billion dollars	Business process management and content management solutions
August 24, 2006	Internet Security Systems (ISS)	Approx. 1.3 billion dollars	Security solutions
February 2, 2007	Softek Storage Solutions	Undisclosed	Data migration standards solutions
June 8, 2007	Watchfire	Undisclosed	Software to verify security and compliance
June 12, 2007	Telelogic	Approx. 845 million dollars	Development of complex systems, including aircraft radar systems
August 23, 2007	WebDialogs	Undisclosed	Online meetings
October 29, 2007	Novus CG	Undisclosed	Storage solutions
November 15, 2007	Cognos	Approx. 5 billion dollars	Information on demand
January 8, 2008	XIV	Undisclosed	Storage technology
January 24, 2008	Net Integration Technologies	Undisclosed	Business server software solutions
February 4, 2008	Arsenal Digital Solutions	Undisclosed	Extensive on-demand/data protection solutions
March 17, 2008	Encentuate	Undisclosed	Main provider of ID and access management software
April 22, 2008	Diligent Technologies	Undisclosed	Online software to delete duplicated data
May 9, 2008	InfoDyne Corporation	Undisclosed	High-speed platform and data feed connector
July 31, 2008	ILOG	340 million dollars	Business rules management system
November 21, 2008	Transitive Corporation	Undisclosed	Cross platform virtualization
July 31, 2009	SPSS	Approx. 1.2 billion dollars	Comprehensive market forecast analysis
August 4, 2009	Ounce Labs	Undisclosed	Software to reduce risks and costs related to security and compliance
December 4, 2009	Guardium	Undisclosed	Real-time monitoring and protection of corporate databases

(*continued*)

Table 7.1 (continued)

Release date	*Target company*	*Cost of acquisition*	*Target company business*
February 12, 2010	Initiate Systems	Undisclosed	Data coordination software to share information between medical facilities and government institutions
February 22, 2010	Intelliden	Undisclosed	Automated solutions for networks
May 11, 2010	Cast Iron System	Undisclosed	Cloud integration software, appliances, and services
May 31, 2010	Sterling Commerce	Approx. 1.4 billion dollars	Network management
June 22, 2010	Coremetrics	Undisclosed	Web analysis
July 8, 2010	BigFix	Undisclosed	Management and automation of security and compliance updates
August 5, 2010	Storwize	Undisclosed	Real-time data compression technologies
August 16, 2010	Datacap	Undisclosed	Software to support improving business processes, reducing printing-related costs and human error, standards for regulations and laws, and others
August 19, 2010	Unica Corporation	Approx. 480 million dollars	Marketing solutions
September 21, 2010	OpenPages	Undisclosed	Identifying risks and managing compliance activities
September 27, 2010	Netezza	Approx. 1.7 billion dollars	Business information analysis
October 1, 2010	BLADE Network Technologies	Undisclosed	Network switching and related software
October 22, 2010	PSS System	Undisclosed	Information governance, policy analysis, automation, execution, and automated deletion of information for large volumes of digitized business information
October 27, 2010	Clarity Systems	Undisclosed	Financial governance software
March 24, 2011	TRIRIGA	Undisclosed	Facilities and real estate management software and solutions provider
September 7, 2011	Algorithmics	387 million dollars	Financial risk management

(*continued*)

Table 7.1 (continued)

Release date	*Target company*	*Cost of acquisition*	*Target company business*
October 11, 2011	Q1 Labs	Undisclosed	Security and intelligence software
October 19, 2011	Platform Computing	Undisclosed	Cluster management software for a decentralized computing environment and grid management software
December 8, 2011	Cúram Software	Undisclosed	Public services support
December 12, 2011	DemandTec	440 million dollars	Consumer behavior analysis
December 19, 2011	Emptoris	Undisclosed	Procurement management solutions

IBM press releases

known that IBM puts in place an in-house team with experience in acquisition and integration after each acquisition.

Nor is it the case that all its acquisitions in the United States were successes. For example, as in the case of Tyco, after actually conducting as many as 800 acquisitions in fields such as electronic parts, pharmaceuticals, and finance, there are instances where the acquired business stalled in the subsequent management, including 150 businesses that ended up being sold after the management and administration became complex, and businesses were repeatedly spun off. Thus, it is not the case that as many acquisitions as possible should be carried out.[5] Tyco was merged by Johnson Control in 2016.

Exiting Commodities Businesses

During the 10 years under discussion, IBM withdrew from businesses it judged to be commodities because they relied on scale and competed solely on price. This decision also played a major role in its achievement of profit growth.

Even when looking only at the major businesses that IBM withdrew from, in 2002, it sold its HDD business to Hitachi, in 2005, its PC business to the Lenovo Group of China, in 2007, its digital printers business to Ricoh, and in 2012, its POS business to Toshiba TEC (Table 7.2). These were all profitable businesses that had significant market share, particularly in the United States, but they were nevertheless sold, not because

Table 7.2 Businesses from which IBM has withdrawn

	Main business from which it has withdrawn	*Purchasing company*
2002	HDDs	Hitachi
2005	PCs	The Lenovo Group
2007	Digital printers	Ricoh
2012	POS terminals	Toshiba TEC

IBM needed cash, but because IBM determined them to be commodities in light of its own strategy.

We tend to think that IBM forecasts a long way into the future and is skilled at selling businesses for a profit, but I would like to conduct a more in-depth analysis of IBM's strategy.

IBM is a company that has grown by creating its own markets through the introduction of original products across its 100-year history. Rather than entering into a market created by another company as an imitator, it has developed its businesses by becoming known for providing the solution that its customers are looking for and for always being at the frontline of the market.

Even when IBM withdrew from a business, it did not simply sell it for a profit. Rather, it selected a leading company to sell the business to, and then subsequently, while maintaining a relationship with the acquiring company as a partner, it stayed in the field and evolved into areas with high added value.

For example, let us consider the case of IBM's sale of its retail store solutions (RSS) business to Toshiba TEC for 850 million dollars. As only around five years has passed since this sale, it is too early to determine if this was a good deal for IBM, for Toshiba TEC, or for both companies. Also, sales of POS terminals and registers to distribution and retail businesses is the core business and cash cow for Toshiba TEC, so it does not seem appropriate to call this business a commodity. At the time of the sale, IBM's POS terminals held the leading share of the global market, so it was an extremely enticing target for Toshiba TEC. With this acquisition, Toshiba TEC would obtain sales channels to deliver its terminals to major retailers in the United States, such as Walmart and Toys "R" Us.

So, why did IBM sell its RSS business even though it had an extremely high-quality customer base in the United States and was achieving sales of 1.15 billion dollars?[6] The strategy of IBM cannot be correctly understood if one assumes that the reason was simply because POS terminals are hardware.

At the time the sale was announced, Mr. Craig Heyman, the general manager responsible for industry solutions in the IBM Software Group, commented,

> A new strategy is required for the dynamically changing retail market, and we believe the current transaction will not only create the world's leading POS company, it will also create an important business partner in our Smarter Commerce initiative, which is strategically important to IBM. We consider that retail businesses will place their trust in both companies, which have an abundance of experience in multi-channel commerce in order to meet the needs of customers who demand a seamless shopping experience, whether online, stores, mobile, or social.

At the same time as the acquisition, Toshiba TEC concluded an additional agreement that would last for several years to be a premium partner in the Smarter Commerce initiative business partner program promoted by IBM. According to IBM, this agreement would enable it to integrate its portfolio of enterprise-level Smarter Commerce solutions at each of its stores and services from its data centers with Toshiba TEC's solutions for frontend retail.

As its frontend (store front) business, which included POS terminals, was becoming a commodity, IBM decided not to maintain this product within the company and that the best course was to sell it to Toshiba TEC, a leading manufacturer, and then utilize Toshiba TEC as a partner.

Mobile payments are starting to become widespread in this field. PayPal of the United States, which provides a dedicated app for credit card payments by smartphone and a dedicated card reader, has established a joint venture with SoftBank and launched sales targeting small-scale retail stores. Similarly, Rakuten is providing its Rakuten Smartpay mobile payment service, and in the United States, Square, established by the founder of Twitter, is opening member stores. Once the payment functions of smartphones and other such devices are further enhanced, it is possible that the role of POS terminal hardware, which is currently centered on cash and credit cards, will change.

The percentage of the total retail market provided by online shopping using the Internet and mobile devices is increasing. Not only frontend, but also such multi-channel commerce is growing in importance among Japanese retailers. IBM saw this change as an excellent opportunity to sell its solutions to retailers, and at the same time, it led to its decision not to maintain its frontend business, which is centered on POS terminals. In

2016, Toshiba TEC announced its impairment loss of 69.6 billion yen upon the business they purchased from IBM. And Toys "R" Us is in process to liquidate its business by closing 735 stores in 2018. The same approach can also be seen for the sale of its digital printer business.

In 2007, IBM sold its digital printer business, which at the time of the sale was achieving sales of 1 billion dollars, to Ricoh for 725 million dollars. Through this acquisition, Ricoh obtained a lineup of digital printing devices, an area in which its own product lineup was weak, and a powerful customer base in North America. Mr. Palmisano, the CEO at the time of the sale, said,

> IBM and Ricoh have both benefited from a strong relationship for many years, and this agreement is a natural extension of that relationship. In addition to its proven track record in the print industry, Ricoh will provide the investment necessary for the InfoPrint Solutions Company to continue to innovate and grow, which will benefit current and future customers. The eventual transfer of the IBM Printing Systems Division to Ricoh enables IBM to continue to refine its focus on its strategic businesses and the clients of those businesses.

Thus, even after the sale, IBM would maintain a relationship with Ricoh as its business partner.

In the 2002 sale of its HDD business, the contrast between the buyer and seller was clearly apparent. At that time, Hitachi was pursuing scale and acquired IBM's HDD business for 2.05 billion dollars. However, soon after, the unit price of storage fell significantly, and the business recorded a loss for five years after the acquisition. The Hitachi head office ended up spending additional funds on it. Hitachi held the HDD business for a long time, and the business had become a heavy burden by the time Hitachi finally sold it to the major US HDD manufacturer Western Digital. The fact of the matter is that Hitachi felt a sense of relief following the sale of the HDD business, for which market conditions fluctuate often.

Most likely, even if IBM had not sold the HDD business, it would not have been able to avoid a deterioration in its results, which would have affected its overall profit growth. Through this sale, IBM did not have to allocate the management resources that would have been required for its restructuring.

IBM sold its PC business to the Lenovo Group of China for 1.75 billion dollars. IBM mainly operates businesses for corporations, but its PC business was familiar to consumers and for a long time, the PC was a representative product of IBM. Before he was appointed CEO, Mr. Palmisano had been responsible for the PC business and had been involved with its restructuring. As the well-known PC brand, Think Pad, was its representative product, IBM tried everything it could think of to improve profits in this business. All things considered, IBM did well to keep the business running until 2005.

Meanwhile, in 2011, Lenovo had paid only 18 billion yen to acquire the controlling stake (51%) in NEC's PC business. The ability of managers to assess a business is expressed by the timing of the decision and is embodied by the valuation at the time of the sale.

In 2013, Lenovo had overtaken Hewlett Packard of the United States to capture the leading share of the global PC market for the first time. However, following the rise of smartphones and tablets, PCs are no longer the main information terminals, and they can be described as one of the products for which the term "commodity" is most suitable.

IBM determined to be commodities those businesses in which it was forced to pursue scale owing to price competition, and it withdrew from them while carefully selecting the companies to sell them to. It would sell these businesses to leading companies when these businesses were still profitable, and even after the sale, it would maintain a relationship with the acquiring company as a partner.

What is interesting when comparing IBM to Japanese companies is the timing of the decision to exit a business. Specifically, it would exit these "commodity" businesses at a time when they were still one of its main businesses with a large market share and also generating profits. We can understand that these were attractive businesses to acquire in the global market at that time from the fact that the acquiring companies were Japan's leading companies.

The difference in the timing of IBM's and NEC's decisions to exit their PC businesses caused the great difference in the selling price at the time. By not hesitating to withdraw from this business, IBM avoided the significant costs that would have been required for restructuring to keep up price competition in the PC business.

However, no matter how much sense it makes in terms of corporate strategy, it is not easy for managers to divest a main business that still generates profits.

I myself have frequently witnessed hesitation among managers and resistance within a company when Japanese companies are considering selling, and actually conducting the sale of, a business with which it has a long history. Even in IBM, which is one of the most sophisticated companies in the United States, it is likely that there were some managers that were hesitant about or opposed to the divestiture, even more so as it is known to be a company that value its employees. It would be impossible to consistently execute a strategy of converting to highly profitable businesses and divesting main businesses that have been deemed to be commodities without the firm conviction of top management on the importance of achieving sustainable profit growth.

Over these 10 years, IBM's total sales increased by only 30%, but its operating profit margin rose greatly, from 9% to 20%. This was because it acquired businesses with high profit margins at the same time as exiting from "commodity" businesses.

One of the keys of IBM's success was that it conducted the acquisitions and divestitures in parallel. Their significant improvement in the operating profit ratio cannot be achieved solely through conducting acquisitions while continuing to hold businesses with low profit margins; on the other hand, it would also seem unlikely that profit growth could be realized solely by divesting business.

Long-Term Commitment by Top Management

We saw that among the success cases involving Japanese outbound acquisitions, the president at the time of the acquisition conducted long-term management. Similarly, over the 10 years from 2002 to 2011, the only CEO at IBM was the career company man Mr. Palmisano.

Mr. Palmisano joined IBM in 1973 in a data entry position, and at the start of the 1990s, he worked at IBM Japan, before being appointed as the head of the PC business in 1996 at the age of 44. After experiencing its golden period in the 1970s and 1980s, in the 1990s, IBM invited Mr. Gerstner from outside of the company, who carried out restructuring. Many senior managers left IBM during this period, and Mr. Palmisano was one of the few managers who survived unscathed and remained with the company.

In the 10 years that Mr. Palmisano was its CEO, IBM's operating profit margin improved for nine consecutive years, and free cash flow also increased by 10 billion dollars. During his term of office, once they had been deemed to be commodities, he did not hesitate to exit businesses, even if he had been responsible for them in the past, such as with the sale of the PC business.

Mr. Palmisano's 10 years as CEO can be described as 10 years in which IBM utilized M&A to achieved profit growth. As the top management, Mr. Palmisano said that during his period of office, he would constantly ask himself the following five questions[7]:

- What should a company do in order to continue to survive even after the founder has retired?
- What should be done when there are conflicting elements for the organization?
- What should be done to deal with the commoditization of businesses?
- What meaning does the nationality of a company have in a global era?
- As a leader, how do I continually maintain a long-term viewpoint?

What did IBM, which had a 100-year history, need to do to survive as a company? Mr. Palmisano himself demonstrated leadership by ascertaining which businesses were undergoing commoditization and taking a long-term view to evolve the company into a highly value-added business, even when this goal conflicted with the organization that served as the company's core. Further, the fact that he consistently executed more than 100 acquisitions and divestitures shows that he realized the embodiment of this approach in practice as well.

It is likely that among the acquired software businesses, there were some companies that did not live up to his expectations, and also that within the businesses IBM exited, there were some that he hesitated to sell due to objections within the company. He would have found selling the main businesses particularly painful, especially having worked at IBM for his entire career.

However, if we imagine that he had not boldly conducted these acquisitions and divestitures, what kind of company would IBM have become? It would have continued to pursue scale and market share, with businesses such as those of PCs, HDDs, and printers remaining as its main business. Constantly subjected to price competition, it would have expended management resources to carry out endless restructuring to maintain slim profit margins. In this situation, even if it had acquired a number of software businesses, their contribution to overall profit would likely have been limited, as they would have been solely to promote marketing its hardware products. Unquestionably, its operating profit margin would not have reached its current high level of 20%.

This description corresponds to that of Japan's electrical appliance manufacturers today, which do not achieve profit growth because they maintain large-scale but unprofitable business with long holding histories.

7.5 The Three Key Approaches that Serve as Successful Lessons

The path IBM took during these 10 years shows that M&A can be an effective method of executing a strategy. The approach of this *monozukuri* (manufacturing excellence) company of conducting acquisitions while maintaining a strong balance sheet has many points in common with the management of Japanese companies. Next, we will consider three points in particular from IBM's M&A that should serve as lessons for Japanese companies.

Keep a Watchful Eye on the "Denominator" (Revenue Scale)

IBM did not pursue scale over these 10 years. Rather, it positioned as commodities those businesses in which it was forced to engage in price competition and chase market share, issued warnings to itself, and selected a course of exiting commodity businesses.

If the aim is to achieve profit growth through acquisitions, it is necessary to keep a watchful eye on the "denominator." This is because for businesses that maintain a large "denominator" (a business segment with a large revenue component) that does not generate profits, the effects of acquiring a profitable business will be limited, even if it is an extremely profitable business. Indeed, the positive impact on total profits will be diluted even if sales trend upwards following the acquisition. Furthermore, when you continue to struggle with the improvement of profitability for a large "denominator," you cannot sufficiently allocate management resources to the highly profitable business that you have purchased and added. There are companies that explain an overseas acquisition as generating synergy with their own low-profit businesses, but it is often the case that the acquired company becomes a less profitable business instead.

IBM also initially considered software businesses to be tools in order to sell hardware, which was its mainstay business. However, if it had acquired and added all those software businesses while continuing to hold on to its

PC and HDD businesses, it seems unlikely that it would have been able to achieve current level of profit growth. This assumption is not only from the theoretical viewpoint but also because it would have been difficult in the first place to operate these software companies as core businesses if management was still maintaining the hardware business as the primary business in practice.

When considering how to realize profit growth from overseas acquisitions, first, an answer to the "denominator" question is required. Success cannot be achieved while maintaining a large "denominator" that does not produce profits. Even after going to the trouble of acquiring an excellent company, the benefits will be buried by a large, poorly profitable "denominator" and it will not be possible to draw out the acquisition's positive effects. Thus, the first lesson is to address the issue of a "denominator" that prevents the generation of profits at the same time as conducting the overseas acquisitions.

Recently, this has at last started to be seen among Japanese companies. For example, Hitachi, after it recorded a loss of 787.3 billion yen in 2009, decided to withdraw from the flat panel TV business and to sell its HDD and overseas air conditioner businesses. The stock market appreciated this move as Hitachi began to take its "denominator" into consideration, and the company's share price rose.

However, Hitachi's operating profit margin finally exceeded 7% only in fiscal year 2017, and such attempts of other Japanese companies are still underway.

Acquire Companies to Create Business "Clusters"

Another point we should pay attention to in IBM's acquisitions is their continuity and supplementary nature. Rather than attempting to solve management issues in one fell swoop with sporadic acquisitions, the company has achieved profit growth by repeatedly acquiring software businesses and creating business "clusters."

In the IT sector, the technique of connecting multiple computers and making them function as a single system is called "clustering." The word refers to gathering multiple items of the same type. IBM has formed a "cluster" of solutions for corporate and urban management by acquiring more than 130 software businesses. Through the acquisitions of DemandTec and Emptoris in the Smarter Commerce field, it created a "cluster" of solutions relating to companies' value chains. It also created a "cluster" of solutions in the big data and business analytics fields through the acquisitions of companies such as Cognos, SPSS, and Netezza. Furthermore, it has used acquisitions to expand its functions in the security field, where there are significant demands from corporate clients.

When IBM conducts an acquisition, it always asks itself the following three questions when evaluating a target company[8]:

- Does it build on or extend a capability IBM already has?
- Does the company have scalable intellectual property?
- Can it take advantage of our reach into 170 countries?

IBM improves its own capabilities by repeating acquisitions and "spinning" businesses to form original "clusters," thereby enabling it to provide new solutions to its customer base.

10 Years of Strategy Commitment

IBM implemented its strategy, of placing solutions at the center of its business, consistently over a period of 10 years to an almost tedious extent. Its CEO, career company man Mr. Palmisano, led IBM to success by tenaciously focusing on improving earnings per share and profit margin, and by stabilizing the long-term strategy.

How might IBM have developed if Mr. Palmisano had been replaced during this period? For example, consider if the new top manager had decided to change the focus from the software business and instead insisted on reverting to hardware products. In this scenario, IBM would probably have kept its PC and HDD businesses, aimed to increase market share and scale, and pursued acquisitions of competing computer manufacturers. In fact, in the second half of the 1990s, IBM negotiated for the acquisition of Apple, and in 2002, Hewlett Packard conducted a merger with the major computer company Compaq.

Alternatively, if he had been replaced with a top manager who advocated business diversification, it is possible that this new manager would have quickly changed IBM's course away from the existing system integration businesses and steered a course to finance and other businesses like GE. Either of these strategies are choices that are entirely realistic based on the management environment US companies faced up to the middle of the 2000s.

There are many Japanese companies that use overseas M&A as a means of executing a growth strategy. However, can a strategy that is grounded on acquisitions be sustained over the long term, and can an environment be provided in which managers can consistently execute this strategy over 10 years? As we understand from the case of IBM, M&A leads to success when company managers have strong commitment to a “10-year project.”

What are the differences in M&A between IBM and Japanese companies? In the case of Japanese companies, it has frequently been an industry consolidation or a reach for market share that became the trigger for the acquisition.

There are also cases where they started to consider the acquisition only after an overseas company in the same industry was put up for sale. It is the same for the case of a withdrawal, as Japanese firms often failed to act until there was an offer to purchase or until it was too late to do anything; in many cases, they hesitated on divestiture even after the company fell into a deadlock.

With such a mindset, a decision becomes a matter of whether or not to seize an opportunity that has appeared in front of their eyes, rather than conducting M&A with an eye to a long-term strategy.

On the other hand, IBM’s M&A are not due to industry consolidation or an effort to gain market share. Rather, they are a means for IBM to attempt to evolve into highly profitable businesses without pursuing scale by focusing on its own profit growth. Moreover, it has not attempted to solve its management issues in one fell swoop through a large-scale acquisition; instead, it improved the competitiveness of its system integration services by forming “clusters” of businesses through repeated acquisitions. Further, by conducting acquisitions and divestitures concurrently, it improved its business structure and achieved profit growth at twice the speed.

Japanese companies do have a stable balance sheet and they are able to implement a long-term strategy. Across all industries in Japan, many companies have advocated converting to high-profit businesses and evolving into solutions-oriented companies in their management plans. What IBM has done to achieve profit growth is not necessarily anything new. However, IBM’s relentless focus on profits would be the most useful lesson for Japanese managers.

Notes

1. General Electric annual report, 2011.
2. IBM annual report, 2011.
3. IBM annual report, 2011.
4. IBM100-Tracing 100 years of IBM (2011).
5. Wall Street Journal, October 3, 2012.
6. IBM press release, April 17, 2012.
7. IBM "THINK Forum Japan," September 11, 2012.
8. IBM annual report, 2012.

Reference

Itami. N (2006) *The gap between Japanese and U.S. companies' profit margins.* Tokyo: Yuhikaku Publishing (in Japanese).

CHAPTER 8

What Should Be Done to Succeed?

8.1 Due Diligence Is No Guarantee of Success

While there are only a few Japanese success stories, there have been companies, such as Kuraray and Terumo, that have grown over time to become world-class businesses through the use of outbound acquisitions. IBM, which has transformed itself into a highly profitable company, is a case of a company that emphasizes manufacturing excellence while continually reviving itself by conducting a series of M&A. In this chapter, we will search for commonalities among the successful examples discussed in this book and answer the question "What should be done to succeed in outbound acquisitions?"

When managers are considering a deal, rather than ascertaining how not to fail, they should ascertain how to succeed. This is because an acquisition, which requires enormous investment and effort, is meaningless if it simply avoids failure. However, currently, when a company considering an acquisition is conducting its due diligence in investigating the target company, it places too much emphasis on mitigating risk and avoiding failure. Thus, there is a gap between what managers should be trying to ascertain and what they actually ascertain.

Currently, an acquiring company tends to ask "how to" questions when conducting due diligence tasks. These questions help to identify problems in the target company, how to determine the value to avoid paying too much, and how to negotiate contract to minimize risk after the acquisition.

S. Matsumoto, *Japanese Outbound Acquisitions*,
https://doi.org/10.1007/978-981-13-1364-6_8

In these tasks, the acquiring company can be advised by and receive detailed reports from experts, such as accountants, bankers, and lawyers. There are many specialty books on due diligence and negotiating contracts for M&A. These tasks are familiar to companies that have been involved in a number of deals, and while the respective techniques are all important at the time a transaction is executed, they are merely tasks meant to prevent failure. No matter how assiduously they are carried out, they are no guarantee of profit growth after an acquisition.

On the other hand, "What should be done to succeed?" is not a "how to" question.

When speaking of management after an acquisition, there are experts who point to the importance of post-merger integration (PMI), a concept that refers to the acquiring company sharing its strategy and integrating with the target company, in areas such as organizational management and operational processes, to realize synergistic effects. Integration tasks after an acquisition are also preparation in order to facilitate the subsequent management of the target company. However, even among experts, there is no clear answer to the question "What should be done post-PMI?" This is because what lies ahead is not simply another "how to" question, but rather a question relating to the acquiring company's management itself.

For companies, ultimately, an outbound acquisition can be a strategy for beating out local competition, supplementing and expanding the beachhead obtained through the acquisition, working toward sustainable profit growth. However, in actuality in many cases, a deal is decided upon while the acquiring company is distracted by the processes and tasks at the time of the acquisition, and it does not pay enough attention to management after the acquisition. To a certain extent, this situation is unavoidable because the history of outbound acquisitions by Japanese companies is still relatively short at 30 years, so success stories remain few and far between. However, I think that the reason there are still so many failures is that the acquiring companies lacked a long-term management perspective. This is because being able to prepare an appropriate transaction at the time of the acquisition is not the same as being able to manage effectively after the acquisition.

"What should be done to succeed in overseas M&A?" Rather than focusing on the techniques and processes of an acquisition transaction, it is necessary to focus on post-acquisition management. When we of acquisitions, we often lapse into specialist and technical discussions, and managers sometimes lose sight of the overall picture. Therefore, in this chapter, we will move away from technical terminology and instead consider "ways of fighting" to ensure sustainable profit growth is achieved after an overseas acquisition is conducted.

It would seem easier to understand what should be done for success by asking oneself specific questions such as where, with whom, with what, and how long to battle after an acquisition.

Using research on actual battles, the book *The nature of failure: Organizational theory research on the Japanese imperial military* (Tobe et al. 1984) provides lessons on corporate management and strategy. This well-known book traces the nature of the failure of the Japanese military by comparing the Japanese and US military forces approaches to battle during the Second World War in the Pacific theater.

For example, this book describes how the Japanese Navy air fleet achieved major successes overseas with its attack on Pearl Harbor followed by its sinking of the British battleship *Prince of Wales* in a naval battle off the coast of Malay. The book then analyzes the Japanese military's "ways of fighting" after these victories. Through these attacks, the Japanese military showed the world that its aircraft carriers had become a main unit of its maritime forces, replacing the battleships that had been its primary unit up to that time. However, subsequently, it was unable to escape its traditional way of thinking, *taikan-kyoho-shugi* ("big ships, big guns"), about decisive naval-gunnery battles between large-scale battleships. Conversely, following the attacks, the US military suspended its plans to construct large-scale battleships and instead focused its resources on producing aircraft and aircraft carriers; its aim was to quickly convert to an aircraft based military force. The US military made a comeback from the disastrous defeat at Pearl Harbor by enhancing its mechanized units and reviewing its structure. It would seem that upon the start of the war, the US military learned more from the Japanese successes than the Japanese military did.

In *The nature of failure*, the factors cited for the failure of Japan's military include strategic thinking focused on short-term decisive battles, ambiguous strategic objectives, and failure to adapt to changing conditions. Conversely, it points out that the US military had a grand design for waging a long-term war all the way up to an invasion of the Japanese mainland.

The ways of fighting by the Japanese and US militaries after the start of the war were clearly distinguishable. *The nature of failure* was published in 1984, nearly 40 years after the end of the Second World War, at a time in which Japanese companies were growing by focusing on exports. However, even today, 30 years later, the lessons from the book's discussion of the ways of fighting and nature of failure would still seem to provide suggestions to Japanese companies not just for their strategies, but also for their post-acquisition management overseas.

Next, we will search for the points in common among the successful outbound acquisitions in terms of post-acquisition management based on three viewpoints: (1) where the main battleground should be; (2) the battle location (business area), or where the war will be waged locally; and (3) the timeframe, or whether to pursue a short-term decisive battle or a long-term war.

8.2 Where and with Whom to Fight After an Acquisition

A question of where the battlefield should be.

Recently, phrases such as "global management" and "global human resources" have become key words in the business world. In fact, companies in industries such as retail, beverages, and food, which up until five years ago had been described as part of the domestic sector, are also seeking opportunities for growth overseas today. The background to this goal is that they are concerned about the tapering off of demand in their respective mature domestic markets upon which they have solely relied. They are advancing not only into Western countries but also into emerging countries in Asia. Furthermore, their overseas business development involves not only adding local production facilities but has expanded to include creating business opportunities in new markets. There are many managers who, at the same time as announcing an overseas acquisition, state that their objective is to accelerate the global expansion of their business.

However, it is dangerous to wrap an overseas acquisition in the cause of global business. Acquiring a company overseas is not in itself global business.

If the acquisition is in the United States, competition will be waiting in the US market; likewise, if it is in France, there will be competition in the French market, so first of all, a battle will be waged locally. Toyota and Coca Cola, which can be said to be leading global companies, arrived at their current forms only after repeatedly gaining control over the markets of individual countries and regions. It is not the case that they conducted global management from the start. A major reason companies conduct an overseas acquisition is to complement local capabilities in the target country and region. You cannot become a global company through acquisition alone.

In fact, companies that have succeeded with outbound acquisitions have focused on, to a considerable extent, becoming "local champions" after the transactions.

For example, Terumo, after it acquired the artificial heart-lung systems business of the US-based company 3M, transferred the divisional headquarters for this business from Japan to the United States. Further, in order to sell an entire artificial heart-lung system to hospitals in the United States, it made additional acquisitions of local businesses, such as those producing cannulas and blood circuits (tubes), so it could offer a full product lineup to these hospitals. Even before the acquisition, Terumo independently possessed superior technologies and products; for example, it had been the first company in the world to develop a hollow fiber artificial lung. However, after the acquisition, it prioritized being the winner not just in Japan, but also in the local market: the United States, the world's largest market for cutting-edge medical devices. In the 1990s, Terumo withdrew from the business of general-purpose products like blood-collection tubes, as it had been unable to compete with major local companies like Johnson & Johnson. From this experience, it selected the artificial heart-lung system to be the main battleground for its business in the United States and used local acquisitions to get on track to profit growth.[1] Having learned from its experience of withdrawing from a business in the United States, it would seem to have decided on a way of fighting based on a clear strategic objective.

In JT's acquisition of RJRI, there is no evidence that it pursued synergy effects with its domestic tobacco business after the acquisition. Rather, JT avoided bringing the management practices of the former state-owned company into the acquired tobacco business in Europe as much as possible. Before the acquisition, its overseas division was located in its Tokyo head office, but after the acquisition, the headquarters of its overseas business was relocated to the RJRI head office in Switzerland. JT used this Swiss office to build a beachhead into Europe. It subsequently realized high profit growth by establishing Europe as its main battlefield, including through the additional acquisition of the major UK tobacco company Gallaher Group, and aimed to become a "local champion."

After it made its wiring harness joint venture a subsidiary in the United Kingdom, Sumitomo Electric Industries (SEI) acquired the in-house wiring harness businesses of the European auto manufacturers Fiat and Volkswagen. Up to that time, SEI's main customers in its European business had been Japanese auto manufacturers like Toyota, but with these additional acquisitions, it added local auto manufacturers to its customer base. With the goal of being the winner in the European market in mind, it realized that horizontal integration to expand its local customer base was essential. If its head office in Japan had looked only at its main customers, Japanese auto manufacturers, it seems unlikely that it would have had this idea of acquiring the in-house businesses of European auto manufacturers. This is a success story of SEI setting Europe to be its main battleground after the acquisition.

On the other hand, there are also cases in which companies did not decide where the main battleground was. While this may seem like a win-win approach for both home and away, a vague strategy in which the battleground is unclear will result in failure.

In many cases, this failure occurs due to the company's overconfidence in their capability to run a local business. I myself have seen many instances of the acquiring company first attempting to change the target company after the acquisition based on its own strengths. In the case of Japanese companies, often they set to work first on improving the acquired company's production sites and quality control. When the head office sends a production manager to local sites, they compare the local factories to their own company's cutting-edge domestic factories and then initiate improvements at these local factories. While these improvements may bring the production sites close to the level of their Japanese counterparts, it is uncertain whether this outcome will be a positive for the target company. As a result of "polishing up" these factories to a level above that which is required locally, the capital investment becomes a heavy burden and the target company's price competitiveness may be damaged. It would seem that in the first place, rather than production, the priority issues for the target company are aspects such as strengthening marketing and sales.

Examples of failure in the steel industry in the United States are the acquisitions of National Steel by NKK and Florida Steel by Kyoei Steel, in which both acquiring companies provided generous technical assistance from Japan after the acquisitions. However, both companies stuck with their acquisitions over the long term, and ultimately, National Steel and Florida Steel went bankrupt and NKK and Kyoei Steel were forced to sell them. Both NKK and Kyoei Steel possessed advanced technologies in their industry, but once their target companies fell into difficulties, they were unable to rebuild the companies. The rapid increase in imports and labor costs, such as pension obligations, became major problems, and there were limits to the extent they could improve results by only providing assistance to production sites from Japan. These are cases in which target companies started to lose money in local battlegrounds and, although there were attempts to repair the situation from Japan, eventually the acquiring companies had to give up and were forced to withdraw.

There are also cases of overseas acquisitions that ended in failure even after purchasing a "local champion" business. Ryobi acquired the household power tools business of Singer Corporation, a prestigious US company. At the time of the acquisition, this was an excellent business that supplied its products under the Craftsman brand to Sears, the biggest retailer in the United States.

Ryobi was itself a major household power tools company in Japan and had previously entered the United States with its industrial electric tools business. However, when the Craftsman business started to decline due to the performance of Sears, which it relied on for sales of household power tools after the acquisition, it tried to make up for this shortfall by exporting these products to Japan and Australia from the United States. However, ultimately, its efforts proved in vain in the local market and Ryobi decided to withdraw from the business in the United States. Once you have captured a beachhead that appears to be strong, it is difficult to defend it when it starts to shrink. There are only a handful of successful cases in which an overseas business was reinvigorated from Japan, despite every possible step being taken.

A point in common among the successful cases of overseas acquisitions is a way of fighting that makes the local market the main battleground and gives the greatest priority to becoming the "local champion." The successful companies postponed the pursuit of so-called global management, such as generating synergy effects with the domestic business and developing into other regions, they did not "sound their own horn" from the beginning, and they were not overconfident about what could be done from Japan. Rather than focusing on cross-border synergy effects with the business in Japan, they prioritized defending and growing the acquired company in its local market.

When a company finds that the acquired overseas business remains in an inferior position locally after the acquisition, it will lose focus and purpose in the battle. Once the overseas beachhead achieved through the acquisition starts to decline, the acquiring company's only options are to invest a great deal of time and effort into repairing it or to give up and withdraw. For example, the benefit of domestic synergy effects obtained in the short term after the acquisition will not continue over the long term if the local business they acquired deteriorates.

In post-acquisition management, it would seem necessary to ensure that no ambiguity remains about the location of the main battlefield, and to thoroughly implement measures to achieve the strategic objective of being the winner locally.

8.3 What to Compete with After an Acquisition?

A question of the battle location (business area) in the local market.

After obtaining an overseas beachhead through an acquisition, how should a company battle in local market? An approach frequently seen among Japanese companies is leaving the acquired local business as it is and providing support from Japan for the areas in which they can extend. As these companies have invested significant amounts of money, which means they value the business, they tend to think that the target company would continue performing well as per the plan without much trouble. This is a passive approach.

One of the backgrounds to this approach is that Japanese companies tend to think the overseas industry in which they invested is developing along the same path as the equivalent industry in Japan. This tendency is particularly strong for acquisitions in emerging countries. However, if the country is different, then even for a company in the same industry, the management environment will be significantly different, including the customers, network of suppliers, and government regulations. The consolidation and growth process of the industry will differ from Japan. For example, NTT DoCoMo was attracted by the growth potential of India's mobile phone market and invested 260 billion yen in an Indian mobile phone company in 2008. However, it decided to withdraw after just five years upon finding itself continually at the mercy of excessive price competition and the policies of the Indian government. Explaining this defeat, NTT DoCoMo commented that "While we think India will continue to grow, the growth potential for us is not as high as we initially anticipated."[2] It misjudged its way of fighting in the local market because it thought that its Japanese domestic success could be standardized.

Companies that succeeded in overseas acquisitions were able to flexibly correct the location of the battle (business area) after the acquisitions.

Kuraray repeatedly conducted acquisitions to become the world leader in Poval resin. The Poval resin business it acquired from Clariant in Europe provided Kuraray's mainstay product, PVA resin, but also added a product, PVB resin.

Subsequently, it acquired locally a PVB film business for construction-use glass and vehicle windshields, with the targeted German film manufacturer having been a Clariant customer for 50 years. Kuraray did not have a PVB business domestically, but through forward-vertical integration in Europe, it established an integrated production structure for PVB resin and film and expanded into business areas in the downstream. After that, Kuraray acquired MonoSol, a US manufacturer of PVA films for packaging for detergents and pesticides, and a vinyl acetate business from DuPont, further expanding its business areas to industrial resin and film.

By vertically and horizontally expanding its Poval business overseas, it went beyond the optical field, which was its area of expertise in Japan, and built a wide-ranging customer base that included automotive and construction customers. We can see Kuraray's grand strategy of achieving sustainable profit growth in its way of fighting by adding businesses that it did not have in Japan (refer to Fig. 8.1).

Ricoh increased awareness of its own brand across Europe by acquiring Gestetner, a long-established UK office equipment distribution company. Before the acquisition, up to the first half of the 1990s, the Ricoh brand was not known locally in Europe, and it had resigned itself to being an original equipment manufacturer (OEM) to local distribution companies. Ricoh had established a production base in Europe owing to the trade friction between Japan and Europe that time, but it relied on local companies to sell their products under the brand of someone else. However, after acquiring Gestetner, it launched new office equipment under the Ricoh brand and was able to get sales of its own brand on track. It then steadily achieved sustainable profit growth by also becoming involved in the sales of consumables and maintenance services in Europe through the distribution companies it acquired. Its strategic objective for Europe, of establishing bases to expand its business, was clear, and it used the acquisition of Gestetner to establish a beachhead into Europe by increasing sales of the Ricoh brand. It seems unlikely that it would be enjoying its present success in Europe if it had limited itself to local production without expanding into base businesses such as maintenance services.

IBM has acquired more than 100 software companies and has created a new market in the field of providing solutions for corporate and public

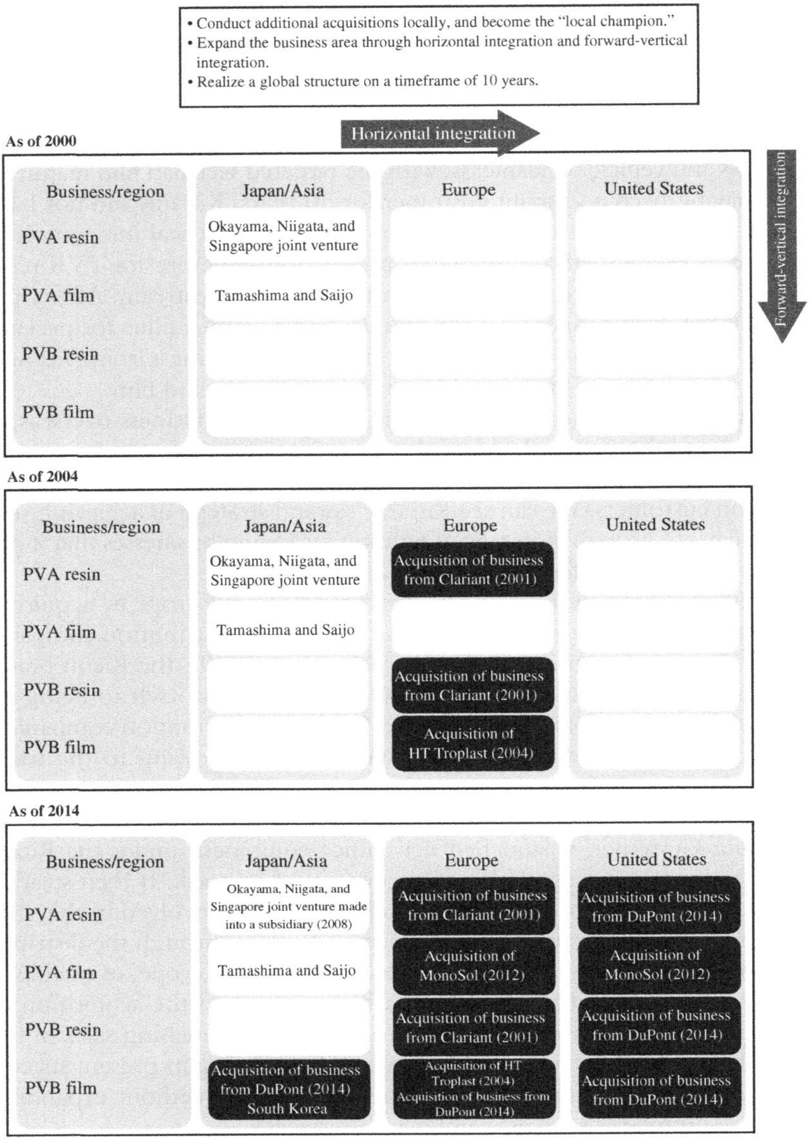

Fig. 8.1 Ways of fighting for an overseas M&A (Kuraray's vinyl acetate business) (*The darkly shaded cells are parts that complemented Kuraray's lineup through M&A*). (Prepared by the author from Kuraray press releases and annual reports)

service organizations. It has a long history of having a powerful sales force for corporate customers, so the sales force recognized what was needed to fight on the frontline.

Initially, IBM positioned software only as a means to sell its hardware products. However, it developed its software business through acquisitions and then switched to a sales approach focused mainly on solutions instead of computers. With this shift, IBM has achieved sustainable profit growth.

From the IBM example, we also understand that the key to success is adapting to a changing business environment and flexibly correcting and expanding the battle location (business area).

In contrast, there are examples of failed overseas acquisitions in which companies excessively stuck to their own business area. In its acquisition of the US-based MCA, Matsushita Electric Industrial targeted synergy effects between the hardware and software businesses. Specifically, it thought that incorporating Universal's movie contents would increase the sales of its own Audio Visual (AV) products, high-quality TVs and videos. Of course, it also seems that Sony's acquisition of Columbia Pictures spurred its acquisition of MCA.

Matsushita entrusted the post-acquisition management to MCA's executive team and waited for the expected synergy effects to arrive for its AV business, but the MCA executive team's priority was surviving in Hollywood.

For example, on a number of occasions, MCA's top management proposed to Matsushita the acquisition of TV broadcasting companies in the United States. The US media and entertainment industry in the early 1990s, which was undergoing deregulation and consolidation, had been swept by a wave of M&A, so it is easy to imagine how the MCA management team argued it was necessary to acquire these broadcasting stations in order to survive in the fierce Hollywood competition.

If seen from the MCA point of view, from the beginning, it seemed not to be convinced of the idea that Matsushita's TVs and videos would sell via synergy effects with its movie contents. Even if it cooperated with this objective, it was only to the extent of occasional product placements of Panasonic AV equipment in the TV detective show *Colombo*, which was also popular in Japan. However, Matsushita stuck to the idea of generating synergy effects for its AV equipment business and would not approve the course correction that MCA was proposing for the local business area, of acquiring broadcasting stations in Hollywood. By looking at Sony's situation after its acquisition, it should have been clear that movie content would not generate synergy effects for its AV equipment business, but Matsushita stuck resolutely to this idea at that time. It ended up repeatedly changing its strategy after replacing its president at the time of the acquisition, and finally it sold MCA.

For its acquisition of MCA, Matsushita was ambiguous on where it should fight (the battle location), and its grand strategy about synergy itself was also wrong.

A point in common among the successful cases is that they flexibly corrected and expanded the business area by conducting local vertical and horizontal integration. In contrast, many of the failures are cases in which the acquiring company was bound by its own existing business area and standards and was unable to adapt to the local environment and changing conditions.

The key to guiding an overseas acquisition to success is not to hesitate to correct the battle location and to adapt to the local business environment.

8.4 A Short-Term Decisive Battle or a Long-Term War?

A question of the timeframe for post-acquisition management.

In an overseas acquisition, how should the timeframe for post-acquisition management be set? Should the timeframe accommodate a short-term decisive battle or a long-term war?

The nature of failure depicts how the Japanese military used many surprise attacks based on its strategic focus on short-term decisive battles, and the US military, which was superior in terms of supplies, reversed its initial defeats by rebuilding its structure.

The US military had a long-term grand design, up to an invasion of the Japanese mainland, and it also adapted flexibly to the changes in the war. Conversely, the Japanese military, even if it had individual strategies for separate battles, lacked an overall strategy to defeat United States, and despite the changes of environment during the war, it was unable to correct mistakes in its strategies once they were decided. Inherently, Japan did not have a grand design like the United States, and instead its thinking was focused on short-term decisive battles using large-scale battleships in Pacific oceans. This shows the critical importance of setting a timeframe when thinking of the way to fight.

There are M&A that involve a short-term decisive battle. For example, a private equity firm will use leverage to acquire a target company and immediately conduct large-scale restructuring. At the stage when its performance is improving, the firm will sell the acquired company for a gain. For private equity, success involves executing this series of tasks as quickly as possible.

On the other hand, the objective of strategic investors conducting outbound acquisitions is to achieve sustainable profit growth, so a long-term war is required. In the first few years after an overseas acquisition, investors must go through and escape from the pitfalls that lay hidden within the expected benefits. For example, it takes time to generate cross-border synergies, so the possibility of profit growth over the short term is limited.

In fact, as we have seen in the Japanese success cases, the president at the time of the acquisition subsequently managed the company for at least 10 years. This long-term management expresses a stability of a strategy, executed over the long term, after an acquisition. Also, in the case of IBM, which has evolved to become a highly profitable company by focusing on the solutions business, Mr. Palmisano served as the CEO for 10 years, and he simultaneously withdrew IBM from "commodity" businesses while conducting a series of acquisitions of software businesses. A point shared in common by the successful cases is that the post-acquisition management took place on a long-term timeframe. Next, I would like us to consider ways of fighting from two aspects of time: "time" you buy through an acquisition and management "time" required for success.

Acquisitions to Buy Time

"Buying time" is one of the benefits of an overseas acquisition that management of acquiring company often cites. I have already described the pitfalls around this benefit that an acquiring company can fall into when thinking on a short timeframe. So, how many years should be considered when "buying time" through an acquisition? Looking at the overseas acquisitions we have considered so far, inherently, it would seem realistic to consider that profit growth that would take 20 years to achieve if conducting a business independently could be achieved in around 10 years through acquisition. Company managers who think that what would normally take three years would take one year using an acquisition only think about the time required to start production and set up local sales networks, but they do not consider the time needed to achieve profit growth.

In an overseas acquisition, it is better to think that it will take 10 years for a company to obtain the results it expects.

For example, when Seven & i announced that it would be acquiring Southland in order to rescue it, many were skeptical about the possibility of a turnaround of 7-Eleven in the United States. 7-Eleven's performance was extremely poor that time, and the critical commentary was that the convenience store business in the United States may have already peaked. In fact, after the acquisition, Seven & i had to invest additional funds in order to carry out restructuring.

Conversely, those at the time who were optimistic about the turnaround thought that if Japanese-style convenience store management, such as the logistics and POS (point-of-sale) systems devised by 7-Eleven Japan, could be transferred to 7-Eleven in the United States, its performance would most likely improve. This was an understandable logic when viewed from the Japanese perspective.

If Seven & i had set a timeframe of three years for post-acquisition management, most likely it would have impatiently sent a lot of managers from Tokyo and tried to implement a Japanese-style in the 7-Eleven stores in the United States. In the case of a short timeframe, its approach would have been to first push onto the other party those aspects it was good at and try to generate synergy effects.

However, Seven & i did not do this. On the contrary, it focused on a turnaround of 7 – that was rooted in the United States. After Seven & i carried out a thorough restructuring, including closing unprofitable stores, it spent time and effort on the local community-centered approach of opening franchise stores. As a result, the ratio of its own stores to franchise stores reversed, and by 2012, 20 years after the acquisition, the ratio of franchise stores had risen to 70%.

These efforts became the driving force behind its turnaround of 7-Eleven in the United States, and it got on track to profit growth. This is an example of how placing the post-acquisition management on a long-term timeframe can lead to success.

Bridgestone acquired tire production bases and retail networks in the United States through its acquisition of Firestone. It had to go through significant restructuring in its first 10 years of post-acquisition management, but over the course of 20 years, its North American business became a pillar of Bridgestone's earnings. If we look at its acquisition of Firestone on a timeframe of only three or five years, it would appear to be a deal that utterly failed to pay off. After the acquisition, it faced one problem after another; GM, Firestone's main customer, terminated its tire supply contracts right after the acquisition; Firestone's tire retail stores in the United States kept losing money; a labor dispute occurred on the closure of a factory; and the bail out of Firestone required additional borrowing, which in turn damaged Bridgestone's balance sheet. Based on those conditions at that time, most likely nobody would have been surprised if Bridgestone had given up on Firestone after about five years and sold it or withdrawn from the business in the United States. If it had done that, there is no doubt it would have become a classic example of how not to conduct an overseas acquisition. However, when viewing the development of Bridgestone's North American business on a timeframe of 10–20 years, we can see that it achieved profit growth in North America within 20 years, which could not have been possible from a greenfield approach, and it is worthy of praise.

After Nippon Sheet Glass acquired Pilkington of the United Kingdom, it was hit by the headwind of the European financial crisis. The slumping results in the Pilkington business caused the Nippon Sheet Glass to also record a net loss for three consecutive years up to 2013. Anchored by a group of banks, it has somehow managed to continue to own Pilkington up to the present time. However, if we looked again at this deal after 20 years has passed from the acquisition, or in other words by 2025, its evaluation may be different from that at the present time. Nippon Sheet Glass may end up being proud of this deal if it realizes profit growth in Europe within 10 years, which would conventionally have taken 20 years to realize.

Time Required for Post-acquisition Management

A point in common among the successful cases is that the managers themselves are deeply involved in post-acquisition management over the long term. It is often the case that once they have completed the planned PMI, managers at the acquiring company think it is sufficient to entrust the business to local managers. However, while PMI is probably a necessary task for integration immediately after an acquisition, profit growth will not be achieved only by integrating the organizations and systems. Post-acquisition management is conducted not by local management, but by the acquiring company itself. It is necessary to be aware that managers must spend an enormous amount of time on the "fight" following an overseas M&A.

Shin-Etsu Chemical chairman Chihiro Kanagawa served as the head of Shintech, its US PVC subsidiary, for over 35 years, from the time he was appointed in 1978, up to the present day. At the time he was appointed, he was also the managing director of the parent company, and subsequently, even when he became Shin-Etsu Chemical's president and chairman, he continued to serve as a head of Shintech.

It is often the case that upon being made the president of the parent company, the president will then ask another to head the subsidiary, but even today, Mr. Kanagawa also serves as Shintech's chairman and keeps watch over its work sites. Over the past 30 years, he grew the PVC resin business to a world-leading position by increasing production capacity through acquisitions; by establishing new plants adjacent to Western chemical manufactures in the United States, such as its raw materials supplier Dow Chemical; and by consistently implementing streamlined management.

When it comes to overseas post-acquisition management, there are physical distances with the acquired company, and there are also distances between the strategy of the parent company in Japan and the operations of local work sites. Top management of acquiring companies need to fill in the gap between the two, and that requires long-term commitment. Mr. Kanagawa's long-term commitment to both the headquarters and local operations over 35 years provides lessons for other managers conducting overseas acquisitions on how to deal with the issues of distance and time that must be addressed.

Although there are many Japanese companies with a corporate policy of *genchi-genbutsu* ("go and see," meaning go to the local place to see how the work is done), upon conducting an overseas acquisition, they become strangely reticent with this approach and back away, leaving the local operations up to local management. Points common to the successful cases of outbound acquisition are that the managers advocated a long-term strategy and they themselves implemented that strategy into operations. Sharing the timeframe and having the managers who served as the commanders participate deeply in the management after the acquisition over the long term are essential to success.

Notes

1. Nikkei Business, December 9, 2013 edition.
2. Nihon Keizai Shimbun, April 26, 2014.

Reference

Tobe. R, Y. Teramoto, S. Kamata, T. Suginoo, T. Murai, and I. Nonaka (1984) *The nature of failure: Organizational theory research on the Japanese military*. Tokyo: Diamond, Inc. (in Japanese).

PART III

Lessons from Failure and Success

CHAPTER 9

Three Lessons for Top Management

Many of the outbound acquisitions by Japanese companies have ended in failure. In an overseas acquisition, once a mistake has been made in selecting the target company, it will not achieve profit growth no matter how much management resources are invested after the acquisition.

Also, even if the target was right, if the post-acquisition management was poor, the value that was dearly obtained through the acquisition will wither away. Such failures will result in a major loss for the acquiring company when the acquired business is sold or withdrawn from.

On the other hand, we have also seen successful cases of overseas acquisitions that resulted in long-term profit growth and the development of the acquired business into a world-leading business. Additionally, there are companies like IBM, which conducted 130 acquisitions in 10 years, that have greatly improved their profitability. The success or failure of an M&A will have a major impact on the financial performance of the acquiring company.

Among Japanese companies, there are those that spent a lot of time and effort before the acquisition to ensure that it would not fail by, among other things, thoroughly carrying out due diligence (DD) and negotiations. However, it is meaningless for an M&A to simply not fail because the company invested significant financial resource in the growth. Thus, in order to make an overseas M&A a success, the acquiring company must have management capabilities that go beyond transactional skills and tasks like DD, negotiation, and even PMI.

S. Matsumoto, *Japanese Outbound Acquisitions*,
https://doi.org/10.1007/978-981-13-1364-6_9

So, what should be done in order to make an overseas acquisition a success? I have noted that we can learn some lessons from the ways of fighting after an acquisition common to the successful overseas M&A we have considered up to this point. The consequences of the deals provide the following three lessons for today's company managers.

1. Avoid subscribing to typical theories about the benefits of cross-border acquisition.
2. Pursue sustainable profit growth through acquisition rather than seeking immediate financial gains and share price increases.
3. Redefine your business through acquisition and conduct divestitures in parallel.

In this final chapter, I want to highlight three lessons for overseas M&A. I would like the readers to refer to these lessons for the deals on which they are currently working.

9.1 Lesson 1

Avoid subscribing to typical theories about the benefit of acquisitions. Evaluate a deal based on the possibility of long-term profit growth.

The "Tunnel of Pitfalls" Is Waiting After the Acquisition

Being lured by short-term benefits into conducting an overseas M&A will lead to failure. At the time the acquisition is announced, many managers speak of the benefits of an overseas M&A, such as "buying time" through the acquisition, joining the top ranking companies for global market share, obtaining an excellent local management team, generating synergy effects with the domestic businesses, and taking advantage of the strong yen (a sense that the target was undervalued due to the strong yen). However, lying in wait beside these benefits are pitfalls into which the acquiring company can easily fall.

In practice, after the acquisition proposal appears and top management becomes motivated to conduct it, there have been cases in which companies are in a rush to accumulate the benefits and synergy used to justify the acquisition. However, even if the significance of the acquisition is "retro-fitted" after it has been conducted, soon after the acquisition, this sort of "rush job" will be exposed. For example, there have been cases in which companies have ended up saying, "Even though three years have passed, the estimated synergy has not being generated," "The operation was entrusted to local managers, but the financial performance has been worsening. We finally had to send executives from Japan to restructure the company," or "After we came to rank second for global market share, there was a recession in the sector and the business we acquired became excess personnel and production facilities." In these situations, far from "buying time," the acquiring companies had to take time-consuming detours to turnaround the overseas business, and owing to the strong yen, they may have come to regret leaping into the acquisition.

If you subscribe to the typical theories about the benefits of overseas acquisitions and assume that the anticipated benefits will be realized soon after the acquisition, you may fall into a deep pitfall.

For example, even if the deal was carefully considered in advance, a few years after the acquisition, the acquiring company may become concerned about the gap between its perceptions about the target company before the acquisition and its actual condition after the acquisition. It may, therefore, embark on restructuring. In Chap. 4, we called this period the "tunnel of pitfalls." As long as the acquiring company is pursuing benefits, this tunnel is unavoidable.

The pitfall is particularly deep when the acquiring company does not have the advantage of scale for its sales or production capacity compared to the target business. Caution is required when the two companies' respective scales are antagonistic or when the scale of the target company is larger. The acquiring company may have set its sights on buying time or obtaining global market share, but the greater the expected benefit, the deeper the pitfall. Two examples are Nippon Sheet Glass' acquisition of Pilkington and Daimler's acquisition of Chrysler, which bought large-scale businesses and fell into these traps post-acquisition.

It is said that Mr. Shigenobu Nagamori, the president of Nidec, a Kyoto based leading motor supplier, which has realized profit growth through repeated acquisitions, sent a "love letter" to a company it was targeting, saying "We want to buy you," even though the other company had no intention of being bought. In addition, Mr. Nagamori, using expressions suitable for a Kyoto manager, spoke of acquisitions and scale as follows:

> The scenery of the city of Kyoto seems completely different from the third station and the fifth station on Mount Hiei. The higher up you go, the better the scenery becomes. Similarly, for companies, the scenery will not change as long as a certain scale is not achieved. When viewed from below, even when saying 'We will acquire that company,' it is easy to fail. However, when viewed from above, it tends not to end in failure. (Nihon Keizai Shimbun 2008, 319)

Nidec increased its scale over a period of many months and years through domestic acquisitions, such as of Sankyo Seiki and the Hitachi subsidiary Nihon Servo. After that, in 2006, it acquired the in-vehicle motors business of Valeo, a prestigious French automotive parts manufacturer, and then in 2011, the motors business of Emerson Electric.

The ideal is to, at all times, keep your own company's profit growth as the main strategy and to attract deals from this position, but there are few companies that are able to do this. However, even if a company cannot achieve this ideal, it should try to anticipate post-acquisition management and not only see the benefits through rose-tinted glasses, but also be aware of the pitfalls that lay in wait along with them.

Pass on Deals in Which You Cannot Expect to Become a "Local Champion"

What sort of target company should be selected in order to achieve profit growth? An acquisition can be said to be a success once it starts to generate profits exceeding the cash flow projection the acquiring company used when it valued the target company. Therefore, the acquisition price or valuation of the target business should reflect a confidence that the acquiring company will exceed projected profits rather than just reflect the validity of the current market price.

When considering the possibility of profit growth, it is better to pass on deals for which you do not expect to be a winner in the local competition after the acquisition. There are many examples of failure in which, even though the acquiring company had no way to become a "local champion" in the country, the acquisition was conducted; it still entered that country through an acquisition because the country or region had a large population and was considered an emerging market. NTT DoCoMo's failure upon entering the Indian mobile phone market is a good example.

With an acquisition, you can obtain a beachhead to enter an overseas market, while additional acquisitions will supplement and enhance functions locally. To become a "local champion," it is essential to combine the beachhead with additional acquisitions. However, caution is required when acquiring a local company that is operating at a loss as a beachhead, even if it is a leading local brand, because if that company stumbles in its post-acquisition turnaround, the vital beachhead will retreat and the acquiring company will not be able to open up the local market. As the beachhead was large and expensive, a lot of time and effort needs to be spent on repairing it. In fact, even leading companies such as Seven & i and Bridgestone struggled in their efforts to turnaround local companies such as 7-Eleven and Firestone, and they required many months and years before finally achieving profit growth. It is difficult enough to turnaround a company domestically, so it is an extremely tough task to do so overseas when you are not fully familiar with local practices. It is better to avoid beachhead-type acquisitions that are premised on turning around a target company, even if it has a significant local market share.

Also, when acquiring a middle or smaller sized overseas company, it is necessary to ascertain the options that can feasibly be deployed after the acquisition and determine how realistic they are; for example, deciding whether or not you can compete against local competitors, including by conducting additional acquisitions for horizontal or vertical integration.

When acquiring a middle or smaller sized company, a situation may continue for a long time in which you are unable to compete with other local companies or other foreign capital that entered the market ahead of you, and you gradually come to lose sight of the objective of the acquisition.

There is also the danger of overconfidence in the abilities of post-acquisition management, that if some sort of support is provided from Japan, the situation of the acquired business can be turned around. Even if the acquired business is strengthened in the field in which the acquiring company excels, such as production and quality control, this will not immediately improve financial results. When conducting an overseas acquisition in which there is no prospect of being the local winner, ultimately, the acquiring company will have to maintain and keep restructuring the business after the acquisition. When this local business is not strong, the expected synergy with the acquiring company's business in Japan will not be generated.

SoftBank, which has achieved success in taking on NTT DoCoMo in its domestic mobile phone business, acquired Sprint, the third-largest mobile phone company in the United States when they deal took place. This acquisition was that of a beachhead into the United States. Sprint was recording a loss, but SoftBank restructured after the acquisition and its results have been improving.

For SoftBank's planned additional acquisition of T-Mobile, the fourth-ranked company in the United States, it ultimately did not receive approval from the US authorities and the negotiations ended. However, SoftBank President Masayoshi Son has asserted they do not intend to settle for third place, and they are aiming to be the "local champion" in the US mobile phone market.

So, how will SoftBank develop its fight in the future against its major US rivals Verizon and AT&T? We should keep an eye on the consequences of the deal.

DD and PMI Are Tasks Only to Prevent Failure

Japanese companies proceed cautiously when conducting an outbound acquisition. They use accountants, lawyers, and experts in personnel and even environmental surveys to conduct DD and identify problems in the target company before they execute a transaction. They also keep in mind the advice of experts when negotiating the contract, and immediately after the acquisition, they carry out the integration of the target.

Overseas acquisitions became full-fledged in Japan 30 years ago, so today's Japanese companies have become familiar with the M&A process, and recently, it has become more common for a company to have its own in-house M&A team. However, DD, contract negotiations, and PMI are all tasks done to prevent failure, and conducting them is no guarantee of success after an acquisition. In fact, many of the failure cases spent a lot of money on DD before the acquisition and PMI after the acquisition.

For example, in the event that the target company is a major Western company or its subsidiary or business division, since careful management and administration have been in practice, it will be in a good condition and will rarely show any major management problems. However, even acquisitions of companies for which the DD found no problems can become major failures once the acquiring companies has fallen into the pitfalls regarding the benefit of gaining global market share and synergy effects, as we discussed.

Also, when inviting external experts and reviewing the target company's personnel system and business processes, there are cases in which the local, competent managers have resigned, and the company has lost its competitiveness. Even if the company conducted PMI well, it will come to nothing if the acquisition itself performs badly.

An overseas acquisition, into which considerable management resources are invested, is meaningless if it does not achieve profit growth above the target company's planned profit. Merely not failing is not an acceptable outcome. A picture of a beautifully integrated organization may be drawn in the PMI. However, while it may be possible to avoid major turmoil simply by conducting post-acquisition management, success will not necessarily be realized.

Japanese companies do their best to avoid failure and pay close attention to ensuring there are no flaws in the process. However, it should be noted that these tasks are carried out with asymmetrical information between them and the existing seller, and that the seller's sole objective is to extract the most favorable possible conditions for the sale. It is a mistake to think the operation of the target company will continue to be fine just because it has been reviewed by external advisors. Rather, it is necessary to think of DD and PMI, Post Merger Integration merely as "tasks that, to a small extent, will reduce the possibility of failure."

When conducting an overseas M&A, what is most important is to evaluate the possibility of profit growth post-acquisition, and there is no external expert to ascertain this other than the acquiring company itself. The risk of failure after the acquisition grows larger when leaving the evaluation to someone else or by doing it halfheartedly yourself.

9.2 Lesson 2

Think about the post-acquisition strategy and synergy on a 10-year timeframe.

Do Not Be Bound by Achieving a Win-Win Outcome with the Domestic Business

There are companies that ascribe numerical values to the expected synergy effects when they announce an outbound acquisition. In many cases, the accumulation of synergy effects that were identified in the process of evaluating the target becomes the grounds for conducting the acquisition. However, being bound by short-term synergy effects will lead to failure.

When looking at cross-border synergy effects, it is better to think that the acquiring company needs to spend a considerable amount of time and effort before it actually generates synergy and results in profits. The synergy effects typically cited are "using local sales channels to increase the sales of our own company's products" and "aiming to reduce costs through carrying out joint purchasing," but these sorts of effects will not be realized immediately. If the company can increase sales of its home products easily overseas, then the company should be able to open up the local market with exports, without having to conduct an acquisition. Also, even if the two companies have parts and materials in common for their respective products, as their countries and customers are different, the specifications and quality standards will also be different, so it will not be easy to unify those purchases. There are also cases in which there are no suppliers able to supply parts or materials globally in the first place.

We can also clearly understand from examples of sales in Japan following an acquisition of a foreign brand that it is not easy to sell your own company's products outside Japan even if you have local sales channels there. Suntory Beverage & Food Limited acquired Orangina, which is "the national soft drink of France" and a leading brand in Europe. Suntory began sales of Orangina in Japan, aiming for cross-border synergy effects. On paper, it estimated that by combining Suntory's strong domestic sales network with Orangina's strong brand and proven track record in Europe, it would be able to quickly generate synergy. However, upon taking a Japanese viewpoint, we can quickly understand that even a "national brand" of France will not necessarily sell well in the Japanese domestic market. In fact, Suntory has been investing in a large-scale marketing campaign domestically for this product. Similarly, a product that is popular in Japan will not necessarily immediately sell well elsewhere via the overseas sales channels obtained through an acquisition. Unless companies invest resources over the long term in post-acquisition management, the cross-border synergy effects will not be realized.

When prioritizing achieving a short-term, win-win outcome in Japan, inevitably, the acquiring company will become impatient and force its acquired business to follow those areas that are the acquiring company's strengths. In many cases, Japanese companies lend a hand starting from the manufacturing process and quality control. They introduce their cutting-edge equipment from Japan into local factories and attempt to locally produce and sell their own products. In itself, this approach is not necessarily bad. However, when the products are improved to a level above that which is required by the local market as a result, the target company is robbed of its source of price competitiveness. The reason for the overseas acquisition in the first place should be that the acquiring company saw no prospects for achieving profit growth in the target destination by independently developing its business. Thus, when the acquiring company pushes its own ways of working onto the target business in post-acquisition management, it can end up losing everything.

Following its acquisition of Nycomed, Takeda Pharmaceuticals expected to generate synergy worth 30 billion yen a year by the third year after this acquisition due to the increase in sales in emerging countries and Europe. However, it was unable to achieve these goals.

Because it failed to achieve the anticipated synergy and also stop losing money in after the acquisition of Nycomed, Takeda Pharmaceuticals appointed a foreign manager to be its president for the first time since its foundation 230 years ago. Christophe Weber, who was headhunted from major UK pharmaceutical company GlaxoSmithKline to lead the company, said "The pharmaceuticals market has different characteristics depending on the country. Upon understanding this, we will make Takeda a globally leading company."[1]

The mistake it made post-acquisition was that it pushed to sell Takeda's products using Nycomed sales channel in Europe, but that did not happen in a short period of time. In addition, Takeda was not able to complete the planned restructuring, including reducing the number of Nycomed employees. It is important to be aware that it takes time to generate cross-border synergy and that the source of the synergy effects is not necessarily found in the acquiring company's domestic business.

Do Not Entrust the Target Company to Local Management

It is better not to entrust local management with the running of the target company after an acquisition, as it may not go well. An acquisition is an opportunity to take control of the company and business. If you intend to simply be silent, like a shareholder, it would be better to purchase shares as investor rather than going to the trouble of acquiring the company; the probability of failure will be less.

The acquiring company often says that "We decided on the acquisition because the management team of the target company is excellent, and we can count on them." This idea is dangerous. In foreign companies, the better the managers, the lower their loyalty to their company. The job market outside Japan has more mobility, and talented managers move once they find a better opportunity. Even if the acquiring company is satisfied that it has successfully built good relationships with the current management team of target in the negotiations process before the acquisition, these managers may all quit soon after the acquisition, leaving the acquiring company bewildered.

It is necessary to be especially cautious when the seller is a private equity firm. The managers installed by private equity firms are competent executives who are skilled in corporate restructuring. They have been entrusted by the private equity firm to raise the target company's value by improving financial performance, and they are promised significant financial rewards if the private equity firm successfully exits after three to five years. Their own value as professional managers rises if they find a good buyer and a high sales price, which brings significant gain to the investors. After the sale, they will be assigned to the next target company. I myself have met a number of these professional managers, and while they are extremely capable at their jobs, they have no particular feelings of loyalty toward the companies they manage, especially after acquired.

The CEO of Pilkington, which was acquired by Nippon Sheet Glass, was even promoted to be the president of the parent company in Japan, but he resigned only one year and two months after his appointment. After its first foreign president resigned, Nippon Sheet Glass subsequently invited another foreign manager from outside the company to serve as president, but he also resigned after one year. In the end, after recording a net loss for three consecutive fiscal years, it settled on appointing a Japanese career company man as president.

There are also companies that say, "We do not have many personnel who have managed overseas businesses, and this is the first time we have acquired a large foreign company, therefore we will entrust its management to local managers." This idea is even more dangerous. If the company publicly admits that it does not possess the required abilities to manage an overseas business, it is certain that it will stumble in the local management post-acquisition. This hands-off approach of doing nothing is not a problem when the business is going smoothly. However, once financial performance starts to deteriorate after having entrusted management to the local staff, ultimately, the only option is to dispatch senior managers from Japan to try to get the situation under control. In Bridgestone's acquisition of Firestone, it entrusted operations to managers in the United States, as it had no one within Bridgestone able to conduct management overseas at that time. However, in the end, it was the managers it dispatched from Japan that turned around Firestone by carrying out a severe restructuring.

Renault's investment in Nissan Motor Company has been called the most successful inbound transaction and alliance in Japan. Mr. Carlos Ghosn arrived at Nissan's Tokyo headquarters from Renault in 1999 and he was CEO and president of Nissan until 2017. He did not entrust management locally (in Japan) even after he was appointed CEO of Renault. He continued to concurrently serve as the president of Nissan. Incidentally, before it invested in Nissan, Renault had no presence in Japan, and furthermore, Mr. Ghosn had no experience managing a company in Japan. With his long-term commitment, Nissan recovered from its crisis in 1999 and it has been delivering significant profit growth.

Mr. Son, the president of SoftBank, which has been actively involved in acquisitions in the United States for more than 20 years, said after its acquisition of Sprint:

> There is a reason I told the employees of Sprint, the company we acquired in the United States, that 'We need to work hard to become one team.' It is the lesson I learned in advancing into the United States through the previous acquisitions of COMDEX, the hi-tech trade fair, and publishing company Ziff-Davis. I flew alone and acquired the companies, and fundamentally, I left the management up to U.S. managers. I thought that 'We should not interfere too much.' However, this meant we were little more than an investor, and from this position, it was difficult to take the major leap of changing their management. Of course, there were some positive outcomes, as we came to know the Internet world and it led to our investment in Yahoo! of the United States. However, even so, deep feelings of regret still linger (about this series of acquisitions). Although we obtained a map and compass for the Net age, our commitment was halfhearted. Therefore (in the acquisition of Sprint), I did not hesitate to loudly express my opinions. I raised my voice and gave them a good talking to.[2]

Genchi-genbutsu is essential to general management and Japanese managers respect that. The same can be said for post-acquisition management overseas. After the acquisition, the only option is to manage that which you see in front of you.

Implement Large-Scale Outbound Acquisitions Only Under a CEO Who Can Commit to Long-Term Management

One of prerequisites to success in achieving profit growth through overseas acquisition is a corporate strategy that is stable over the long term. The post-acquisition management will not go well if the senior managers who decided the deal are replaced in the short term.

In the successful cases involving Japanese companies, the president at the time of the acquisition continued in the top position for at least the next 10 years. For better or worse, the true colors of the top management are attached to the acquisition. In many cases, the position of the target business and its priority within the acquiring company is reconsidered after the top management who decided on the acquisition is replaced. Despite the fact that the business after the acquisition is finally on track, a change of business policy means the investment plan has to be reviewed again from scratch. In the most extreme cases, new management may sell the acquired business. If managers are not confident that they themselves will be responsible for the management for at least 10 years after the acquisition, it is better to forget the idea of conducting a large-scale overseas acquisition.

I imagine that among the readers, there are those who respond to this and say that Japanese companies do not decide on an acquisition from the top down, and even if the top management is replaced, the strategy will not change that much because most of senior managers are career company men.

However, deals in which it is uncertain who made the decision and acquisitions in which the managers themselves feel no affinity toward the acquired company will be problematic. If the management after the acquisition falters, nobody takes responsibility, and no new investment is carried out. These sorts of deals will not be a success.

In an overseas acquisition in which there is both a physical distance and a management philosophy of "distance," conducting long-term management is still essential in order to weave together the strategy of the acquiring company and the local operations acquired. In the successful cases, the CEOs conducted management and kept an eye on the target company's performance for at least 10 years after the acquisition, such as Mr. Suzuki at Seven & i, Mr. Wachi at Terumo, Mr. Wakui at Kuraray, Mr. Hamada at Ricoh, and Mr. Kanagawa at Shin-Etsu Chemical. After the acquisitions, they restructured the target companies, used additional acquisitions to expand the businesses vertically and horizontally, and grew their acquisitions to be globally leading businesses. At IBM, Mr. Palmisano, who used M&A to achieve incredible profit growth, served as CEO for 10 years, which enabled IBM to stably implement its strategy of prioritizing its solutions business.

After a large-scale acquisition overseas, the top management must themselves execute a consistent strategy and continue investing, including in roll-up acquisitions, for at least 10 years until profit growth is achieved. Without this sort of commitment from top management, the overseas M&A will not be a success.

9.3 Lesson 3

Redefine your business through acquisition and conduct divestitures in parallel.

Redefine Your Business

One of the points shared in common among successful overseas acquisitions is that they generated synergy effects from additional acquisitions in the region. The successful companies adapted to the local environment, which was different to their domestic environment, they were not bound by their existing business area, and they did not hesitate to correct and expand their businesses.

For example, JT and SEI solidified their local customer bases in the European market by repeatedly conducting horizontal acquisition and integrations. Through forward-vertical acquisition and integration, Kuraray developed a unified production structure in Europe and the United States, from Poval resin through to film for vehicle windshields and construction-use glass. Terumo used acquisitions to complete the necessary lineup of products to sell its artificial heart-lungs as a system, thereby supplementing sales to hospitals in the United States. Ricoh acquired distribution companies to expand its business in Europe and included maintenance services and sales of consumables, which became its foundation for profit growth overseas. In each of these cases, they were not bound by the framework of their domestic business but continued to expand its coverage through roll-up acquisitions.

Because M&A takes place more frequently outside of Japan, if you do not act quickly you will be left behind in industry consolidation. Also, if your ideas originate only from headquarters in Japan, you will lose the initiative in approaching local customers. What is most important in post-acquisition management is adapting flexibly to changes in the local environment. To achieve this, it is critical for acquiring companies to have the ideas, human resources, and funds together in order to conduct a series of additional acquisitions in targeted regions.

While Japanese companies usually have the funds, they often lack the ideas and human resources to identify opportunities and evaluate them. There have been failures in which the local management at an acquired company suggested acquiring another company to the Japanese company, and the Japanese company provided the funds for the acquisition without fully understanding what it was investing in. Simply increasing revenue or scale through additional acquisitions is not always a good thing, and having in place the human resources able to carefully investigate and evaluate a local proposal is essential to success.

When AEON acquired the US luxury apparel company Talbots, in the beginning, its financial performance was well above expected, and it contributed to the consolidated results of the AEON Group. After the acquisition, AEON entrusted US management to the local managers, while it devoted itself to the Talbots franchise business in Japan.

However, when Talbots' business in the United States began to deteriorate, Talbots proposed to AEON the acquisition of J. Jill, a major US casualwear company, with the idea to turn around its own business. The funds needed for the acquisition totaled 60 billion yen, which AEON itself provided.

Unfortunately, AEON had no human resources to evaluate the idea of the synergy effects between luxury apparel and casualwear in the USA and to determine whether it would lead to a turnaround of Talbots or not. As a result, this additional acquisition further deepened the wounds it had already suffered and three years after the acquisition it sold J. Jill. After that, AEON gave up on Talbots. AEON should have examined the reason why J. Jill's shareholders chose to sell the company in order to adapt to changes in the business environment. Funds alone are insufficient for correcting and expanding the local business domain, and success cannot be achieved unless the ideas and human resources are also in place.

IBM conducted acquisitions at a pace exceeding 10 per year over a 10-year period, yet during this time, its free cash flow continued to increase. IBM's powerful corporate sales force worked on the frontline, and so they understood the solutions required by customers, while IBM's in-house specialist M&A team completed the series of negotiations and integrations. This case is one in which the funds, ideas, and human resources were all in place and profit growth was realized through roll-up acquisitions.

One of the real thrills of an overseas acquisition is developing the local business through post-acquisition management. A company should not hesitate to correct the business area in order to adapt to changes in the business environment. Also, outbound acquisitions should not stop at obtaining a beachhead into the local market, and it is important to evolve locally while complementing the functions of the local business through additional acquisitions. The beachhead may shrink if the local business is bound by the acquiring company's domestic standards and policies.

If You Acquire One, Dispose of Another

If you are aiming to achieve accelerated profit growth through outbound acquisitions, it is vital to also address the task of reviewing and correcting your business portfolio. When conducting an acquisition, it is necessary, at the same time, to look at an existing business to withdraw from. Even if a company acquires a highly profitable business overseas, its impact on the financial performance of the company as a whole will be diluted if the company keeps a business that has been slumping for many years.

Anyone can conduct an acquisition as long as the funds are available but exiting is a difficult decision. The fact that withdrawing from a low-profitability business will effectively improve profits can be understood without having to use a complicated formula, but even so, there are companies that are unable to make those decisions. However, maintaining a large-scale, low-profitability business or simply becoming larger in scale through acquisitions will not be a successful strategy for achieving profit growth.

There is a tendency among some companies to think of overseas acquisitions as simply adding new business to its existing businesses, and that they themselves do not have to change. This is equivalent to choosing to abandon the dynamism of cross-border acquisitions. The dynamism of outbound acquisition comes from a company redefining its core business and evolving by incorporating the new overseas business into a new whole. The reality is that in many cases, while thinking that "one plus one equals three" applies to the synergy effects from the acquisition, the acquiring company either leaves the management after the acquisition up to local managers, or attempts to forcibly align the target company with itself. Both are approaches in which the acquiring company turns its back on changing itself and therefore, fails to realize the dynamism of cross-border M&A.

The fact that there are many failures among the acquisitions by white knights rescuing the target company or of a joint venture following the withdrawal of the joint venture partner is because the acquiring company is swayed by the situation at the other company and does not think sufficiently about its own business portfolios. Following an acquisition proposal from Aquascutum's management in the UK, Renown agreed to acquire it as a white knight. However, after the acquisition, it was unable to take the steps to restructure Aquascutum and increase sales outside Japan as it had expected. While being unable to change itself, its financial performance slumped, and ironically Renown was itself rescued by a Chinese company acting as a white knight.

After Mitsubishi Motors Corporation's joint venture partner with Volvo was incorporated into the Ford Group, it made NedCar of the Netherlands into a subsidiary, but this acquisition was at the convenience of the other party. After the acquisition, Mitsubishi Motors planned to increase plant utilization by bringing in production of compact cars with Daimler, which it had invited to be a major shareholder. However, this alliance with Daimler also came to nothing, and in the end, all Mitsubishi Motors was left with was surplus production facilities in the Netherlands. Although both Renown and Mitsubishi Motors struggled to maintain these loss-making businesses over the long term, they eventually sold the businesses.

On the other hand, the successful cases include companies that boldly redefined their businesses. In the same year that Kuraray embarked on the acquisition of a Poval resin business in Europe through an acquisition, it withdrew from the rayon business, which was its original business. It attempted to redefine itself from a company that was focused on textiles to one focused on chemicals. Kuraray had previously attempted to diversify its business due to the recession in the textile industry, and it tried its hand at businesses such as beverages and real estate, but none of these attempts had gone well. Its subsequent acquisitions and withdrawals make it clear that it has placed its center of gravity on the chemicals business, particularly on poval resin.

Before Terumo acquired 3M's artificial heart-lung systems business, it withdrew from underperforming general-purpose products, such as blood-collection tubes in United States, including closing plants. This case is one of correcting the battle location in which to fight in the US market, and subsequently, it got on track to profit growth in the United States by focusing on its medical devices business.

SEI used domestic and outbound acquisitions to grow its automotive wiring harness business to a global scale. On the other hand, despite the fact that its automotive brakes business was profitable, its revenue was close to 60 billion yen, and the business had a more than 40-year history in Japan, SEI sold the business to Aisin Seiki and withdrew from the industrial brakes business. Thus, SEI conducted both acquisitions and withdrawals within the same automotive business.

IBM has achieved extraordinary profit growth by conducting acquisitions at the same time as withdrawing from businesses such as PCs, HDDs, and printers that it judged to be "commodities." It has evolved into a highly profitable company not by pursuing scale, but instead correcting and redefining its business domain. For example, if IBM had kept its PC and HDD businesses till today, even though it kept adding solution business through acquisitions, it would likely not have achieved an operating profit margin of close to 20%. Conversely, if IBM had only conducted restructuring and reduced the scale of its existing businesses without acquisitions, it would probably not have achieved its current highly profitable form either and it may not even exist today.

Succeeding in an outbound acquisition requires that the acquiring company focus on the wisdom needed to achieve profit growth in that region, not on increasing its scale as a whole. Inherently, an M&A is a tool to redefine the acquiring company's business domain, and if a company hesitates in transforming itself, even after having spent tremendous money and effort to bring an overseas company into their group, then all it will have achieved will be the painful task of inserting foreign matter into its corporate body.

Finally, I would like to introduce you to a comment made by IBM's Mr. Palmisano in 2012 on the occasion of passing on the baton to his successor. Reflecting on his 10 years as CEO, he told shareholders

> This is a fundamentally different IBM than existed a decade ago – one that is delivering historic results despite a global economic downturn even as it more fully exemplifies the company's century-old character.[3]

Even within the 100 years of its history, during which its business evolved from sales of meat scales to its current business founded on its "Smarter Planet" vision, its evolution within these 10 years are worthy of special mention, even more so when considering that its results had only just recovered from a slump at the start of these 10 years. It seems unlikely that this accelerated growth through M&A would have been realized without a manager who constantly considered his company's survival in the distant future and executed a consistent strategy.

If you hesitate to change your own company, the acquisition will not be a success.

Notes

1. Nikkei Veritas, April 14, 2014 edition.
2. Nihon Keizai Shimbun, January 4, 2014.
3. IBM annual report, 2011.

Reference

Nihon Keizai Shimbun, ed. (2008) *Challenges facing Nidec's Nagamori-ism*. Tokyo: Nikkei Business Publications, Inc. (in Japanese).

Afterword

Shigeru Matsumoto

When I was a M&A banker, I was delighted when I closed deals after spending lots of hours and efforts for negotiation. However, I was even more delighted when the client told me that the management after the acquisition was going well.

I was told this just the other day by a client that acquired an automotive supplier in Europe. The acquisition led to a large-scale order from General Motors (GM). My client has cleared GM's strict quality demands by cooperating with the acquired company's product development and sales teams. It began supplying brake hoses to Chevrolet, a global strategic vehicle of GM, with an annual production of 1 million vehicles in Europe, North America and Asia.

Through this acquisition, my client obtained production bases in Europe, and it expanded customer base beyond Japanese car makers. The deal negotiations took place in the middle of the European financial crisis during which the Greek government bonds had crashed. Thus, a fierce debate repeatedly took place within the company, on whether or not to go ahead with the acquisition, but in the end, they went ahead. They were well prepared to run the business and then became a global supplier to generate synergy with this acquisition.

Going forward, the number of Japanese companies conducting outbound acquisition is likely to increase and the size of the deals will grow larger. Not only large companies, but also medium-sized companies are actively conducting acquisitions overseas. We will see even more frequently the impact of a successful or failed acquisition on their financial performance.

S. Matsumoto, *Japanese Outbound Acquisitions*,
https://doi.org/10.1007/978-981-13-1364-6

While some companies will proudly declare their success in post-acquisition management, there will be more companies who end up withdrawing from or selling the business they purchased with loss. Thus, the consequences of overseas acquisition may determine the future of company.

"Why do acquisitions fail?"

"How do we fight to make it a success in post-acquisition management?"

I felt that there were many things that managers conducting an acquisition needed to learn from actual successes and failures in the past, yet I could not find a book that provided a comprehensive collection of such case studies. I decided to write this book to fill that space.

As someone who has worked as an advisor for 15 years on the frontline of cross-border M&A and also as a business school professor, I feel proud that I have been able to complete this book in the absence of any similar publication. I hope that all its readers will find some useful suggestions from the consequences of these Japanese outbound acquisitions as well as the lessons derived from the case studies described in this book. I would also be delighted to receive your feedback.

In order to write this book, I completely rewrote the results of the research I conducted as part of the Ph.D. program at Kobe University so that it would be suitable for business practitioners, scholars, and students. I would like to thank Professor Kazuhiro Mishina of Kobe University for his guidance. I was extremely fortunate to meet Professor Mishina, who is one of the leading researchers in the field of strategy.

"Those who are unfamiliar with failure cannot understand the weight of success."

Among the many things Professor Mishina said to me, this has remained the longest in my memory. I used his words as guidelines when writing this book.

I also received valuable advice from Professor Nobuyuki Isagawa of Kyoto University, a leading researcher in corporate finance. Professor Isagawa also plays a role in the training of new investment bankers in Japan. Finally, I would like to express my thanks to Jacob Dreyer and Anushangi Weerakoon at Palgrave Macmillan. I was able to complete the marathon of writing it through their encouragement as they ran alongside me.

Beautiful Summer in Kyoto, 2018 Shigeru Matsumoto

Acknowledgment

This work was supported by JSPS KAKENHI Grant Number JP17K03977.

Shigeru Matsumoto

S. Matsumoto, *Japanese Outbound Acquisitions*,
https://doi.org/10.1007/978-981-13-1364-6

Appendix

Table A.1 List of sources for Material 3 at the end of Chapter 5

Acquiring company	*Target company*	*Acquiring company data source*	*Target company data source*
Matsushita Electric Industrial	Music Corporation of America	Matsushita Electric Industrial annual securities report, March 1992	Matsushita Electric Industrial annual securities report, March 1992
TDK	Silicon System	Nihon Keizai Shimbun, June 6, 1996	Nihon Keizai Shimbun, June 6, 1996
Mitsubishi Electric	Apricot's computers business	Mitsubishi Electric annual securities report, March 1990	Nikkei Sangyo Shimbun, March 13, 1990
NEC	Packard Bell	NEC annual securities report, March 1998	Nikkei Sangyo Shimbun, February 22, 1999
	Packard Bell's European business	NEC annual securities report, March 1999	Nikkei Sangyo Shimbun, February 22, 1999
Fujitsu	Amdahl	Fujitsu annual securities report, March 1997	Nikkei Sangyo Shimbun, August l, 1997
Hitachi Koki	DataProducts	Hitachi Koki annual securities report, March 1990	Nikkei Sangyo Shimbun, April 17, 1990

(continued)

S. Matsumoto, *Japanese Outbound Acquisitions*,
https://doi.org/10.1007/978-981-13-1364-6

Table A.1 (continued)

Acquiring company	*Target company*	*Acquiring company data source*	*Target company data source*
Toshiba	Dominion Semiconductor	Toshiba annual securities report, March 1999	Nihon Keizai Shimbun, July 7, 1999
Matsushita Kotobuki Electronics Industries	Quantum's magnetic tape business	Nihon Keizai Shimbun, May 2, 1997	Nihon Keizai Shimbun, May 2, 1997
Akai Denki	Konwa	Akai Denki annual securities report, November 1994	Nihon Keizai Shimbun, June 30, 1995
Yuasa Battery	Exide's industrial battery division	Yuasa Battery annual securities report, March 1991	Nihon Keizai Shimbun, November 10, 1991
NISSEI Electric	Arcotronics	Nikkei Sangyo Shimbun, July 10, 1990	Nihon Keizai Shimbun, January 30, 1990
Mitsubishi Kasei	Verbatim Corporation	Nikkei Sangyo Shimbun, March 23, 1990	Nikkei Sangyo Shimbun, March 23, 1990
Mitsubishi Corporation	Aristech Chemicals	Nihon Keizai Shimbun, January 17, 1990	Nihon Keizai Shimbun, January 17, 1990
Settsu	Uarco	Settsu annual securities report, March 1988	Settsu annual securities report, March 1989
Dainippon Ink and Chemicals	Reichhold	Dainippon Ink and Chemical annual securities report, March 1987	Nihon Keizai Shimbun, June 25, 1987
	Spencer Kellogg	Nihon Keizai Shimbun, July 13, 1989	Nihon Keizai Shimbun, July 13, 1989
	Kopper's unsaturated polyester business	Nihon Keizai Shimbun, July 13, 1989	Nihon Keizai Shimbun, July 13, 1989
	Jotun Polymer	Nikkei Sangyo Shimbun, July 15, 1997	Nikkei Sangyo Shimbun, July 15, 1997
Nippon Sanso	Thermos Corporation	Nippon Sanso annual securities report, March 1989	Nippon Sanso annual securities report, March 1990

(*continued*)

Table A.1 (continued)

Acquiring company	*Target company*	*Acquiring company data source*	*Target company data source*
Ishihara Sangyo	SDS Enterprise	Ishihara Sangyo annual securities report, March 1990	Nihon Keizai Shimbun, October 16, 1990
Fuji Film	Crossfield	Nikkei Sangyo Shimbun, June 2, 1995	Nikkei Sangyo Shimbun, June 2, 1995
Yamanouchi Pharmaceuticals	Shaklee	Nihon Keizai Shimbun, May 14, 1989	Nihon Keizai Shimbun, May 14, 1989
Shionogi & Co., Ltd.	Eli Lilly's capsule business	Nihon Keizai Shimbun, February 21, 1992	Nihon Keizai Shimbun, February 21, 1992
Chugai Pharmaceutical	Gen Probe	Nikkei Sangyo Shimbun, November l, 1989	Nikkei Sangyo Shimbun, November l 1989
Fujisawa Pharmaceuticals	Lyphomed	Fujisawa Pharmaceuticals annual securities report, March 1989	Nikkei Sangyo Shimbun, August 22, 1989
Seibu Saison	InterContinental Hotels	Nikkei Sangyo Shimbun, October 1, 1988	Nikkei Ryutsu Shimbun, October 4, 1988
Kyotaru	RAI	Nihon Keizai Shimbun, January 25, 1990	Nihon Keizai Shimbun, January 25, 1990
	Paragon Steakhouse	Nikkei Ryutsu Shimbun, April 24, 1990	Nikkei Ryutsu Shimbun, April 24, 1990
JUSCO	Talbots	Nikkei Ryutsu Shimbun, October 2, 1990	Nikkei Ryutsu Shimbun, October 19, 1989
Renown	Aquascutum	Renown annual securities report, December 1989	Nihon Keizai Shimbun, April 24, 1990
Sogo	Paragon	Sogo annual securities report, February 1989	Nikkei Ryutsu Shimbun, September 26, 1989
Kawasaki Steel Corporation	LNP Engineering	Nikkei Sangyo Shimbun, October 17, 1991	Nikkei Ryutsu Shimbun, September 20, 1991

(*continued*)

Table A.1 (continued)

Acquiring company	*Target company*	*Acquiring company data source*	*Target company data source*
NKK	National Steel	NKK annual securities report, March 1990	Nihon Keizai Shimbun, April 19, 1991
Kyoei Steel	Florida Steel	Nikkei Sangyo Shimbun, July l, 1992	Nikkei Sangyo Shimbun, July 1, 1992
Komatsu	Union Carbide's polycrystalline silicon business	SUMCO annual securities report, March 2005	Nikkei Sangyo Shimbun, November 21, 1996
NSK	UPI	NSK annual securities report, March 1990	Nihon Keizai Shimbun, January 18, 1990
JUKI	Union Special Corporation	JUKI annual securities report, March 1988	Nihon Keizai Shimbun, May 7, 1989
Nippon Electric Glass	OI NEG	Nippon Electric Glass annual securities report, March 1993	Nihon Keizai Shimbun, September 29, 1993
Asahi Glass	Hankuk Electric Glass	Asahi Glass annual securities report, March 1999	Nihon Keizai Shimbun, October 31, 1999
Ryobi	Singer's household power tools business	Ryobi annual securities report, March 1989	Nihon Keizai Shimbun, July 6, 1988
Furukawa Electric	Yates I	Nippon Keizai Shimbun, November 11, 1989	Nippon Keizai Shimbun, November 11, 1989
Mitsubishi Motors	NedCar	Mitsubishi Motors annual securities report, March 2000	Nikkei Sangyo Shimbun, June 20, 1996
Aoki Construction	Westin Hotels	Aoki Construction annual securities report, March 1989	Aoki Construction annual securities report, March 1989
Daishowa Paper	Reed International's North American paper business	Daishowa Paper annual securities report, March 1989	Nikkei Sangyo Shimbun, June 14, 1988

(*continued*)

Table A.1 (continued)

Acquiring company	*Target company*	*Acquiring company data source*	*Target company data source*
SoftBank	Interop	Nihon Keizai Shimbun, February 9, 1995	Nihon Keizai Shimbun, February 9, 1995
	Interface	Nihon Keizai Shimbun, February 9, 1995	Nihon Keizai Shimbun, February 9, 1995
	Ziff-Davis Publishing	Nikkei Sangyo Shimbun, November 10, 1995	Nikkei Sangyo Shimbun, November 10, 1995
	Kingston	Nihon Keizai Shimbun, August 15, 1996	Nihon Keizai Shimbun, August 15, 1996
Footwork	Harry Hamaha	Quarterly report, fiscal year ended March 1991	Nikkei Kinyu Shimbun, October 13, 1992
Suntory	Kentwood Springwater	Nihon Keizai Shimbun, October 15, 1985	Nihon Keizai Shimbun, January 8, 1988
Shin-Etsu Chemical	Robin	Nihon Keizai Shimbun, October 2, 1999	Nihon Keizai Shimbun, October 2, 1999
Kuraray	Clariant AG's Poval resin business	Nihon Keizai Shimbun, July 10, 2001	Nihon Keizai Shimbun, July 10, 2001
Seven & i	Southland (7-Eleven Hawaii)	7-Eleven Japan company information	Nihon Keizai Shimbun, November 15, 1989
Japan Tobacco	RJ Reynolds	Nihon Keizai Shimbun, March 10, 1999	Nihon Keizai Shimbun, March 10, 1999
SEI	Lucas SEI Wiring System	Nikkei Sangyo Shimbun, December 10, 1999	Nihon Keizai Shimbun, July 8, 1999
Ricoh	Gestetner	Ricoh annual securities report, fiscal year ended March 1996	Nihon Keizai Shimbun, July 14, 1995
Toray Industries	Rhône-Poulenc's polyester film business	Toray Industries annual securities report, fiscal year ended March 1997	Nikkei Sangyo Shimbun, May 14, 1996

(*continued*)

Table A.1 (continued)

Acquiring company	*Target company*	*Acquiring company data source*	*Target company data source*
Seven & i	Southland	7-Eleven Japan company information	Nihon Keizai Shimbun, March 22, 1990
Terumo	3M's artificial heart-lung systems business	Terumo company history	Nihon Keizai Shimbun, April 16, 1999

References

Agrawal, Anup, Jeffrey F. Jaffe, and Gershon Mandelker, 1992. "The post-merger performance of acquiring firms—a re-examination of anomaly." *The Journal of Finance* 47 (4):1605–1621.

Agrawal, Anup, and Jeffrey F. Jaffe. 1999. "The post-merger performance puzzle." Working Paper, University of Alabama.

Aguilera, Ruth, and John Dencker. 2004. "The role of human resource management in cross-border mergers and acquisitions." *International Journal of Human Resource Management* 15 (December):1355–1370.

Ambrosini, Véronique, Cliff Bowman, and Richard Schoenberg. 2011. "Should acquiring firms pursue more than one value creation strategy? An Empirical Test of Acquisition Performance." *British Journal of Management* 22 (1):173–185. https://doi.org/10.1111/j.1467-8551.2010.00693.x

Andrade, Gregor, Mark Mitchell, and Eric Stafford. 2001. "New Evidence and Perspectives on Mergers." *Journal of Economic Perspectives* 15 (2):103–120.

Andrade, Gregor, and Eric Stafford. 2004. "Investigating the economic role of mergers." *Journal of Corporate Finance* 10 (1):1–36.

Asquith, Paul, Robert Bruner, and David Mullins. 1983. "The gain to bidding firms from merger." *Journal of Financial Economics* 11 (1–4):121–139.

Baker, Malcolm, Xin Pan, and Jeffrey Wurgler. 2009. "A reference point theory of mergers and acquisitions," AFA 2010 Atlanta Meetings Paper. https://doi.org/10.2139/ssrn.1364152

Barney, Jay. 2001. *Gaining and Sustaining Competitive Advantage*. Second Edition Pearson Education. (in Japanese)

Barney, Jay B. 2003. *Corporate strategy theory* (Volumes 1, 2, & 3) (Masahiro Okada, trans.) Tokyo: Diamond, Inc. (in Japanese)

S. Matsumoto, *Japanese Outbound Acquisitions*,
https://doi.org/10.1007/978-981-13-1364-6

Bradley, Michael, Anand Desai, and E. Han Kim. 1988. "Synergistic gains from corporate acquisitions and their division between the stockholders of target and acquiring firms." *Journal of Financial Economics* (21) 1: 3–40.

Brock, David. 2005. "Multinational acquisition integration: The role of national culture in creating synergies." *International Business Review* 14 (3):269–288.

Bruner, Robert. 2002. "Does M&A Pay? A review of the evidence for the decision-maker." *Journal of Applied Finance* 12 (Spring/Summer):48–68.

Cannella, Albert, Jr, and Donald Hambrick. 1993. "Effects of executive departures on the performance of acquired firms." *Strategic Management Journal* 14 (S1):137–152. https://doi.org/10.1002/smj.4250140911

Capron, Laurence. 1999. "The long-term performance of horizontal acquisitions." *Strategic Management Journal* 20 (11):987–1018. https://doi.org/10.1002/(SICI)1097-0266(199911)20:11<987::AID-SMJ61>3.0.CO;2-B

Capron, Laurence, and Nathalie Pistre. 2002. "When do acquirers earn abnormal returns?" *Strategic Management Journal* 23 (9):781–794. https://doi.org/10.1002/smj.262

Capron, Laurence, and Mauro Guillen. 2008. "National corporate governance institutions and post-acquisition target reorganization." *Strategic Management Journal* 30 (8):803–833. https://doi.org/10.1002/smj.768

Carnes, Thomas A., Ervin L. Black, and Tomas Jandik. 2001. "The long-term success of cross-border mergers and acquisitions" SSRN https://doi.org/10.2139/ssrn.270288

Cartwright, Susan, and Richard Schoenberg. 2006. "Thirty years of mergers and acquisitions research: Recent advances and future opportunities." *British Journal of Management* 17 (S1):Sl–S5. https://doi.org/10.1111/j.1467-8551.2006.00475.x

Chandler, Alfred D. 2004. *Organization in accordance with strategy*. Translated by Yuko Ariga. Tokyo: Diamond, Inc. (in Japanese)

Datta, Deepak, and John Grant. 1990. "Relationships between types of acquisition, the autonomy given to the acquired firm, and acquisition success: An empirical analysis." *Journal of Management* 16 (1):29–43. https://doi.org/10.1177/014920639001600103

Datta, Deepak, George Pinches, and V. K. Narayanan. 1992. "Factors influencing wealth creation from mergers and acquisitions: A meta-analysis." *Strategic Management Journal* 13 (1):67–84. https://doi.org/10.1002/smj.4250130106

Datta, Deepak, and George Puia. 1995. "Cross border acquisitions: An examination of the influence of relatedness and cultural fit on shareholder value creation in US acquiring firms." *Management International Review* 35 (4):337–359. http://www.jstor.org/stable/40228285

Deans, Graeme K., Fritz Kroeger, and Stefan Zeisel. 2003. *Winning the Merger Endgame: A Playbook for Profiting from Industry Consolidation*. New York: McGraw-Hill.

Dos Santos, Marcelo B., Vihang R. Errunza, and Darius P. Miller. 2008. "Does corporate international diversification destroy value? Evidence from cross border mergers and acquisitions." *Journal of Banking and Finance* 32 (12):2716–2724. https://doi.org/10.1016/j.jbankfin.2008.07.010

Drucker, Peter. 1981. "The five rules of successful acquisition," *The Wall Street Journal*, October 15.

Eisenhardt, Kathleen. (1989), "Building theories from case study research," *The Academy of Management Review* 14 (4):532–550.

Eisenhardt, Kathleen, and Melissa Graebner. 2007. "Theory building from cases: Opportunities and challenges." *Academy of Management Journal* 50 (1):25–32.

Franks, Julian, Robert Stulz, and Sheridan Titman. 1991. "The post-merger share price performance of acquiring firms." *Journal of Financial Economics* 29 (1):81–96. https://doi.org/10.1016/0304-405X(91)90014-B

Garr, Doug. 2000. *IBM Redux: Lou Gerstner and the Business Turnaround of the Decade*. Translated by Keiko Watarai. Tokyo: Tokuma Shoten Publishing Co. (in Japanese)

Ghosh, Aloke. 2001. "Does operating performance really improve following corporate acquisition?" *Journal of Corporate Finance* 7 (2):151–178. https://doi.org/10.1016/S0929-1199(01)00018-9

Gugler, Klaus, Dennis C. Mueller, B. Burcin Yurtoglu, and Christine Zulehner. 2003. "The effect of mergers: An international comparison," *International Journal of Industrial Organization* 21 (5):625–653. https://doi.org/10.1016/S0167-7187(02)00107-8

Haspeslagh, Philippe, and David Jemison. 1991. *Managing Acquisitions: Creating Value Through Corporate Renewal*. New York: Free Press.

Healy, Paul M., Krishna G. Palepu, and Richard S. Ruback. 1992. "Does corporate performance improve after mergers?" *Journal of Financial Economics* 31 (2):135–175. https://doi.org/10.1016/0304-405X(92)90002-F

Heyward, Mathew L. A. 2002. "When do firms learn from their acquisition experience? Evidence from 1990–1995." *Strategic Management Journal* 23 (1):21–39. https://doi.org/10.1002/smj.207

Hitt, Michael, Jeffrey Harrison, R. Duane Ireland, and Aleta Best. 1998. "Attributes of successful and unsuccessful acquisitions of US firms." *British Journal of Management* 9 (2):91–114. https://doi.org/10.1111/1467-8551.00077

Hofstede, Geert. 1983. "The culture relativity of organizational practices and theories." *Journal of International Business Studies* 14 (2):75–89. https://doi.org/10.1057/palgrave.jibs.8490867

Inoue, Kotaro, and Hideaki Kato. 2006. *M&A and share price*. Toyo: Keizai, Inc. (in Japanese)

Isagawa Nobuyuki, Hidetaka Kawakita, and Hidenori Sugiura. 2008. *Japanese companies' corporate finance*, Tokyo: Nikkei Publishing, Inc. (in Japanese)

Itami, Noriyuki. 2006. *The gap between Japanese and U.S. companies' profit margins.* Tokyo: Yuhikaku Publishing. (in Japanese)

Jensen, Michael C., and Richard S. Ruback. 1983. "The market for corporate control: The scientific evidence." *Journal of Financial Economics* 11 (1–4):5–50. https://doi.org/10.1016/0304-405X(83)90004-1

Jensen, Michael C. 1986. "Agency cost of free cash flow, corporate finance and takeovers." *American Economic Review* 76 (2):323–329. http://www.jstor.org/stable/1818789

Jensen, Michael C. 1988. "Takeovers: Their causes and consequences." *Journal of Economic Perspectives* 2 (1):21–48.

Kanagawa, Chihiro. 2011. *Managers must fight precisely because there is a crisis!* Tokyo: Keizai, Inc. (in Japanese)

Kaplan, Steven, and Michael Weisbach. 1992. "The Success of Acquisitions: Evidence from Divestitures." *The Journal of Finance* (47) 1:107–124. https://doi.org/10.1111/j.1540-6261.1992.tb03980.x

Kaplan, Steven, Mark Mitchell, and Karen Wruck. 1997. "A clinical exploration of value creation and destruction in acquisitions: Organization design, incentives, and internal capital markets." Working Paper No. 450. Chicago: The Center for Research in Security Prices. https://doi.org/10.2139/ssrn.10995

Kavanagh, Marie H., and Neal M. Ashkanasy. 2006. "The impact of leadership and change management strategy on organizational culture and individual acceptance of change during a merger." *British Journal of Management* 17 (S1):S81–S103. https://doi.org/10.1111/j.1467-8551.2006.00480.x

King, Major David R., Dan R. Dalton, Catherine M. Daily, and Jeffrey G. Covin. 2004. "Meta-analysis of post-acquisition performance: Indications of unidentified moderators." *Strategic Management Journal* 25 (2):187–200. https://doi.org/10.1002/smj.371

Lang, Larry H. P., René M. Stulz, and Ralph A. Walkling. 1991. "A test of the free cash flow hypothesis: The case of bidder returns." *Journal of Financial Economics* 29 (2):315–335.

Luttwak, Edward. 2014. *Edward Luttwak's strategy theory.* Translated by Yasuhiro Takeda and Katsuya Tsukamoto. Tokyo: The Mainichi Newspapers Co. (in Japanese)

Maksimovic, Vojislav, Gordon Phillips, and N.R. Prabhala. 2011. "Post-merger restructuring and the boundaries of the firm." *Journal of Financial Economics.* (102) 2:317–343. https://doi.org/10.1016/j.jfineco.2011.05.013

Martynova, Marina, Sjoerd Oosting, and Luc Renneboog. 2006. "The long-term operating performance of European mergers and acquisitions." European Corporate Governance Institute Working Paper No.137. SSRN https://doi.org/10.2139/ssrn.944407

Mayrthofer, Ulrike. 2004. "The influence of national origin and uncertainty on the choice between cooperation and merger-acquisition: an analysis of French and German firms." *International Business Review* 13 (1):83–99. https://doi.org/10.1016/j.ibusrev.2003.07.002

Mishina, Kazuhiro. 2004. *The logic of strategy failure.* Tokyo: Keizai, Inc. (in Japanese).

Mishina, Kazuhiro. 2007. *The causes of strategy failure* Tokyo: Keizai, Inc. (in Japanese).

Mishina, Kazuhiro. 2008. "Basic strategy and profit growth: An empirical analysis of 1,013 Japanese companies." Kokumin Keizai Zashi 197 (3):12–23. (in Japanese)

Mitchell, Mark, and J. Harold Mulherin. 1996. "The impact if industry shocks on takeover and restructuring activity." *Journal of Financial Economics* 41 (2):193–229. https://doi.org/10.1016/0304-405X(95)00860-H

Miyajima, Hideaki, ed. 2007. *Japan's M&A.* Tokyo: Keizai, Inc. (in Japanese)

Morosini, Piero, Scott Shane, and Harbir Singh. 1998. "National cultural distance and cross-border acquisition performance." *Journal of International Business Studies* 29 (1):137–158. https://doi.org/10.1057/palgrave.jibs.8490029

Nihon Keizai Shimbun, ed. 2008. *Challenges facing Nidec's Nagamori-ism.* Tokyo: Nikkei Business Publications, Inc. (in Japanese).

Porter, Michael. 1987. "From competitive advantage to competitive strategy." *Harvard Business Review* (May-June):43–59.

Ravenscraft, David, and F. M. Scherer. 1989. "The profitability of mergers." *International Journal of Industrial Organization* 7 (1):101–116. https://doi.org/10.1016/0167-7187(89)90048-9

Roll, Richard. 1986. "The hubris hypothesis of corporate takeovers," *The Journal of Business* 59 (2, Part 1):197–216. http://www.jstor.org/stable/2353017

Schoenberg, Richard. 2006. "Measuring the performance of corporate acquisitions: An empirical comparison of alternative metrics," *British Journal of Management* 17 (4):361–370. https://doi.org/10.1111/j.1467-8551.2006.00488.x

Servaes, Henri. 1991. "Tobin's Q and gain from takeovers." *The Journal of Finance* 46 (1):409–419. https://doi.org/10.1111/j.1540-6261.1991.tb03758.x

Singh, Harbir, and Cynthia Montgomery. 1987. "Corporate acquisition strategies and economic performance." *Strategic Management Journal* 8 (4):377–386. https://doi.org/10.1002/smj.4250080407

Sudarsanam, Sudi, and Ashraf A. Mahate. 2006. "Are friendly acquisitions too bad for shareholders and managers? Long-term value creation and top management turnover in hostile and friendly acquirers." *British Journal of Management* 17 (S1):S7–S30. https://doi.org/10.1111/j.1467-8551.2006.00476.x

Suzuki, Kazunori. 2002. "M&A and corporate performance." *Securities Analysts Journal* 40 (12):17–29. (in Japanese)

Suzuki, Kazunori. 2008a. "Motivations for M&A and effects on companies seen from prior theoretical and empirical research in the United States." *Securities Analysts Journal* 46 (2):5–17. (in Japanese)

Suzuki, Toshifumi. 2008b. *Challenges: My yearning*. Tokyo: Nikkei Publishing, Inc. (in Japanese)

Teerikangas, Satu, and Philippe Very. 2006. "The culture-performance relationship in M&A: From Yes/No to How." *British Journal of Management* 17 (S1):S31–S48. https://doi.org/10.1111/j.1467-8551.2006.00477.x

Tobe, Ryoichi, Yoshiya Teramoto, Shinichi Kamata, Takao Suginoo, Tomohide Murai, and Ikujiro Nonaka. 1984. *The nature of failure: Organizational theory research on the Japanese military*. Tokyo: Diamond, Inc. (in Japanese)

Wachi, Takashi. 2004. *Moving people while valuing people*. Tokyo: Keizai, Inc. (in Japanese)

Williamson, Oliver E. 1980. *Markets and hierarchies*. Translated by Mari Asanuma and Akira Iwasaki. Tokyo: Nippon Hyoron Sha. (in Japanese)

Zhu, PengCheng. 2011. "Persistent performance and interaction effects in sequential cross-border mergers and acquisitions." *Journal of Multinational Financial Management* 21 (1):18–39. https://doi.org/10.1016/j.mulfin.2010.12.004

Index

S. Matsumoto, *Japanese Outbound Acquisitions*,
https://doi.org/10.1007/978-981-13-1364-6